Twenty-seven-year-old Lt. Belton Y. Cooper in Cologne, Germany, near the end of the war.

Death Traps

The Survival of an American Armored Division in World War II

Belton Y. Cooper

Foreword by Stephen E. Ambrose

★
PRESIDIO

To the brave men of the 3d Armored Division who gave their lives so that those of us remaining, by the Grace of Almighty God, could become survivors.

This edition printed 2000·

Copyright © 1998 by Belton Y. Cooper

Published by Presidio Press, Inc.
505 B San Marin Drive, Suite 160
Novato, CA 94945-1340

Library of Congress Cataloging-in-Publication Data

Cooper, Belton Y.
    Death traps : the survival of an American armored division in World War II / Belton Y. Cooper : foreword by Stephen E. Ambrose.
        p. cm.
    Includes bibliographical references (p. 318).
    ISBN 8-89141-670-6 (hardcover)
    ISBN 8-89141-722-2 (paperback)
    1. Cooper, Belton Y. 2. United States. Army—Ordnance and ordnance stories. 3. World War, 1939–1945 Tank warfare. 4. World War, 1939–1945—Personal narratives, American. 5. Sherman tank. 6. United States. Army—Biography. 7. Soldiers—United States—Biography. I Title.
    D793.C66 1998
    940.54'1273—dc21   98-16672
                                        CIP

All photographs courtesy of the U.S. Army Signal Corps
Printed in the United States of America

Contents

Foreword

Belton Cooper's memoir of his World War II service with the 3d Armor Division in Europe is a gem. As a member of the 3d Armored Division Maintenance Battalion, he had liaison duties that took him far and wide, so he saw more of the war than most junior officers, and he writes about it better than most anyone. He takes us into the hedgerows of Normandy, through the Falaise pocket to the Siegfried Line, then to the Battle of the Bulge; over the Rhine, and across Germany.

His stories are vivid, enlightening, full of life—and of pain, sorrow, horror, and triumph. I first read Cooper's memoir in manuscript and quoted from it extensively in my own *Citizen Soldiers*. That is the highest compliment I can pay to a memoir.

Stephen E. Ambrose

Preface

Although there have been a number of great books written on the American Army's campaign in Western Europe during World War II, most military historians have failed completely to understand the enormous impact on American armored troops of having to fight superior German tanks. The campaign in Western Europe was essentially a war of movement, of armored conflict developed to the highest state of the art. Our major weapon for this armored warfare was the M4 Sherman main battle tank. In all the key capabilities of a main battle tank—firepower, armor and mobility—the M4 Sherman was decidedly inferior to the superior German tanks it encountered in battle. This major disadvantage not only resulted in tremendous pain and suffering and losses in personnel and armor, but also delayed the successful conclusion of the War in Europe. Herein lies the primary focus of this book.

My function was to travel with the Combat Command during the day, and assist in coordinating the recovering, evacuation and maintenance of damaged combat equipment. When the Combat Command stopped at night, it would prepare a 360° perimeter defense. Why 360°? Because during the attack, a breakthrough would put them behind enemy lines with little or no infantry support. It was my responsibility to prepare a Combat Loss Report showing all the tank and other vehicle losses during the day. I then took this report back through the bypassed German units, and delivered it to the Ordnance Battalion, thirty to sixty miles to the rear. The next morning I would return to the Combat Command with tanks and other replacement equipment lost forty-eight hours prior to this date.

Thus, we had new replacement vehicles within a forty-eight hour period after taking severe losses.

To me, one of the greatest tragedies of World War II was that our armored troops had to fight the Germans with a grossly inferior tank compared to the heavy German panzer units. Before we went into Normandy, we had been led to believe that the M4 Sherman main battle tank was a good tank, thoroughly capable of dealing with German armor on an equal basis. We soon learned that the opposite was true. The 3d Armored Division entered combat in Normandy with 232 M4 Sherman tanks. During the European Campaign, the Division had some 648 Sherman tanks completely destroyed in combat and we had another 700 knocked out, repaired and put back into operation. This was a loss rate of 580 percent.

In addition to this staggering battle loss rate of 580 percent in our main battle tanks, we also experienced extremely heavy wear and tear due to the everyday operation of the equipment. From where we landed on Normandy Beach, across France, around Paris, through Belgium, through the Siegfried Line, back and forth during the Battle of the Bulge, across the Rhine Plain, around the Ruhr (Rose) Pocket, and deep into Germany was approximately 1,460 miles. I believe the only way for a unit to survive these staggering losses and extreme wear and tear was because of the superior maintenance and supply system which we had available operating in the field at that time. In a reinforced heavy armored division, like the 3d Armored Division, out of some 17,000 troops, we had an ordnance maintenance battalion of over 1,000 men. In addition to this, if you consider the total number of maintenance soldiers in the maintenance companies of the two armored regiments and the armored infantry regiment, plus the maintenance units in the three armored field artillery battalions, the tank destroyer battalion, the antiaircraft battalion, the combat engineer battalion, the signal troops and all the other remaining maintenance personnel in the division, this gives an additional 1,000 maintenance soldiers. The reinforced heavy armored division had some 4,200 vehicles both combat and wheel vehicle types. Each vehicle had a driver and an assistant driver who did first echelon maintenance such as checking tires, tracks, spark plugs, belts and putting in gas and oil and other lubrication. Thus out of

17,000 men approximately 10,400 were involved either directly or indirectly in maintenance. This amounts to some 61 percent of the entire division personnel. It was only through the super human effort of these maintenance people plus an extremely efficient ordnance supply system that enabled the division to survive under such extremely adverse conditions.

When the 3d Armored Division was organized in the spring of 1941, the initial cadre came primarily from the southeastern states, such as Alabama, Tennessee, Georgia, Mississippi, Florida, Louisiana and Texas. A high percentage of these men came from rural backgrounds and had some experience with farm machinery, such as tractors and cultivators. The second large cadre of personnel came from the midwestern states of Illinois, Indiana, Michigan, Ohio, and Pennsylvania. A number of these men came from industrial backgrounds and had experience with industrial machinery in manufacturing. The maintenance battalion picked the best mechanics, machinists, and welders from these two groups. These men were given additional training by experienced ordnance noncommissioned officers, some of whom had seen service in World War I. In addition to this, many of the best qualified men were sent to the tank maintenance school at Fort Knox or the ordnance armor school at Aberdeen Proving Ground. Practically all our ordnance mechanics had had some three years experience in maintenance work, prior to getting into combat.

Once in combat, it was virtually impossible to get replacement tank maintenance mechanics, and equally difficult, if not more so, to get trained replacement tank crews. As a result, it was necessary for the ordnance maintenance battalion to develop a two fold function. We not only did the maintenance, repair, and replacement of the shot up tanks, but we actually became involved in the training of new tank crews. After severe tank losses and comparable losses in the crews, the armored regiments ran out of good tank crews. It was necessary for the ordnance to take raw infantry recruits who had just come off the boat from the United States and train them to be tank crews. In some cases the training time amounted to only several hours or maybe a day at the most. These inexperienced crews in turn suffered more severe losses due to their lack of training. This is one of the great tragedies of World War II, and most historians have completely failed to understand this point. Had it not been for the ordnance maintenance crews and the maintenance crews of the armored regiments, the division could not have survived, and been maintained as a viable combat unit until the end of the war. Herein lies the secondary focus of this book.

In order to carry out this job effectively, it was necessary for the maintenance companies to operate in extremely far forward positions with the combat commands. These maintenance companies were responsible for their own security because of the fact that often they would have to drop off crews and set up VCP's (vehicle collection points) after the combat command had moved on. Each maintenance company had three 57mm antitank guns for its own protection. These antitank guns were manned by maintenance personnel who had been trained by the main antitank section back in the headquarters company. These forward maintenance elements not only took care of our combat command, but often did maintenance for the various infantry divisions attached to the corps. These infantry units had no forward maintenance, and would have been completely helpless without the vehicles and weapons maintained by the forward maintenance units in the combat command.

Thus it may be seen that the VII Corps, which was the most powerful armored corps in the First Army, which in turn made it the most powerful armor corps in Western Europe, depended heavily on the forward maintenance of the 3d Armored Division, and without this help they would not have been able to accomplish many of their remarkable long movements and envelopments. Herein lies a third major focus of this book.

Introduction

All personal memoirs of the war are written from the author's perspective. As my perspective was a relatively limited one, I feel this should be explained in the beginning.

Before entering combat, and as part of my training as an Ordnance Officer, I attended the Armored Force School at Ft. Knox. This not only provided me with a practical background in tank and vehicular maintenance, but also provided me with a theoretical background in armored war tactics. This knowledge of American Armored Force Doctrine proved particularly valuable later in combat, and gave me an appreciation of how German armored superiority forced American tank commanders to disregard doctrine and improvise new tactical solutions.

There were sixteen armored divisions in the American army during World War II. Out of this number, only the 2d and 3d remained heavy armored divisions. Later combat experience proved that the heavy armored division could sustain much heavier losses than the light ones, and thus be more effective in major operations. For this reason, the 2d and 3d Armored Divisions teamed up and worked side by side in every major operation from Normandy to the end of the war in Europe.

As the spearhead of the First Army in all these major operations, the 3d Armored Division destroyed more German tanks, inflicted greater enemy losses, and participated in the capture of more prisoners than any other American armored division. In accomplishing this distinction, the 3d Armored Division lost more American tanks than any other American armored division. Of the three combat commands in the 3d Armored Division, Combat Command B destroyed more German tanks and lost more American tanks than any other combat command. As the ordnance liaison officer for Combat Command B of the 3d Armored Division, I believe I have seen more battle damaged American tanks than any other living American.

After each fire fight, the maintenance group would go forward and try to locate the damaged vehicles. Unless we could locate the knocked out tank by its map coordinates and at the same time get the "W" number on the tank as well as determine the extent of the damage, it was difficult to obtain a replacement tank through the military supply bureaucracy.

Once the extent of damage to a vehicle had been determined, a quick decision was made whether it could be repaired by the combat maintenance facilities, or whether it would have to be left for the army ordnance depot to pick up later. In this latter event, a request could be made for a replacement vehicle. If the tank was in a mine field, we would have to get the engineers to come up and clear a path, in order for recovery vehicles to get to it. If not, we could make immediate plans to evacuate the tank to a VCP.

In preparing combat loss reports day after day, I became intimately familiar with weaknesses and inadequacy of our main battle tank, the M4 Sherman. I also learned about the weapons and tactics the Germans used to knock out our tanks.

After dark, it was my responsibility to carry the combat loss report to the division maintenance battalion headquarters located some thirty to fifty miles to the rear. Because the information in this report would have been extremely beneficial to the enemy, should it have fallen into their hands, it could not be sent by radio, but instead had to be carried by personal messenger.

I put the report and other sensitive documents in a small plywood box, which was located in the back seat of my Jeep. I also kept a Thermite incendiary grenade inside the box. In the event of ambush the plan was to set off the grenade and abandon the Jeep in hope that the documents would be burned up and destroyed.

The area between the combat command columns and the division trains was known as the "void," and travelling through the void was called "running the gauntlet." During the day, an armored division combat command would bypass many enemy units. Since the American infantry units following the combat command would sometimes not come forward for a day or more, there were probably no friendly units between the combat command and the division rear. It was logical to assume that any units we met on the road at night would probably be Germans.

Thus, it was necessary to travel with extreme caution. We could not even use our blackout lights or flashlight to look at a map. It was necessary to memorize the road junctions with the map as we came forward during the day.

My driver and I would generally leave the combat command VCP after midnight. The windshield of our jeep was lowered flat against the hood and covered with a canvas cover to protect against reflection of flares or moonlight. We did have a small angle iron wire cutter mounted on the bumper. This was protection against wires which the Germans would sometimes run across the road to decapitate Americans riding in jeeps or motorcycles.

We worked out a technique by which we could travel with a reasonable degree of safety. In Europe, most of the highways had trees growing on both sides of the road, and at night there was a discernible amount of starlight shining between the trees, even if it was cloudy. My driver would look up at an angle of approximately 30 degrees, and I would look straight down the highway to discern any remote objects, or possible German roadblocks, as far away as possible. We were able to stay fairly well in the center of the road, and drove at a top speed of sixty-five miles per hour, which was as fast as the Jeep would go.

When we arrived at the division maintenance battalion headquarters I would report to the maintenance battalion shop officer and give him the combat loss report. I would give him all of the information I knew on the tactical situation as well as the location of the knocked out tanks and other vehicles. Although the vehicles being replaced were actually those that had been destroyed two days before, the fact that we brought fresh vehicles every twenty-five hours enabled the Combat Command to maintain a reasonable degree of its combat strength.

In order to travel the thirty to fifty miles between the Combat Command and the division maintenance battalion headquarters in the dark of night, I needed to know my location in both terms of map coordinates and my positional relationship to other American units. In order to lead the replacement tank convoy back to the Combat Command, I had to know not only where I was going, but also where the Combat Command was going. I, therefore, had to know more about the overall tactical situation facing the division than most junior officers.

It soon became obvious from reading combat loss reports on a daily basis that one could reconstruct a diary of the activities of the Combat Command. The information gathered from this material plus personal observations, conversations with other soldiers, and research in other documents (listed in the bibliography) provided a wealth of information for preparing this book. Conversations with other soldiers immediately after an operation, discounting the fact that most soldiers tend to exaggerate, provided a lot of interesting information. By combining information from many conversations from other soldiers who had diverse viewpoints with my own observations, I could obtain a fairly good picture of what was actually happening.

In conclusion, I feel that I was fortunate to be in a particular position to observe the American Army's campaign in Western Europe during World War II because I was a survivor. I came on active duty in June 1941 at Camp Polk with a cadre group of some 400 officers. During the next three years of training in the states and in England, I got to know many of them, and became close friends with some of them. Of those assigned to positions closer to combat than I was—in the infantry, tanks, combat engineers, or as artillery forward observers—not a single one made it from the first battles in Normandy to the final battles in Germany without being killed or wounded. I had to tell this story because they could not.

With the exception of certain well known ranking officers, some names have been changed.

Acknowledgments

I would like to acknowledge several people who hepled me write this book, not necessarily in the order of their importance.

While still in Germany, I confided my thoughts to my buddy, Lt. Earl Binckley, who continually prodded me to tell my story. Dr. James Tent, professor of history, University of Alabama, was encouraging and introduced me to Dr. Stephen E. Ambrose. Dr. Ambrose reviewed my manuscript and used it as a reference for his book, *Citizen Soldiers*. As a result of this, Dr. Ambrose graciously consented to write the foreword for this book.

Dr. Russell Weigley, professor of military history, Temple University; Lt. Col. Lee Clark, Commandant of the Armored Force School, Fort Knox; John Purdy, director of the Patton Museum; Bill Hanson, director of the Armored Forces School Library; Colonel Elder, CO of the 16 Cavalry Regiment; Hanes Dugan, historian of the 3d Armored Division; Clarence Smoyer of E Company, 32d Armored Regiment.

My family: my wife Rebecca; my sons, Belton, Lloyd, and Spencer; and Lloyd's wife, Tish, were patient, helpful, and encouraging. My secretary, Betty Hartwell, did much of the typing.

Mike Bennighof, a doctoral candidate in history, did an excellent job of editing my original manuscript. The photographs were furnished courtesy of Ernie Nibbelink, Earl Binckley, Clarence Smoyer, and Marvin Mischnick. I am indebted to Sheila Criss for producing the maps. Deborah Baxter Swaney provided considerable help with proofreading the manuscript. I am indebted to Bob Kane, Richard Kane, and E. J. McCarthy of Presidio Press for their guidance and professionalism.

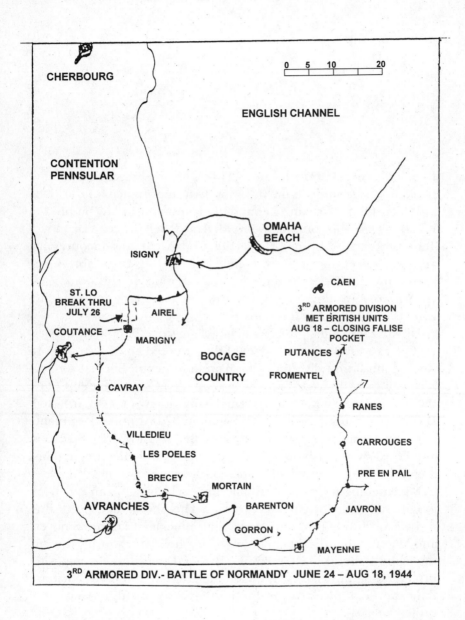

CHERBOURG

ENGLISH CHANNEL

0 5 10   20

CONTENTION
PENNSULAR

OMAHA
BEACH

ISIGNY

CAEN

ST. LO
BREAK THRU
JULY 26

AIREL

3RD ARMORED DIVISION
MET BRITISH UNITS
AUG 18 – CLOSING FALISE
POCKET

COUTANCE

MARIGNY

BOCAGE

PUTANCES

COUNTRY

FROMENTEL

CAVRAY

RANES

VILLEDIEU

CARROUGES

LES POELES

PRE EN PAIL

BRECEY

MORTAIN

AVRANCHES

BARENTON

JAVRON

GORRON

MAYENNE

3RD ARMORED DIV.- BATTLE OF NORMANDY JUNE 24 – AUG 18, 1944

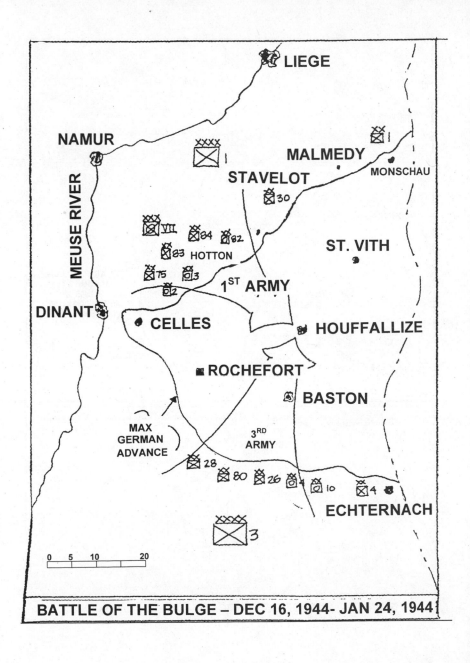

BATTLE OF THE BULGE – DEC 16, 1944- JAN 24, 1944

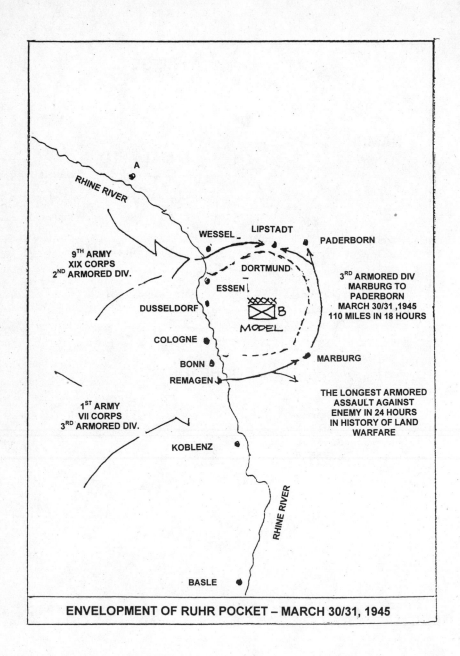

RHINE RIVER

A

WESSEL

LIPSTADT

PADERBORN

9TH ARMY
XIX CORPS
2ND ARMORED DIV.

DORTMUND

3RD ARMORED DIV
MARBURG TO
PADERBORN
MARCH 30/31 ,1945
110 MILES IN 18 HOURS

ESSEN

DUSSELDORF

MODEL

B

COLOGNE

BONN

MARBURG

REMAGEN

1ST ARMY
VII CORPS
3RD ARMORED DIV.

THE LONGEST ARMORED
ASSAULT AGAINST
ENEMY IN 24 HOURS
IN HISTORY OF LAND
WARFARE

KOBLENZ

RHINE RIVER

BASLE

ENVELOPMENT OF RUHR POCKET – MARCH 30/31, 1945

1
Reflections

On Board the LST to Normandy

My feelings were somewhat ambivalent as I stood on the deck of the landing craft and looked down at the gently rolling seas of the English Channel. Although the water was not particularly rough, the heavily laden landing craft seemed to have a roll frequency in sync with that of my stomach. We had been advised to take seasick pills about two hours before embarking, but because I had spent ten days crossing the entire ocean without using pills, I felt certain I would not need them to cross the narrow Channel.

Earlier in the evening, when we had loaded on the landing craft, we were immediately shown the officers' country mess, where I proceeded to load up on buttered toast, doughnuts, and coffee. This now was my undoing, and I regretted having waited until getting out to sea before taking the pills.

In addition to being seasick, I felt thoroughly confused. My concern and apprehension about the future were somewhat offset by the excitement of participating in the largest invasion of all time. But I was also teed off. Watching all the surrounding ships made me realize that I should have chosen the navy; instead, I was an ordnance liaison officer in the 3d Armored Division.

During my first two years of college at the Virginia Military Institute (VMI), I took army ROTC in the artillery branch. At the beginning of my junior year, I transferred to the University of Michigan to study naval architecture and marine engineering, which had been my lifelong ambition. Because the University of Michigan did not have a naval ROTC at the time, I decided to enter the army

ROTC ordnance branch, which was the closest thing to artillery offered by the university. Although I received full credit for my ROTC studies, I had to take additional hours to graduate. By fall 1941, a new naval ROTC program had been started at Michigan, but by this time I had already received my commission as a second lieutenant in the Army Ordnance Department Reserve.

The naval ROTC unit started offering ensign's commissions for senior naval architects in the Bureau of Ships, pending graduation. I immediately submitted my transcript and took the physical exam to apply for a commission; I was accepted based on my graduation in February 1942.

But a problem surfaced during my interview with the naval commanding officer. He told me it was not possible to have simultaneous commissions in the army and the navy; I would have to resign my army commission in order to accept my navy commission. I agreed at once and requested that he contact the War Department and have me transferred to the navy. But it wasn't that simple. According to regulations, the navy could not request that the army transfer me; I would have to resign. However, he would be glad to provide a letter showing that I had been offered the commission as an ensign.

Here began my enlightenment about the government's bureaucratic machinations. One could not simply turn in a resignation. Instead, certain forms had to be requested from the War Department, filled out in triplicate, and sent back to the department. I immediately requested such forms, then waited.

In early June 1941, I received a telegram from the War Department and eagerly opened it in anticipation of good news about my requested transfer. I was shocked when I read the contents.

TO BELTON Y. COOPER SECOND LIEUTENANT ORDNANCE DEPARTMENT RESERVE stop. CONGRATULATIONS, YOU ARE HEREBY ORDERED TO REPORT TO ACTIVE DUTY TO THE EIGHTEENTH ARMORED ORDNANCE BATTALION THIRD ARMORED DIVISION CAMP POLK LOUISIANA ON JUNE 22ND 1941 stop. YOU ARE TO BE RELIEVED OF ACTIVE DUTY IN ORDER TO RETURN

TO YOUR HOME IN HUNTSVILLE ALABAMA BY JUNE
22ND 1942 stop.
SINCERELY HENRY L.STIMSON SECRETARY OF WAR.

Although I did not know then that circumstances would extend
my active duty and postpone my graduation until June 1946, I was
upset that my plans to design the world's first unsinkable battleship
were shot square in the rear end. It appeared incomprehensible to
me that the government would insist that I remain a maintenance
officer in an armored division when every year only ninety naval architects graduated as opposed to some twenty thousand mechanical
engineers, who could have easily filled this position.

It was sometime past midnight on July 3, 1944, when we cleared
the breakwater at Weymouth, England. I was impressed with the skill
of the U.S. Navy in keeping the LSTs in a somewhat orderly formation. In the darkness, I could barely see the shadowy forms of the
ships in front and to the rear of ours.
All of a sudden, my seasickness became acute.
"Cooper, what the hell are you doing?" asked one of my buddies.
"I'm feeding the fish, damnit. What the hell does it look like?"
Had I not grabbed my helmet, I would have lost it also to the briny
deep. I sat down on the deck in a cold sweat and waited for the next
spasm. Fortunately, the queasiness passed.

Crossing the Atlantic
It was only natural that I would compare the trip across the Channel to crossing the Atlantic on the troop ship *John Erickson.*
We sailed from New York on September 5, 1943, in the largest
troop convoy that had yet been assembled in World War II. The German submarine wolfpack attacks on American convoys had peaked
in the spring of 1943 and now seemed to be abating. The navy took
no chances, however, because the German battleship *Tirpitz* was
known to be in Norway along with several cruisers and submarines.
The convoy consisted of nine transports carrying the 3d Armored
Division and the 101st Airborne Division, which would play a major
role in the battle of Normandy and the following breakout, as well

as numerous separate artillery, medical, and service units. The convoy also included nine navy tankers, loaded with fuel and supplies for the upcoming invasion, and an escort consisting of the battleship *Nevada* and nine destroyers.

I was standing on the deck at the stern as our ship passed down the Hudson Channel. Some two thousand troops were also on deck enjoying the sunshine of a clear September day. Looking aft, we could see the Statue of Liberty as her head disappeared over the horizon. This final vision of New York had a profound effect on me and probably all the other troops. I'm sure that many were wondering if or when we would see our country again.

I was assigned to a cabin with five other first lieutenants. The cabin, about ten feet square, contained two stacks of three bunks each and had a small adjoining toilet and saltwater shower. Although we were crowded, our accommodations were luxurious compared to those of the enlisted men, who slept in the holds in bunks stacked five high. I had an upper bunk on the starboard side next to a blacked-out porthole. I was comfortable and had no trouble sleeping, despite the fact that my lieutenant buddies loved to shoot craps and play poker well into the night.

On day five, halfway across the Atlantic, I was asleep in my bunk about midnight when I was suddenly awakened by the sound of a remote explosion followed immediately by two similar explosions. I jumped out of my bunk and tore out down the hall barefooted and in my long underwear. I was followed by my buddies, who had been shaken out of their lethargy following a late-night poker game.

As we passed through the double blackout curtains onto the deck, we saw a fully lighted ship on the horizon. My first thought, although not entirely logical, was that one of the ships in the convoy had been torpedoed and had turned on the lights to allow the troops on board to escape. It soon appeared that the ship was dead in the water, because the convoy proceeded and the ship disappeared to our rear. There were no further explosions or other unusual activities, and we finally drifted back to our cabins and went to sleep.

There was great excitement and much speculation on board the next morning. The GI rumor mill was going full tilt. The most logical explanation, from the naval officer in charge of our gun crew, was that the lighted vessel was a hospital ship returning to the States from England. Such ships, which were painted white with a large red cross on the side, traveled fully lighted at night so as not to be mistaken by German submarines; in fact, the Allies notified the Germans when these ships were on the high seas. According to the Geneva Convention, the ships, as noncombatants, were allowed to proceed under the protection of the International Red Cross.

When a hospital ship approached a convoy, the convoy would open up and let it pass through. Knowing this, German submarines would surface at night and follow the hospital ship closely so that the propeller of the submarine could not be detected separately from the propeller of the hospital ship. The submarine would safely enter a convoy and then attack. In an attempt to counter this, Allied navies would drop several depth charges behind any hospital ship that approached a convoy.

Each of the men sleeping in the holds of our ship had a space approximately two feet by two feet by six feet for himself and his duffel bag. The bag, about eighteen inches in diameter and thirty-six inches long, held all of a soldier's personal gear. Obviously, the soldier was crowded in his bunk. Under the double loading arrangement, soldiers spent twelve hours in their bunk and the next twelve hours on deck. They would bring their duffel bags with them wherever they went, because they might not return to the same bunk.

Each section of the deck was patrolled by military police (MP). One day, a private had just come up on deck, placed his duffel bag against the door of a storage locker, and settled down with one of his buddies to spend the rest of the day in the sunshine. He had no sooner gotten comfortable than the MP sergeant came by and told him he couldn't block the entrance to the door. So the private moved himself and his bag to the only other place available—by the rail.

A few minutes later a young second lieutenant came by and noticed the soldier lying against the rail underneath the lifeboat. The lieutenant told him that he was blocking the way to the lifeboats, not a good idea in the event of an emergency.

"The MP sergeant told me to move over here," said the private, "because I couldn't block the entrance to the door."

"I don't care what the sergeant told you," the lieutenant replied. "You'll have to move back. You can't stay here."

The private moved his duffel bag back against the door. No sooner had he gotten settled and started talking with his buddy than the MP sergeant came by again.

"Soldier, I thought I told you to move that bag against the rail."

"Sergeant, I moved it there and some second lieutenant told me it wasn't safe to be on the rail and to move back here."

"I don't care what some damn shavetail told you," replied the MP sergeant. "I'm in charge of this deck, and you'll move that thing back over there like I told you in the first place."

The frustrated young soldier moved back against the rail. Sure enough, a few minutes later the lieutenant came by again.

"Soldier, I thought I told you to move that barracks bag away from this rail."

"Lieutenant, I did, but the sergeant told me to move again."

The young lieutenant was feeling his oats. "Move that damn bag away from the rail. I don't want to tell you again, do you understand?"

"Yes, sir. I do."

The soldier moved back against the door with his bag. "I've had it up to here," he told his buddy. "If I have to move this damn bag again, it's going in the ocean."

Shortly, the MP sergeant came back down on the deck. When he saw the soldier with his bag against the door, he was infuriated.

"Damnit, soldier, this is the last time I'm gonna tell you to move that bag over to the rail."

"Sergeant, that won't be necessary," the soldier replied. "You'll never have to tell me again."

With that, he stood, picked up his bag, walked calmly across the deck, and tossed the bag over the rail into the waves. The MP sergeant looked stunned. All the enlisted men in the vicinity started applauding and hollering, "Go soldier, go, go."

At a special court-martial convened that afternoon, the soldier was tried and convicted for destruction of government property.

Aboard the LST in the English Channel, I felt much better after a brief nap in my bunk. As far as the eye could see in any direction, there were ships. Most of the combat vessels had either gone east to Gold Beach to support the British or west to Utah Beach to support the American VII Corps. Because the beachhead was about ten miles inland from Omaha Beach, there was no threat of direct fire from artillery.

The LSTs circled in slow, lazy patterns as they awaited the signal to come onto the beach. This was D + 28, so all the fighting had long since cleared the beach itself. There was still threat of aircraft, but I was assured that we had adequate protection.

A few moments later, a lone Me109 came screaming down the beach. Although the combat vessels were gone, it seemed as though hundreds of giant hoses sprayed liquid antiaircraft fire in long, arched trajectories as the tracers tried to seek their target. Yet the plane continued on its path until it was out of sight. I found out later that it was a reconnaissance plane that repeated this operation several times a day. Although I had seen enemy reconnaissance planes in the searchlight beams over England at night, this was my first view of the enemy in actual combat. It was indeed an exciting Fourth of July.

I had a bet with my buddy Ernie Nibbelink, who was on the LST next to us, as to who would be the first to go ashore. We were all off the Fox Orange section of Omaha Beach, awaiting the beach master's signal. The captains of the LSTs apparently also had bets as to who would go ashore first.

Immediately after the signal, the ships broke formation and headed for the beach. As our ship approached, it trimmed aft as much as possible, dropped the stern anchor about two hundred yards from shore, and rammed the beach at top speed. Because an LST is most vulnerable when beached, all due haste was made to unload and get it off the beach as quickly as possible.

We were all down below revving the Jeep engines and ready to debark. I had loaded on the transport as late as possible so that my Jeep would be close to the bow doors and I'd be able to get off before Ernie. He'd apparently had the same thing in mind. As we came down the landing door, his Jeep appeared to be somewhat ahead of mine. However, about thirty feet of water separated the end of the landing door and the beach, which meant that he had to wade. This should have been no problem; we had already waterproofed the vehicles to be able to operate in about three feet of water. But Ernie's Jeep came off the landing door and dropped straight out of sight. It seems that the LST had landed in a shell crater; it had to be pulled out with a bulldozer. Needless to say, I beat Ernie to the beach and won the bet.

The beach operation appeared extremely well organized. The Normandy beaches were receiving an average of thirty thousand troops a day and a greater tonnage of cargo than the port of New York. In addition to this, numerous burned-out hulks of tanks, half-tracks, and other vehicles were strewn up and down the beach, as if a giant child in a temper tantrum had broken his toys and scattered them in disgust.

The traffic control was well planned, and we immediately exited the beach on one of the many roads that had been bulldozed through the sand dunes to the paved roads behind the beach. Yellow tape marked both sides of the sand road and also both sides of the highway that led westward. Signs at all exits from the road and at intermediate points read, "Mines clear to the hedgerows." This was a warning to be extremely careful about pulling onto the shoulder of the road or going into any field that was not guaranteed to be cleared of mines. Numerous Jeeps had hit mines; they were completely destroyed and their passengers were killed. We continued with caution to our first bivouac area, just south of Isigny.

The *Bocage* and the Hedgerows

The area south of the Cotentin Peninsula is the *bocage* country, the ancestral home of the Normans, who invaded England in the eleventh century. Now the process was being reversed.

The area in peacetime had an almost storybook quality. Beautiful, quaint, small villages were scattered throughout the gently rolling hills. The villages were surrounded by fields that were separated by picturesque hedgerows. These hedgerows proved to be a death trap for the American army.

The Normandy countryside has deep, rich topsoil that is free of stones. Due to this lack of stone to build walls, Norman farmers who wanted to divide their land among their sons would plant rows of hedges and trees to separate the fields, which were often only one to three acres in size. The roots embedded themselves deeply and held the soil. Natural erosion over seven centuries of Norman occupation washed away the land, leaving these hedgerows—earth mounds six to eight feet high and ten to twelve feet thick at the base. Reinforced by tree and hedge roots, these natural fortifications could not be penetrated by tanks.

This *bocage* country extended from ten to forty miles inland from Omaha Beach throughout the Normandy area. German generals could not have conceived of a more formidable defense against highly mobile armored and infantry troops. Even the vaunted Maginot and Siegfried lines paled in comparison.

In spite of this terrain, the selection of Normandy as the invasion site proved fortuitous. Northwestern France is separated from the rest of the country by the Loire and Seine Rivers. Access to the area depends on bridges. Normandy and the Cotentin Peninsula are at the extreme northwestern tip of this area. For about six months prior to the invasion, the Allied air forces bombed all the bridges across these rivers. The Germans would rebuild them by night, and Allied aircraft would knock them down the next day.

At the same time, the air forces heavily bombed the Pas-de-Calais area and built up a false concentration of military units in the Thames estuary. This ruse apparently worked well, because it convinced Hitler that the Pas-de-Calais area was the main invasion spot even after the Normandy landings had taken place. Hitler remained convinced that the Normandy invasion was a feint until the night before the Saint-Lô breakthrough. Not until then did he finally release the panzer divisions that had been held in reserve in the Pas-de-Calais area. Fortunately for the Allies, this decision came too late.

The planning and execution of Operation Overlord was brilliant. Naval, ground, and air forces cooperated with precision. Logistics and supplies were well coordinated. It appeared that great lengths were taken to attend to the most minute details. A small booklet entitled "Invade Mecum" (invade with me) was given to platoon leaders before the D-day invasion. It contained detailed drawings of every hamlet and village in the Normandy area, with the location of major buildings in the village, such as the mayor's home, city hall, the public utility building, and the telephone exchange; in some cases it even gave the names of the mayor and the director of utilities. The booklets proved an invaluable source of information to the combat troops.

In spite of all this planning, and even though hedgerows existed in England, somehow the tremendous defensive potential of the hedgerows was completely overlooked. If the G2 and G3 sections were aware of this, it never reached the combat units that had to negotiate these terrible obstacles. The hedgerows were to cost the Americans dearly in lives and equipment.

The maintenance battalion set up its first bivouac in several fields about a mile south of Isigny. The vehicles pulled off the road between yellow taped markers, then circled the edges of the field. It occurred to us that the hedgerows would provide excellent cover. Little did we realize the price we would pay for this camouflage.

Everyone was cautious about mines, particularly antipersonnel mines. After a time, however, we developed a kind of sixth sense about our surroundings.

A dilapidated lean-to against a hedgerow in one corner of the field we entered was occupied by a young Frenchwoman and her little boy. They had fled Isigny when the fighting started and had been here ever since. Although thin, they appeared to be in good health. We fed them and turned them over to the military government, which evacuated them. These French civilians, the first I had encountered, impressed me with their will to survive and their ability to adjust to the most primitive conditions.

Combat Command A: Action at Villiers-Fossard

We had no sooner settled down than we were called for a briefing to inform us of the tactics that the Germans would use to oppose us in the hedgerows. They would run telephone wire completely around the perimeter of each of several fields in a row. As they were driven out of a field into the one behind it, they could hook their telephone clips into the wiring and immediately call for mortar fire in the field they had just left. This ability to get mortar and artillery fire almost instantly would prove to be devastating to our infantry and tanks who had just occupied the field.

At the French village of Villiers-Fossard, south and east of Airel on the Vire River, the Germans had penetrated three thousand yards into the 29th Division area. Combat Command A (CCA), which had come in ten days before Combat Command B, was given the mission of capturing Villiers-Fossard and eliminating the German salient. After three years of training, the division was being committed for the first time.

The combat command was organized in three separate task forces, each consisting of a reinforced tank battalion with infantry and artillery support. The attack started on the morning of June 29 with two task forces abreast and one in reserve. The columns on the right and left of the highway each had one bulldozer tank to get through the hedgerows. The initial penetrations moved rapidly but soon ran into heavy small-arms, mortar, and antitank fire from a German reinforced infantry battalion. The two bulldozer tanks were knocked out early in the operation, leaving only explosives to break through the hedgerows.

It was here that we encountered, for the first time, the deadly combination of hedgerows and the short-range German *panzerfaust*. Operated by a single man without any special training, the *panzerfaust* was an ideal weapon for close-range hedgerow fighting. After the two dozer tanks were knocked out, the only way to get through the hedgerows was by planting explosives and blowing enormous gaps so that the remaining tanks could pass. This, of course, warned the Germans where the next tanks were coming; they concentrated their fire at those points, with murderous effect.

After two days of bitter fighting, CCA accomplished its objective and withdrew. It lost 31 tanks, 12 other vehicles, and 151 men—heavy losses for an operation of this type—but the lessons learned by the combat command would save many lives and much equipment in future operations.

At a critique following this operation, General LeRoy Watson, the division commander, voiced his concern not only about the losses but also about our having left several knocked-out tanks in the fields.

Although the maintenance people of the 32d Armored Regiment had T2 armored recovery vehicles, they explained that some of the knocked-out tanks were actually behind the German lines and others were in no-man's-land between the lines. Burned beyond repair, they were not worth the sacrifice of further lives. Colonel Joseph Cowhey, seeing an opportunity to enhance the prestige of the ordnance maintenance battalion, told the general that if the armored regiments could not recover the tanks with their T2s, he and the maintenance battalion would retrieve them.

As a West Point graduate, Cowhey had stood high enough in his class to be selected for ordnance duty. Having taken considerable pride in this, he apparently became greatly concerned when lower ranking classmates, assigned to the infantry and artillery, were being promoted much faster than he was. He saw the recovery of these tanks as an opportunity to show what a combat ordnance unit could do.

Because the maintenance battalion had no T2 recovery vehicles, Cowhey selected an M25 tank transporter—a large, heavy-duty six-by-six tractor—to do the job. Probably no other vehicle was less suitable. The colonel proceeded down the Isigny–Villiers-Fossard highway with his small task group: the M25 in the lead; followed by the Jeep holding himself, another officer, and a driver; and a three-quarter-ton weapons carrier with a tank maintenance crew.

Except during heavy fighting, the front lines in combat were extremely quiet and calm, as was the case this day. As the small convoy approached the last infantry outpost, the M25's 250-horsepower engine created quite a commotion. The convoy was stopped at the roadblock by an infantryman and cautioned about proceeding further.

At this point, a disheveled-looking soldier emerged from the hedgerows with a Thompson submachine gun. "Who in the hell told you to bring that monster down here!" he yelled.

The colonel got out of his Jeep and came around to the front of the transporter. "I did, damnit!"

"And who the hell are you?" hollered the young soldier as he nervously pulled back the bolt on his Thompson. His helmet net did not camouflage his insignia; he was a captain. He was obviously nervous; his unit had been under heavy mortar fire. He was infuriated that anybody could be dumb enough to bring a large, noisy transporter into this area, which would call additional fire on his men simply to recover worthless, burned-out tanks.

"I'm Colonel Cowhey of the 3d Armored Division, and I've come to recover our tanks."

Apparently unfazed, the captain pointed his tommy gun directly at the colonel. "I'll give you fifteen seconds to turn around that pile of junk and get the hell out of here. If you don't, I'll blow your brains out."

The colonel, who had never been talked to in such an insubordinate manner by a junior officer, yelled to the lieutenant to turn the convoy around and leave. On the way back to Isigny, Cowhey realized that what he had done must have appeared to be a grandstand play, and the captain had risked a court-martial against the chances of being killed in action. Cowhey was so humiliated that he never mentioned the incident. Some felt that, in the long run, it resulted in the survival of other officers and men in the maintenance battalion.

2
First Combat

Combat Command B Actions at Airel, Pont Hébert, and Vents Heights

On the afternoon of July 8, Major Arrington, the maintenance battalion shop officer and my immediate superior, told me to report to Combat Command B (CCB) headquarters at 1700. Each unit in the combat command had its own liaison officer, and we all assembled with the staff to hear the briefing by General Bone, CCB's commander.

In a brief opening statement, the general told us that we were now ready to put to use all those years of training for combat. He felt that the state of readiness was excellent, our morale was high, and the equipment was good. I had a slight twinge of uneasiness when I remembered the disaster our tanks met in CCA's first engagement. However, we had just received a few new M4A1 tanks with 76mm guns, which I felt would give us a better chance against German armor. They were bound to be more effective than the short-barreled 75mm M2.

The G2 briefed us on the enemy situation and gave us a general outline of German positions along the Vire River and slightly north and south of Airel. The G3 then briefed us on the general plan of operation. It appeared that the line north and west of Saint-Lô was highly irregular, and certain positions of high ground should be seized prior to the final assault on Saint-Lô itself, a key communication center for the German 7th Army. Its capture was essential to breaking out of Normandy.

The immediate plan of operations was to capture the high ground north and west of Saint-Lô. The 30th Division had already launched an attack at daybreak across the Vire River at Airel, driven three thousand yards deep, and set up a perimeter defense around the village. Combat Command B was to cross the river at Airel on the night of July 8 and bivouac in this perimeter before attacking at daybreak. This operation was supposed to straighten out the line somewhat and give the American First Army a better position from which to assault Saint-Lô.

After the briefing, I reported to Major Arrington. The convoys began to form on the Isigny–Saint-Lô highway at about 2000. The liaison officer group formed up immediately behind combat command headquarters.

It was strictly a start-and-stop operation, similar to a heavy traffic jam. Maintaining normal intervals between vehicles became impossible as we proceeded farther down the highway and the convoy increased in size. By this time, we had become accustomed to the periodic firing of our own artillery into the German lines. The closer we came to the intersection of the Airel–Le Dézert highway, five miles south of Isigny, the more intense the firing became.

Suddenly, we heard a whirring noise and then *wrack, wrack, wrack* as three incoming German artillery shells landed in the woods about a hundred yards to our right. Prior to this, all the artillery had been outgoing; now a new dimension had been added. The artillery was aimed at us.

When we reached the intersection, we turned right and headed toward Airel. The incoming artillery became much more intense; I wasn't sure whether it was targeting us or the infantry around us. In any event, the column kept bunching up and stretching out in accordionlike fashion as it headed for the bridge at Airel.

I found myself at the head of the liaison group and immediately behind a Red Cross ambulance half-track from CCB. I thought I'd be safe if I stayed close to the half-track. Although the incoming artillery was more frequent, I was somewhat reassured by the briefing at CCB, earlier in the day, informing us that we were not actually going into combat until the next morning.

As we approached the bridge about a hundred yards east of Airel, we came upon an old tavern with an open courtyard. The building was in flames, and two dead young American soldiers were lying naked on the ground near a Jeep. Apparently, they had taken cover from artillery fire in the courtyard; a shell had struck the building and the blast had been deflected directly down on them. It had blown them both out of the Jeep and torn off their clothes. Their horribly burned flesh was splotched red and black. The light from the flames of the burning building danced across their bodies, which looked like surreal painted mannequins. As I turned away I noticed that my driver, Smith, was also choked up. There was no dignity for these young soldiers, even in death. A great sense of revulsion welled up in me, and the sadness was almost overwhelming. At this point, we both felt completely human.

A direct hit by German artillery had blown a large gap in the stone floor of the bridge into Airel. The tanks and half-tracks were being routed across the bridge; the wheeled vehicles were crossing the river on a pontoon bridge about a hundred yards to the north. We came across the pontoon bridge and met up with the column again. The MPs were stopping the columns and merging them by allowing one vehicle from each to pass. Thus, I had to stop and let the ambulance half-track go ahead. When I was allowed to go, I wound up behind one of the medium tanks assigned to CCB headquarters. I wasn't sure whether I had gained or lost in the deal.

The column was on a narrow road that circled north around a small hill in the middle of town. As we started down the road, we were in a defiladed position between two hedgerows. All hell broke loose. I did not know it at the time, but just as we were beginning to cross the bridge, the Germans had launched a counterattack north and south of the town. As the column moved in a slow start-and-stop fashion down the road between the hedgerows, we found ourselves between the American and German units. The Germans were in the hedgerows to the north, the Americans in the hedgerows to the south.

Fortunately, the hedgerows were high, and most of the firing went over our heads. The column slowly snaked up the road toward the top of the hill. Suddenly, a German artillery shell came screaming across the top of the tank and exploded against a tree on the far side of the hedgerow. Although the top hatch was open, the tank commander had his head inside the turret and missed the blast.

Although it was dark on this back road at night, many of the buildings nearby were on fire, and the flames flickered just enough to give us light from time to time. We did not dare use our blackout lights, so we had to be careful not to run up on the vehicle in front of us. This was not a problem for me; the tank we were following was so high and made so much noise that I didn't have much trouble keeping behind it. However, I had to be careful not to be rammed by Lieutenant Foster, the liaison officer from the 23d Armored Engineers, who was in the Jeep behind ours.

As we reached the top of the hill, an MP directed us into a field to the left that turned out to be the CCB headquarters bivouac area. It's unclear why the billeting officer chose this area; it was on a forward slope of a hill under direct German fire, and it was an orchard. Incoming artillery would strike a tree branch and detonate, with a devastating effect to those on the ground.

My driver, Smith, pulled our Jeep as close as possible to the edge of the field, then we got out and started digging a foxhole. The earth was hard chert and extremely difficult to penetrate. We dug as fast as we could with our pick, our trench shovel, and even our helmets. Every time a round of artillery came in, we would stick our heads in the hole. We must have looked like a couple of ostriches with our heads in the sand and our butts completely aboveground.

We found out later that the Germans had managed to hoist a 75mm PAK41 antitank gun into the church steeple about a quarter mile from us. Because the top of the steeple was just about the height of the hill, they could fire directly into our area. Had it not been for the cover of darkness, the entire CCB headquarters could have been wiped out.

After about two hours of hard work, Smith and I were able to dig a two-man foxhole approximately six feet by three feet by twelve to fourteen inches deep—big enough to protect our heads *and* our butts. Close to daybreak, one of our tanks located the antitank gun in the steeple and knocked it out with one shot. This decreased the incoming fire considerably.

At daybreak, CCB moved out and launched a two-pronged attack. As it headed south, we found that our area was relieved considerably from artillery fire. We emerged from our foxhole and looked around to get the lay of the land. At the base of the hedgerow near us were two dead 30th Division infantrymen who apparently had been killed the night before. We called the medics, who in turn called the graves registration people to take away the bodies.

I set out to find Maj. Dick Johnson, who commanded the maintenance company for the 33d Armored Regiment. As the combat command's senior maintenance officer, he was primarily responsible for the immediate recovery and evacuation of our vehicles. It was my job to coordinate the ordnance activities with him. The major was sturdily built, had a good sense of humor, and was well respected by his men for handling his job in a competent manner. As I walked around the bivouac area and called his name, I heard his voice come out from under a light tank: "Cooper, where are you?"

I looked under the tank, and there was the major in his sleeping bag next to the tank crew.

"What the hell are you doing under there, Major?"

"Crawled under here to get rid of those damned airbursts last night. What do you think I'm doing here?"

As I looked under the tank, I noticed a hundred pounds of TNT strapped to the glacis plate; it would be used to blow a breach in the hedgerows.

"Do you realize there's a hedgerow breaching charge strapped to the front of this tank?" I asked.

"If this thing had been ticked off by an airburst, we would have all been blown to kingdom come," the major said as he crawled out from under the tank. "Damn, if I'd known this thing was here, I wouldn't have gotten near it."

We established our first vehicle collecting point (VCP) on the south side of the hill, on the main road coming through Airel toward the Saint Jean de Daye highway. The 33d Maintenance T2 recovery crews started bringing the first vehicles from the initial combat around 0900. The first casualty was an M4 medium tank with the body of one of the crew still inside. According to surviving crew members, they were hit on the Saint Jean de Daye highway. The German gun crew apparently held their fire until the tank was no more than fifty yards away, then let go with two rounds from a 75mm PAK41 ground-mount antitank gun. Because of its extremely low silhouette, the gun could not be seen until a tank was upon it. The first round severed the main drive shaft of the M4, incapacitating the tank. The second round struck the top of the turret with a glancing blow right over the tank gunner's head, killing him.

I got on top of the turret to examine the damage but deliberately didn't look at the body that was still inside. The second round had struck the tank turret at the top of the long radius where the armor varied in thickness between two and a half to three and a half inches and the angle of incidence of the shell to the armor could have been no greater than fifteen degrees. In our ordnance training we had been told that thirty-eight degrees was the critical angle, below which a shell would normally ricochet. This was particularly true for an American shell from an M2 low-velocity tank gun.

Upon examining the front of the tank, I found that the first shot had struck the final drive, which was a large, heavy-duty armored casting that contained the transmission and the differential, which drove the tank tracks. The projectile had struck the tip of the final drive casting in line with the radius of the casting at its thickest point, which was about four and a half inches. The projectile penetrated the armor, passed through about a foot of fifty-weight oil, severed a five-and-a-half-inch steel driveshaft, then passed through another eight to ten inches of oil and a one-inch armored back plate before entering the driver's compartment. By this time the shell had spent itself and nested between the driver's feet under his seat. Because it was an armor-piercing shot, no explosion took place. Even though the second round had ricocheted off the turret, its velocity was sufficient to penetrate the armor in a gash approximately three inches wide and ten inches long. The blast inside the tank killed the gunner; the shot had gone right through his periscope. I realized that we could not repair it in the field, because the mounting had to be machined. We had to evacuate the tank to the ordnance company.

Tragic Inferiority of the M4 Sherman Tank

By this time, a number of tanks had entered the VCP with all manner of damage. Those evacuated from the column on the Saint Jean de Daye–Saint-Lô highway were mostly damaged by tank and anti-tank fire, whereas those coming from the Airel–Pont Hébert highway were mostly knocked out by *panzerfausts*. The German *panzerfaust* could penetrate our tanks with impunity, even through the extra armor we'd put in front of the driver and on the ammunition boxes on the side. These *panzerfausts* were obviously more powerful than our American bazookas.

As the tanks and other armored vehicles were brought into the VCP with broken and twisted bodies still inside, the horror of war began to settle into my being. When a tanker inside a tank received the full effect of a penetration, sometimes the body, particularly the head, exploded and scattered blood, gore, and brains throughout the entire compartment. It was a horrible sight. The maintenance crews had to get inside and clean up the remains. They tried to keep the body parts together in a shelter half and turn them over to graves registration people. With strong detergent, disinfectant, and water, they cleaned the interior of the tank as best they could so men could get inside and repair it.

Often when a tank was penetrated, the shower of fragments would sever the electrical cables. Even though the cables were protected by armored covers, the fragments would cause a short and could set the tank on fire. If the tank crew pulled the fire extinguisher switch before evacuating, the fire would be snuffed out and the interior of the tank would burn only partially. If the crew was unable to do this, the tank would burn up completely, and the tremendous heat would soften the armor and make the tank impossible to repair.

After the repairs were completed, the tank's fighting compartment would be completely painted. In spite of this, the faint stench of death sometimes seeped through. A new crew might hesitate to take a tank assigned to them because they were superstitious about tanks in which their buddies had been killed.

Seeing our mounting tank losses made me realize that our armored forces had been victims of a great deceit, and we in ordnance had been part of that deceit. During my summer at Aberdeen Proving Ground in 1939, we were told that our total annual research and development budget for tanks was only $85,000. I had felt that the tremendous engineering and manufacturing capability of the United States had more than made up for this deficiency in the intervening five years. However, the isolationist Congress during the interwar period had completely decimated the army's technical capability, particularly that of the armored forces. The few imaginative and innovative ordnance engineers who came up with new ideas were quickly discouraged due to budgetary restraints.

A brilliant young tank designer named J. Walter Christy had come up with an entirely new concept in hull and suspension design in the early thirties. The idea involved an ingenious torsion bar suspension system for the bogey wheels that supported the tracks. This suspension system had a greater amplitude of deflection, and thus provided a much easier ride over rough terrain, than did the helicoil system used on our M4 tanks. In addition, the tracks could be quickly removed, and the tanks could travel on the highway as wheeled vehicles at speeds up to sixty miles per hour. It was a radical concept at the time, and the ordnance engineers at Aberdeen were greatly restricted by their less innovative superiors, who did not choose to rock the boat.

Discouraged by lack of American interest, Christy took his invention to Russia, where engineers recognized the tremendous advantages of the system and adopted it. Many German tanks in World War II also used this system to great advantage. In addition to the high deflection of the Christy system, the bogey wheels could be overlapped, which allowed use of a wider track. The resulting greater track bearing area and lower ground bearing pressure per square inch allowed German tanks to negotiate muddy terrain with much greater ease than could American tanks. This shortcoming proved disastrous in several battles. Not until the war was almost over did we realize our error and start using Christy suspension on the new M24 and M26 and all other new tanks to follow.

In spite of the flaws of the M4, we were told that it was a good tank, comparable to the German tanks we would be meeting in northern Europe. Back in the States and also in England, we had received numerous ordnance evaluation reports on German equipment, most dealing with the German PzKw IV, which we usually called the Mark IV. The original Mark IV had a short-barreled gun similar to the 75mm M2 on our M4s; its muzzle velocity was fifteen hundred feet per second. These had been replaced on the PzKw IV by a 75mm KwK41 gun with a much higher muzzle velocity (three thousand feet per second). The Mark IV was a smaller, low-profile tank that weighed only twenty-two tons compared to our M4's thirty-seven and a half tons. It had four inches of armor on the vertical part of its glacis plate and a wider track than the M4, which enabled it to negotiate soft ground more easily than the M4 could.

In the meantime, we began to receive M4A1 medium tanks with a long-barreled 76mm gun with a muzzle velocity of 2,650 feet per second. Considering that the penetrating capacity of the projectile varies as the square of the muzzle velocity, even the Mark IV outgunned both our M4 and M4A1. When we ran into the German PzKw V Panther, a fifty-two-ton tank with three and a half inches of armor on a thirty-eight-degree glacis plate, compared to two and a half inches of armor at forty-five degrees on the M4, we were grossly outgunned. The Panther carried the even more powerful 75mm KwK42 gun, with a muzzle velocity of 3,300 feet per second. The myth that our armor was in any way comparable to German armor was completely shattered. We realized that we were fighting against German tanks that were far superior to anything we had to offer. As a result, many young Americans would die on the battlefield.

This situation had been further aggravated by command decisions made earlier. After arriving in England in January 1944, General Eisenhower had ordered some of the division commanders and staff officers to report to Tidworth Downs, the main ordnance depot for armored equipment in the European theater, where all the latest ordnance equipment available at the time was demonstrated. The operation was code-named for an ordnance colonel from Aberdeen Proving Ground who came over to perform the demonstration.

Many general officers from the U.S., British, and Canadian armies had attended plus a number of high-ranking colonels and other field-grade officers. The maintenance battalion of the 3d Armored Division was stationed at Codford Saint Mary, a short distance from Tidworth Downs. Some of our maintenance people who had been detailed to this demonstration to provide maintenance support for the armored weapons systems told us what they had seen. When I visited Tidworth Downs fifty years later, the post historian told me that no records of the demonstration exist other than to note that it took place.

First to be demonstrated were infantry weapons systems, including small arms, machine guns, and mortars. Particularly impressive was the firepower of the M1 Garand rifle in comparison to that of the German Mauser, of World War I vintage. There was some concern that our .30-caliber machine guns, also of World War I vintage, had a much lower cyclic rate of fire than the German machine guns; however, the Germans had no counterpart for our .50-caliber machine gun. Our 60mm and 81mm mortars appeared comparable to the German weapons, and our 4.2-inch chemical mortar was an excellent weapon for laying down white phosphorus smoke shells.

Artillery was demonstrated next. Although it could not be fired due to lack of range, aspects of various pieces were demonstrated, particularly the unlimbering setup and relimbering preparatory to movement. The 105mm howitzer, the 155mm howitzer, the 155mm rifle (Long Tom), the 8-inch howitzer, the 8-inch gun, and the 240mm howitzer were all of modern design, were completely motorized, and had pneumatic tires for high-speed highway transport. This equipment was equal or superior to the German guns, because the Germans still used a great deal of horse-drawn artillery.

Finally, the armored weapon systems were reviewed. First came the armored artillery. The M7, a modified M3 tank carriage with a 105mm howitzer and a .50-caliber ring-mounted machine gun, proved an excellent weapon. The M12, another modified M3 medium tank chassis, carried a 155mm GPF rifle of World War I vintage. Even though this weapon did not have the muzzle velocity of the newer 155mm Long Tom, it proved to be extremely effective. The 991st Field Artillery Battalion, equipped with these M12 gun carriages, was attached to the 3d Armored Division throughout the European operation.

Next came the antitank weapons. The small 37mm antitank gun, already obsolete, was being replaced by the 57mm antitank gun, which was still inferior to the German PAK41. The 90mm gun was a dual-purpose weapon that had been originally developed as an antiaircraft gun. In addition, it could be lowered to a horizontal position and used as an antitank gun. It was similar to the German 88mm; however, it had a lower muzzle velocity than the 88 and therefore was not as effective an antitank weapon.

Then came the tanks. The M5 light tank was demonstrated first. It had an inch and a half of armor at forty-five degrees on the glacis plate and an inch of armor on the sides. It was equipped with a 37mm antitank gun in the turret, two .30-caliber machine guns, and a .50-caliber ring mount. It had two Cadillac engines driving a hydramatic transmission, which proved to be a good power train that provided considerable mobility and speed.

The M5 was a good, fast light tank, although it was too light to be engaged in firefights with German tanks and was already considered obsolete. It was being replaced by the M24 light tank, which was still in production in the States and would not be received until we were well into Central Europe. Instead, films of this tank were shown. The M24 was between the M5 and the German Mark IV in size, had a wider track system than either of them, weighed approximately twenty tons, and was the first American tank equipped with Christy suspension. It had better armor protection than the M5 and also had a 75mm gun. The muzzle velocity was still too low to be effective against German armor.

Our main battle tank, the M4, was demonstrated next. It had two and a half inches of armor at forty-five degrees on the front glacis plate and an inch and a half to two inches on the side of the hull and on the sponsons. The turret had three to four inches on the front and two inches on the side plus a five-inch mantlet that fitted over the gun tube and raised and lowered with the gun. The tank had two .30-caliber machine guns, one in a ball mount in front of the assistant driver and one in the turret coaxial with the main gun. There was also a .50-caliber machine gun on a ring mount on top of the turret. The tank's main armament consisted of a short-barreled 75mm M2 gun with a muzzle velocity of 2,050 feet per second. The tank had narrow tracks with a ground bearing pressure of approximately seven pounds per square inch on the ground. Theoretically, this was about the same pressure that a man exerted walking on soft ground; it was felt that if a man could walk across the ground, a tank could also negotiate it. This was almost twice the ground bearing pressure per square inch of the German tanks.

The M4A1 was shown next. It was essentially the same tank as the M4 but with an improved high-velocity 76mm gun and a different turret to accommodate it. This was a vast improvement over the M4, but the gun was still less powerful than the German KwK41. By the time we arrived in Normandy, between 10 and 15 percent of our tanks carried the 76mm, and thereafter almost all replacements were 76s.

From our experience in North Africa, it had been belatedly recognized that both the M4 and the M4A1 were inadequately protected. Thus, we had arranged with the British main ordnance depot at Warminster to modify all of our M4 tanks by putting one-inch armor patches over the three ammunition boxes and quarter-inch armor inside the sponsons and also underneath the turret. We also put an additional two-inch armor patch in front of the driver's periscope and the assistant driver's periscope on the front of the glacis plate. All the new tanks coming off the production line in the States already had this modification before they were shipped to England.

The next demonstration opened up a can of worms that placed rank and authority against knowledge and experience, and pitted the narrow interpretation of tactical doctrine against flexible response to meet new, changing conditions. A new heavy tank known as the M26 Pershing had just been developed and was ready for production. There was no working model of this tank in England at the time, but films of it were shown. The tank had been thoroughly tested and approved by both the ordnance and armored forces boards. The Tank Automotive Center in Detroit was prepared to go into full production immediately upon receipt of a go-ahead from Supreme Headquarters, Allied Expeditionary Force (SHAEF). Because of the urgency of this project, a high priority had been granted by the War Production Board to proceed immediately, and schedules had been prepared that would allow these tanks to be delivered in time for the invasion.

The M26 was the first totally new main battle tank that we had. Instead of old hulls modified bit by bit but still maintaining the old disadvantages, the M26 was brand new from the ground up. It weighed forty-seven and a half tons and had four inches of armor at forty-five degress on the glacis plate. The sides had about two inches of armor, and the turret had six inches in front plus a five-inch mantlet. It had a .30-caliber coaxial machine gun in the turret and a .50-caliber ring mount on top. The main armament was a ground-mount 90mm M3 gun with a muzzle velocity of 2,850 feet per second, a muzzle brake, and a special recoil mechanism for mounting in a tank. The tank had a 550-horsepower engine and a hydramatic transmission. The suspension system was a brand-new torsion bar Christy with double bogey wheels on each arm and a wide track. This wider track gave the tank about half the ground bearing pressure of the old M4 and made it comparable to the German tanks in negotiating soft, muddy terrain.

The power ratio of the M26 was approximately 12 horsepower per ton compared to 10 horsepower per ton on the M4; this made the M26 faster and more agile over rough terrain and steep inclines. Its longer track length enabled it to span wider ditches than the M4. In every way it was far superior to the M4. Even though its muzzle velocity was less than that of the German Mark V Panther or the German Mark VI King Tiger, it was still by far the best tank we had at the time.

The M26 tank was greeted enthusiastically by the field officers and combat commanders who had actually fought against the Germans in North Africa. Brigadier General Maurice Rose, who commanded CCA of the 2d Armored Division in Sicily and had encountered the German Mark VI Tiger tank for the first time, felt strongly that we should have the M26 as soon as possible.

However, Lt. Gen. George Patton, who had commanded American troops in North Africa and Sicily and was the highest-ranking armored commander in the European theater, was not enthusiastic about the M26. Undoubtedly one of the best-informed officers on military history in the entire U.S. Army and a stickler for adhering rigidly to regulations, Patton interpreted the Armored Force Doctrine to a T and cited it as his reason for not favoring the M26. He said that the tanks of an armored division were not supposed to fight other tanks but bypass them if possible and attack enemy objectives to the rear. (According to the doctrine, the tank forces should be divided into two groups. The GHQ tank battalions were supposed to be heavy tanks attached to the infantry divisions and would be used to make breakthroughs and penetrate fortified lines. The armored divisions were supposed to penetrate deep behind the enemy lines, destroying enemy artillery and disrupting the enemy reserves and supplies.) Patton felt that because the M4 tank was lighter and required less fuel than the M26, it would be faster and more agile and was better equipped to perform the mission of the armored divisions.

Patton's assumption that the M4 was lighter and would require less fuel was correct, but he did not realize that the M26 had a higher horsepower ratio, was much more agile, and had superior armor and firepower. Apparently, he did not put much faith in the GHQ tank battalions' ability to work with infantry and make the initial penetrations. This lack of faith was well founded; the GHQ tank battalions had never been provided with a heavy tank to perform their mission properly, and the infantry and the tank battalions had never been trained to work together.

It was extremely difficult to argue with Patton, because he was strong, determined, and highly opinionated. He had a long and distinguished career as a professional soldier. He led the American tank corps in World War I, reportedly riding into battle on the front of a light tank. He later commanded the 2d Armored Division during its formative years and built it into a first-class organization. He developed an excellent group of officers who followed him with an almost cultlike dedication. The 3d Armored Division took its initial officer cadre from the 2d Armored Division, and many of the officers who had served under Patton brought with them the same zeal for excellence and military efficiency. Patton's commands in North Africa and Sicily had made him the highest-ranking American officer to command major armored combat operations.

In an excellent argument that the M26 heavy tank should be used, General Rose and other field commanders resisted the higher-ranking Patton. The experiences in North Africa at Kasserine Pass and also in Sicily had convinced them of the superiority of German armor and the need for a heavy tank to offset it. However, Patton persisted in his view; he was not above a hassle. He insisted that we should downgrade the M26 heavy tank and concentrate on the M4.

Patton's rank and authority overwhelmed the resistance of the more experienced commanders, and the decision was made to concur with Patton's view. SHAEF immediately notified Washington to deemphasize production of the M26 heavy tank and concentrate instead on the M4 medium tank. This turned out to be one of the most disastrous decisions of World War II, and its effect on the upcoming battle for Western Europe was catastrophic.

Tree Snipers

By midmorning on July 9, more damaged tanks had come in. Just as the maintenance crews were starting work on them, there was a sudden *crack*, then a *ping*, then a whirring noise. Everybody hit the ground; it didn't take any second guessing to realize that we had come under sniper fire. Command Combat A had already had a number of casualties from sniper fire, and we knew that these marksmen were usually left behind to slow us down.

Although the tank maintenance mechanics had been issued carbines, the crews had placed most of them in the trucks while they were repairing the tanks. As soon as some of the men got up and tried to run to the trucks to secure their weapons, the sniper fire started again. It was finally determined that the sniper was in a tree across the road, although nobody could spot exactly where he was. The tall pines in Normandy were festooned with large bunches of mistletoe, which grew as a natural parasite. There were so many trees and so many bunches of mistletoe that it was difficult to find the snipers who hid there.

Just as the next shot rang out, a half-track from the 36th Armored Infantry came down the road headed toward the Saint Jean de Daye–Le Dézert highway. The infantryman on the .50-caliber ring mount on the half-track saw the maintenance crew on the ground yelling and pointing across the road, and he knew immediately what was happening. He swung the .50 caliber around and let go with a short burst. The top of the tree exploded as the limb, the mistletoe, and the sniper plummeted to the ground. The half-track never stopped.

This ended the sniper fire for the time being, and the crew started back to work. But sporadic sniper fire continued throughout the rest of the day. The only time it subsided was when infantry reserves would approach. We never got used to the fire; we just had to work around it as best we could.

By the middle of the afternoon, the VCP was rapidly filling with more tanks and other armored vehicles. Although a truck or a Jeep would be brought in occasionally, the combat vehicles, particularly the medium tanks, got first priority. We expanded the VCP into the adjacent field to accommodate the increased volume.

In the meantime, B Company of the maintenance battalion, which was attached to CCB, had moved into an area about half a mile across the river and just to the south of Airel. There was a large field next to the VCP, and Major Johnson told me he would like B Company to move there.

As I started down the road in my Jeep, I reflected on the past twenty-four hours. Up to this time, I had been too busy to think. Your mind tends to boggle after a constant series of shocks and trauma, and apparently it reaches a different psychological level. This tends to neutralize all sensations and the mind tends to become inert to further shocks. Thoughts begin to develop in multiple levels with the past, present, and future. The future tends to go away first, and, as the past diminishes, the present becomes a continuum of events moment by moment. I decided that this was nature's way of reducing anxiety and worry and providing a safety valve for maintaining psychological balance. I realized how lucky I was compared to the infantrymen, tankers, artillerymen, and combat engineers, who were constantly exposed to much greater shocks over longer periods of time, and my heart went out to them.

I remembered an observation made by a soldier in the 2d Armored Division who had fought the Germans in North Africa. He said that the difference between the Americans, who had been in combat only a short time, and the British, who had been there for two years, was that the Americans fought today so they could go home tomorrow, and the British fought today and hoped and prayed that they would be alive to fight again tomorrow. I supposed that all soldiers developed this attitude if they survived long enough.

By now the engineers had spanned the gap in the bridge with a treadway to accommodate wheeled vehicles. As I crossed the bridge, I encountered another column of infantrymen coming up single file on either side of the road. From their clean uniforms and neatly shaven faces, I could tell that these young men were going into combat for the first time. There was a combination of excitement and strain on their faces, and I wondered what they were thinking about.

A man marching into combat, knowing full well that his chances of survival are extremely limited, would seem to require an inner strength based on faith in his own ultimate purpose. Although he is terrified, he develops the courage to cope with this terror and is able to function, and through this functioning he is able to survive. I remember reading somewhere, "Courage is fear that has said its prayers."

After crossing the bridge, we proceeded down the road about half a mile, turned right on a small country road, and climbed to the top of the hill where B Company was located. Dead cattle littered the fields on both sides of the road; the bodies were bloated by the hot sun, and the stench was strong.

I immediately went to see Captain Roquemore, commander of B Company of the maintenance battalion. Rock was a tall, slender, lazy-eyed Southern country boy with a slow drawl and an easy, subtle sense of humor.

"Cooper, put it to me," he said. "What the hell is happening over there?"

I told him we had a lot of losses and that Dick Johnson needed help. We went over the maps in detail, and I showed him the areas that Dick had picked out for B Company. Rock concurred and said he would like to move at daybreak. It was already dark by this time, so I decided to spend the night in the B Company bivouac.

My driver, Smith, had already parked the Jeep next to a hedgerow and started digging a foxhole. I pitched in with a shovel. The earth here had been a plowed field and was much softer than that across the river at Airel. The digging was made even easier by the fact that we weren't being shelled.

We dug a two-man foxhole approximately seven feet by five feet by two feet deep. We cut down some small saplings and placed them across the hole, then laid our shelter half tents on top. We covered this with dirt, which we tapered from about eighteen inches in the middle to about six inches on the sides. We left a small entrance at one end. Although the foxhole would not stand a direct hit from an artillery shell, it would protect us from any that landed nearby.

The night before on the hill at Airel, a number of artillery shells had hit close by. From that experience, I concluded that what we had been taught at the bomb disposal school at Aberdeen Proving Ground in January 1943 was true. As long as we could stay below an explosion's blast cone, we had a reasonable chance of surviving. Also, the Germans sent their planes up at night to drop butterfly bombs, small bombs about the size of a hand grenade that are scattered from a large canister and had a considerable effect against personnel sleeping in uncovered foxholes. We'd had a number of casualties in the maintenance battalion back at Isigny due to butterfly bombs.

Thoughts on the Reality of Combat

Smith and I climbed into our foxhole and stretched out on our bedrolls. I took off my boots and helmet, put my pistol under my helmet, and relaxed. I could tell by Smith's deep breathing that he had gone to sleep immediately, but I could not sleep right away. I was excited, concerned, and frightened all at the same time. I thought about those young soldiers marching up the road to go into combat for the first time, then I thought about having to lead B Company across to the VCP tomorrow. Where would we have to go after that? I became extremely nervous and sad. Tears came to my eyes when I thought about the two soldiers we saw who had been blown out of their Jeep. I began to wonder if I had the strength and courage to go through this for who knows how long.

I began to reflect on my whole life and my ideals, particularly my religious views. I thought about my early Sunday school days when I was a child in the Methodist Church in Huntsville, Alabama. I remembered being taught the Twenty-third Psalm. "The Lord is my Shepherd, I shall not want." The words came clearly, and I started crying. I continued saying the words to myself: "Yea though I walk through the valley of the shadow of death, I will fear no evil, for Thou art with me. Thy rod and Thy staff they comfort me."

Then a feeling of calm came over me. I stopped crying and finished the psalm, thinking that something was happening to me, something I did not understand but I knew was real. To quote the Episcopal prayer book, "A Peace which passeth all understanding" came over me. I knew then that I could do what had to be done. I knew there would be terrible times ahead and I would still be frightened and be exposed to a great deal of suffering and devastation.

However, I knew that I would be able to cope with it. This experience would influence my entire life.

More Tank Losses

The next morning, the trip across the bridge at Airel was uneventful. B Company moved into the VCP and immediately prepared to go to work. A steady stream of knocked-out tanks and other vehicles came in all day long. In addition, the 33d Maintenance Company T2 recovery crews reported a number of tanks that had been knocked out and set on fire and were thus beyond repair. They bypassed these and recovered only those that had a reasonable chance of being fixed and put back into action.

An entire platoon of five tanks from the 33d Armored Regiment came under flanking fire on the lower river road near Pont Hébert. The Germans knocked out the rear tank first, which blocked the road. They proceeded to knock out the front tank, then concentrated their fire on the three tanks in the middle. The tank crews returned the fire but were completely overwhelmed by the superior German antitank guns.

The Germans were dug in in the heavy *bocage* hedgerows, and the infantry could not come up fast enough to dislodge them. Whenever the tanks got too far ahead of the infantry, they were exposed to withering flanking fire from antitank guns and *panzerfausts*. The Germans continued their fire until all the tanks were in flames; they knew that once a tank burned, it could not be repaired. Those crew members fortunate enough to escape worked their way back down the river road through enemy lines.

With the ever-increasing vehicle casualties, it became obvious that we had to forget the regulations and adopt a radically new procedure. All of the ordnance logistic training for the invasion of Europe had been based on the assumption that our vehicular casualties, particularly the tanks, would be much lower than what we had encountered in initial combat, so the requirements for ordnance spare parts for armor divisions were grossly inadequate. Although the maintenance battalion had fifty-four two-and-a-half-ton GMC trucks devoted entirely to spare parts, plus a number of other trucks in the maintenance companies of the various armored units, they were not enough. The initial determination of spare parts for an armored division was based primarily on information from line officers in the armored units. If Patton had been so completely wrong about the heavy tank, it was little wonder that the line officers underestimated the combat requirement for spare parts.

Given these assumptions, the procedure was that all repairs were to be made with spare parts available to unit maintenance companies, plus those additional parts carried by the ordnance maintenance company attached to the combat command. Any vehicles that could not be repaired, due to lack of spare parts, were to be left in place, not cannibalized but left at the VCP for evacuation later to the army base ordnance companies.

It became immediately obvious to the maintenance people in the field that it would be a disaster to follow the directive not to cannibalize certain tanks. They would have to do so in order to repair others and get them in operation quickly. The maintenance personnel decided to scrap the regulations and get on with the job of repairing the most vehicles in the least possible time and returning them to combat. One tank in combat was a lot better than two on the dead line waiting for spare parts. Even doubling the number of spare parts trucks available would have been insufficient to handle the tanks damaged in combat.

In addition, there were insufficient resources to handle the administrative paperwork involved in finding spare parts. It was apparent that the damaged vehicles were the best source of parts. Thus, if a tank received a penetration in the turret ring (the point where the turret was attached to the hull), both the turret and the hull would be damaged beyond repair in the field. The tank would immediately be scrapped, and the power train, the engine, the gun, and any other parts would become available for repairing other tanks. These decisions were made at the lowest level by the ordnance platoon leaders. This was as it should have been, and it worked to the advantage of the entire division.

Because we were operating on "double British summertime" (seven hours ahead of eastern standard time), it did not get dark until around 2330, so we had about eighteen hours of daylight in which to work. In addition, some of the maintenance crews erected shelter halves over the back ends of the tanks so they could repair the engines after dark. They worked around the clock and caught little catnaps whenever they could. They felt that this was the least they could do to support their comrades in the tank and infantry units who were on the line all the time.

We had to be extremely careful working under tarpaulins after dark, because the slightest glimmer of light could be seen from miles away by the low-flying German aircraft, which always came after dark. They would reconnoiter our ground positions, particularly in the rear areas where maintenance work was going on; if they saw any signs of activity, they would drop butterfly bombs.

Toward the end of the day, Major Johnson, Captain Roquemore, and I got together to prepare a list of all the vehicles and other ordnance work in the VCP. This list included any spare parts that we would need from the battalion, plus a list of all the vehicles that were damaged beyond repair and had been cannibalized. We also got a list from the T2 recovery crews of any tanks and other vehicles that had been damaged beyond repair and had not been recovered. This list included the "W" numbers of the vehicles, the map coordinates, and, if possible, a brief description of the damage. From this list, I prepared our first combat loss report, which contained information considered too sensitive to send by radio. One of the primary responsibilities of the ordnance liaison officer was to deliver this list personally to the maintenance battalion in the rear.

It was after midnight and completely dark by the time Smith and I started down the road toward Isigny to deliver my combat loss report. Under these conditions we traveled without any light, not even the little cat eye blackout lights. Fortunately, there was an MP at the bridge to see that my Jeep was in the center of the road so the wheels would get on the temporary treads put across the hole in the bridge.

After leaving the bridge, we headed toward the intersection of the Isigny–Airel Road, about a mile and a half away. There were no other vehicles in sight, so we stayed in the center of the road as best we could. As we approached the next road junction, we were signaled to stop by two MPs, who asked where we were going. I told them we were going back to division trains.

The MP corporal in charge said he'd been instructed to warn all vehicles that the Germans had dropped paratroopers between this point and Isigny. The last convoy had come from Isigny about forty-five minutes before; however, this was before the report about the paratroopers. Any convoys returning to Isigny would come in a random fashion, he said.

We decided to wait about half an hour to see if another convoy was coming along. In the meantime, Smith and I discussed what to do. If there were German paratroopers along this road, it would seem that their first objective would be to capture American vehicles for transportation. They would probably try to block the road and ambush us to capture our Jeep intact. I had previously had the rear seat of the Jeep removed and a plywood box installed to carry my combat loss report and other ordnance documents and maps. I kept a thermite grenade next to the box. In the event of impending capture, I planned to pull the pin on the grenade to set all of the documents on fire, then abandon the Jeep.

After waiting a little while longer and seeing no signs of a convoy, I decided we had to take a chance and run the gauntlet—the name we had given the area between division forward and division rear— which varied in width from a few miles to maybe forty to fifty miles. The distance from this road junction to the battalion area in Isigny was about ten miles. The road was straight and narrow and had trees on both sides.

We drove in the middle of the road at top speed, which for the Jeep was sixty-five miles an hour even with the governor taken off. To estimate the center of the road, Smith looked up at an angle of approximately thirty degrees to see the sky between the trees. I looked straight ahead down the center of the road and at the shoulders to see if I could detect anything. After a while, our eyes became accustomed to the darkness, and we were amazed at what we could see even without moonlight. We were no longer concerned about meeting any American trucks on the road, only about the possibility of meeting Germans.

After we had gone about five miles, I saw a light piercing the darkness approximately a quarter mile away. The light was arching slowly up and down, similar to a railroad signal. Smith slowed down. At the same time, I removed the safety on the .30-caliber carbine, which I had previously taken out of the rack on the windshield. We knew that no American soldier could be dumb enough to shine a flashlight in this area; we would not even dare light a cigarette on the beach at night without first getting into a covered foxhole. It must be Germans.

Fortunately, we had rehearsed what we might do in a situation like this. Smith would slow down. If he could see clearly that the road was not blocked, I would open fire and he would accelerate as rapidly as possible to try to get away. If the road appeared to be blocked, we would hit the ditch on the right side of the road, I'd pull the pin on the thermite grenade, and we would jump over the hedgerow and try to get away.

As we approached the source of the light, it went off and I could see the bows of a GMC truck against the starlight. I figured that the Germans had captured the truck and killed the crew and were now trying to get a Jeep. I could see shadowy figures in the dark by the side of the truck. As one of the figures slowly approached the Jeep, I realized that he could not see us well either. I slowly raised the carbine to my shoulder and started to pull the trigger.

When the figure was about ten feet from the Jeep, I heard him say, "Hey, soldier, y'all got a tire tool?"

No German could imitate a deep Southern drawl like that.

"What in the hell are you doing shining that light, soldier?" I demanded. "Don't you realize the Germans have dropped paratroopers along this road?"

"I ain't heard no such report," he replied. He said his truck had a flat tire and he had no tire tools, probably because they'd been traded to the navy on the LST for slabs of bacon.

"Sir, you mean they done dropped them paratroopers way back here?"

Before I could reply, he hollered to his buddy and they jumped into the cab of the truck and took off down the highway, flat tire and all. I was in a cold sweat as I realized that I'd come within seconds of killing an American soldier.

• • •

Major A. C. Arrington was shocked when he saw the first combat loss report. "The Germans are chewing the hell out of those M4 tanks," he said. "They're no damn good. Cooper, you tell Captain Roquemore to forget the regulations and to cannibalize every vehicle he can to get those in the VCP running."

He was glad to hear that the captain was already doing this on his own initiative. Arrington notified Capt. Tom Sembera, the division ordnance property officer, and started immediately securing replacements.

It was amazing how quickly procedures changed once the unit got into combat. Paperwork went out the window and the replacements were made by verbal request. I began to realize something about the U.S. Army I had never before thought possible. Although under garrison conditions it is highly regimented and somewhat bureaucratic, in the field it relaxes and recognizes individual initiative. This flexibility was one of the great strengths of the U.S. Army in World War II.

The next day, July 11, I returned to the VCP with a small convoy of spare parts trucks. One of the most needed maintenance parts was spark plugs. I gathered all I could beg, borrow, or steal and brought them with us. Most of the M4 tanks had R975 Wright nine-cylinder air-cooled radial engines. When the engine was started, the tank usually backfired with considerable noise, which gave away the unit's position and instantly brought enemy fire. Most of the tank crews would idle the engines as slowly as possible when trying to maintain a defiladed position in the hedgerows.

The air-cooled radial engine was a holdover from the Depression years. Lack of funds prompted ordnance to use surplus air force radial engines in tanks. They couldn't have chosen a more poorly designed engine for this purpose, but it was the only one available in quantity when the war started.

Designed for high, constant speeds in an aircraft, the engine had excessive clearance between the cylinder walls and the pistons. When the engine was running at the proper speed in an aircraft, the clearance narrowed and the engine performed satisfactorily. In a tank however, where the engine was run slowly, the excess clearance allowed the engine to pump oil, which fouled the spark plugs.

Each engine had nine cylinders, and each cylinder had two spark plugs. This meant that eighteen spark plugs had to be replaced every time the engine fouled. No special provisions had been made in the overall planning for fighting tanks in the hedgerows, so it was no wonder that the spare parts allotment for spark plugs was grossly underestimated.

In addition to the spark plugs we brought up from battalion, we stripped all the plugs out of the tanks that had been damaged beyond repair. The ordnance shop trucks were equipped with small spark plug sandblast cleaning machines, which were kept busy around the clock. Ordnance soon ran out of blasting sand and sent crews to the beach to get more. It had to be dried and sifted before it could be used, but it saved the day.

The German Counterattack:
Tanks and Infantry in the Hedgerows

That same day, July 11, became one of the most critical in the battle of Normandy. The Germans launched a massive counterattack along the Saint-Lô–Saint Jean de Daye highway in an attempt to capture Carentan and Isigny and split the First Army in two. If this attack was successful, VII Corps would be completely isolated from Omaha Beach, and the Germans could drive the entire First Army back on the beachhead. The results would be disastrous. Combat Command A, which was attached to the 9th Infantry Division, put up a terrific defense in the vicinity of Saint Jean de Daye against attacking tanks and paratroopers. The fighting became so intense that CCA finally brought up some of the 155mm GPFs on M12 chassis from the 991st Field Artillery.

The German assault gun known as the *Jagdpanther*, which had a barbette turret (it did not rotate) with the gun mounted behind a heavy six-inch armored faceplate, was used to make frontal assaults on infantry. The *Jagdpanther*, in conjunction with other Panthers and flanking protection by paratroopers and infantrymen, made an extremely formidable force. The armor was virtually impervious to our M4 Shermans as they advanced up the highway in an almost continuous attack.

At one point, a German tank came through an opening in a hedgerow and encountered an M12 with its 155mm GPF zeroed in on the gap. The 155 let go and struck the tank at the base of the turret, completely decapitating it. The turret and gun were blown off, and the tank stopped in its tracks. In another instance, as the German tank force was approaching the intersection of the Saint Jean de Daye–Airel highway, Lieutenant Colonel Berry, who commanded the 67th Armored Field Artillery, got in a ditch with his forward observer and personally directed the fire for the entire battalion against the German task force.

The 105mm howitzer mounted on the M7 chassis proved to be one of our most effective weapons against German armor. Although the 105mm projectile would not stop a tank if it hit the glacis plate head-on, it had a good chance of penetrating the light top deck armor of the German tanks if it came down on top of the tank at an angle. It appeared that the German tank designers had put most of the weight in frontal and side armor. Even the German Panther and Tiger tanks had only about a quarter inch of armor on some areas of the top deck. The high angle of an incoming howitzer shell would allow it to strike the top deck and explode, thus penetrating and killing the entire crew inside.

If artillery fire was intense enough around a tank, it would kill the infantry, which would slow the tank's progress. Because a tank crew has limited vision when buttoned up inside, it is dependent on the infantry's hand signals to point out targets. If the infantry is not there, the tank slows down and proceeds cautiously or stops completely. Although the howitzer on the M7 was designed for a maximum fire rate of 4 rounds a minute, skilled gun crews could fire 10 rounds a minute. With eighteen guns they could concentrate 180 rounds a minute, or 3 rounds every second, on a given target. This, combined with the fire from the tanks plus the 155mm guns from the 991st, stopped the German advance.

In the meantime, Combat Command B, with task forces headed by Lieutenant Colonel Lovelady at Pont Hébert and Colonel Roysden at Vents Heights, fought against a savage counterattack by the Germans in the south. The Germans had committed the Panzer Lehr Division, a new armored division with new equipment and fresh troops. They were making an all-out attempt to recapture hill 91 in the vicinity of Vents Heights. Task Force Roysden finally took hill 91 with heavy casualties but was driven off by the ferocious attacks of the Panzer Lehr. After regrouping, the decimated task force retook hill 91.

It was during this period that Colonel Roysden's young driver was killed by a sniper; the colonel reportedly sat down and wept. Men in combat often developed a strong sense of personal bonding, regardless of rank. This display of emotion was not considered a sign of weakness but rather a sign of courageous humanity.

After taking hill 91 for the second time, Task Force Roysden was completely surrounded by elements of the Panzer Lehr. On July 16, the 30th Infantry Division broke through and relieved them, which ended the German offensive. Both combat commands then returned to division control, and the division itself was assigned to VII Corps.

The division regrouped and the maintenance people again worked around the clock. New tanks came in to replace those damaged beyond repair. To this point, the division's total losses of M4 Sherman tanks had been eighty-seven, which did not include those repaired and put back into action. These losses after a penetration of only five miles into enemy territory were obviously unacceptable and could not possibly be sustained. The shock of these losses plus those from other divisions was compounded by the realization that an enormous error had been made by Patton at Tidworth Downs in January. Requests immediately went to Washington to reverse this decision and get M26 heavy tanks into the European theater as quickly as possible.

In addition to the loss of tanks and other vehicles, we had lost all nine of our L5 Cub forward observer aircraft, which belonged to the field artillery battalions. Each battalion was equipped with three of these planes, which located enemy positions and directed artillery fire. The design of the plane was such that the pilots flew too low and too far forward, where they were subject to small-arms fire.

With the promise of new planes, the artillery observers asked for additional protection. One of the most feared wounds by men was injury to the genital area. We fabricated two small bucket seats for each plane from quarter-inch armor plate cut out of German halftracks. Each seat was contoured to protect the lower back, buttocks, genitals, groin, and upper part of the legs. The seats, which weighed about eighty pounds, were welcomed by the pilots and forward observers and raised the overall morale. The pilots eventually learned to fly a thousand feet up and a thousand feet back behind friendly lines. If they could maintain this distance safely, they could still observe enemy targets and be reasonably free from flak.

The Gas Attack

During this period, a potentially disastrous event took place that had a dramatic effect on the tactical situation at the time. I have never seen it mentioned in any article or book except the history of the 3d Armored Division.

Early in the evening of July 21, while it was still daylight, I arrived at our battalion headquarters bivouac area to see the sentry wearing his gas mask and whirling his ratchet claxton, the signal for a gas attack. My driver and I had our gas masks in the Jeep, and we put them on immediately. The men in the bivouac area were putting down their tools and scrambling to find gas masks, which were stored in a trailer next to the ordnance shop headquarters. They'd been put there for reissue after we'd stripped them off tanks or other vehicles that had been shot up and abandoned.

The men grabbed the gas masks from the trailer until there was only one left. Two men entered the trailer simultaneously, one from each end. On one end was Lieutenant Reed, a strapping six feet four inches and weighing 250 pounds. (We used to call him Big Reed, from the cartoon "Terry and the Pirates.") On the other end was Major Arrington, about five feet eleven inches and weighing about 160 pounds. They both looked covetously at the mask. Nobody knew exactly what went through their respective minds, but Lieutenant Reed wound up with the mask and the major walked away empty-handed.

Fortunately, the gas attack was a false alarm. It turned out that the Germans had fired a white phosphorus smoke shell into the rear of the battalion area and one of the sentries mistook the smoke for gas and gave the alarm. Other sentries took up the alarm, which quickly spread throughout the entire area. By the time it was dark, things had settled down, but there was an air of nervousness, and everyone kept his gas mask close at hand for the night.

The ordnance companies were equipped with three decontamination trucks in the event of a mustard gas attack. The trucks contained large wooden tanks filled with water and several drums of chloride of lime powder. The procedure was to mix the powder in the water and spray it on any contaminated vehicle. The chloride of lime would release a free chlorine radical, which would neutralize the additional chlorine in the mustard gas and make it harmless. As the result of this false alarm, the drivers of the decontamination trucks checked their equipment carefully that evening, and one driver opened a drum to make sure that it held plenty of chloride of lime.

The crew of the decontamination truck went to sleep in their foxhole, right next to the truck. Later in the evening, a heavy mist began to settle over the bivouac area, and some of the moisture apparently got into one of the drums that had been opened, and a small amount of chlorine was released. Because chlorine gas is heavier than air, it spilled over the side of the drum, down the side of the truck, and into the foxhole. The driver of the truck awakened and smelled the chlorine gas. Needless to say, the events of the previous hours had a great deal to do with what happened next. The terrified driver screamed, then fainted dead away. The assistant driver sharing the foxhole with him woke up, saw the slumped body of his buddy, and, smelling the gas, thought the man was dead. He immediately panicked and screamed, "Gas! Gas!" at the top of his voice.

All hell broke loose. Other soldiers awakened and immediately relayed the gas signal. Some fired three shots, and the sentries whirled claxtons again. One radio operator hollered, "Gas! Gas! Gas!"

In a matter of seconds the alarm spread throughout the entire First Army beachhead, and pandemonium broke out. Men abandoned their fox holes and ran around in the dark screaming and looking for their gas masks. Had the Germans realized what was happening, they could have attacked against a completely disorganized army. After a while, the men realized that this was another false alarm; the sentries' gas patches, which changed color when exposed to gas, did not indicate that any was present.

How could a well-trained, disciplined army have been subject to such sudden hysteria? Perhaps because this generation of young men grew up hearing stories about the terror of gas in World War I.

No one, perhaps even to this day, really knows how profoundly this panic could have affected the security of the army. The next morning, the CCB commander, General Boudinot, called a meeting of all the unit commanders. Boudinot expressed his shock and amazement at the disintegration of discipline among the troops. In all of his years in the army, he had never seen anything like it, and he was not about to put up with any more of it in the future. He gave a direct order from General Bradley, commander of the First Army, which is abbreviated as follows.

In view of the experience of the previous evening, it has been concluded that had the Germans actually used gas, the physical damage to our troops could not have possibly been as disastrous as the pandemonium that resulted from the gas alarm. Thus, you are hereby ordered to instruct all personnel that the gas alarm will be given under no conditions, even in the event of an actual gas attack. All claxtons and other types of gas alarm signals are to be taken up. The gas identifying patches on the sentries will remain, to be used for their personal protection. Any soldier giving the gas alarm, regardless of the circumstances, is to be shot on sight by the closest available soldier.

This was the strongest order I've ever heard given by an army commander. I'm not sure whether General Bradley had the authority to issue it, but the order was effective and was probably necessary at the time. At least it got our attention and we had no more gas alarms.

3
The Breakthrough

Preparation: The Hedge Chopper

The division spent the next few days regrouping. New personnel replacements were integrated into their units. The maintenance battalion continued to work around the clock trying to catch up on some of its backlog. In addition, replacement tanks and other vehicles were coming in across the beach directly from Tidworth Downs.

The tanks had to be refurbished by the maintenance people before being issued to the combat units. The vehicles supposedly had all the equipment on board, but some of it that was still in boxes and other wrapping had to be taken out, cleaned, and installed. This could have been done at the depot and saved the maintenance crews in the fields some time, but because the depot people were not familiar with all the equipment and how it was used, the vehicles still had to be checked in the field regardless of their condition when received. In many cases, tank crews were assigned to the maintenance battalion to help refurbish these replacement vehicles, because only experienced tank crews knew the proper place for all the equipment.

On the afternoon of July 22, Major Arrington ordered me and the other two liaison officers, Lieutenant Nibbelink of CCA and Lieutenant Lincoln of Combat Command R (CCR), and also Lieutenant Lucas from headquarters company, to report with him to witness a demonstration in a nearby field. As we entered the field, we noted a number of high-ranking officers congregating around an M5 light tank. We could tell by the red signs on several Jeeps that there were some general officers among them. As we got out of our Jeeps and started to approach the high-ranking brass, I began to cringe, as I'm sure my lieutenant buddies also did. Major General Watson, our division commander, and Brigadier Generals Hickey of CCA and Boudinot of CCB, and most of the division staff were present.

A tall officer standing in the middle of the group could be identified immediately. He is said to have worn more stars than any other general officer in the army: three on his helmet, three on each side of his collar, and three on each epaulet of his Eisenhower jacket. General Patton had come to witness the demonstration, but because the Third Army had not yet been activated, his presence in Normandy had been kept secret.

Patton was a fine-looking man with rugged features and piercing eyes. In his Eisenhower jacket, brightly polished riding boots, riding britches, and leather belt with a brass buckle and holding ivory-handled pistols, he looked every inch a soldier. Although some felt that he looked overdressed, this was part of his mystique. One could not help but stand in awe of him, and he dominated the conversation by his bearing and presence. Many of our division's officers who had previously served under him looked upon him as a demigod. His aggressive nature and severe disciplinary manner produced an ambivalence in those who served under him; they either hated his guts or worshiped the ground he walked on.

The demonstration that we had come to see was a test of a new device that would attach to the front of the M5 light tank and allow it to breach the hedgerows. The only way a tank could currently get through the hedgerows was with a bulldozer tank in front of it, and the division had only four of these.

A young soldier from a nearby engineering battalion had come up with the idea for this new device based on his experience back home as a farmboy clearing hedgerows with a bulldozer. The device was fabricated steel with ten- to twelve-inch-long pointed spikes welded perpendicular to the base channel. This weldment was attached to the towing clevis brackets on the front end of the tank transmission. Previously, tanks that rammed hedgerows simply reared up backward, because the thickly embedded roots reinforced the hedgerow mass. The spikes on the new device embedded themselves in the hedgerow and prevented the tank from rearing up. At the same time, they cut some of the reinforcing roots, and the inertia of the tank moved the entire hedgerow mass out of the way.

The test worked beautifully the first time: The tank went through the hedgerow without a problem. The possibilities were immediately recognized. Instead of waiting for bulldozer tanks, it was now possible to breach the hedgerows at many places simultaneously. When Patton nodded his approval, we knew it was a go situation. General Watson called Colonel Smith, the division chief of staff, and told him to make plans to have the hedge choppers installed at once. Colonel Smith and the G3 estimated that the division required fifty-seven of the devices. Because a major assault was scheduled for the next day, everything was of the utmost urgency.

Without any idea of how many man-hours it would take to fabricate these units or even how long it would take to get the steel, Colonel Cowhey told General Watson that he would have fifty-seven hedge choppers built and installed on the tanks by 0700 the following morning. Based on this commitment, the division made its plans for the next day's assault. Everyone realized that this quick commitment by Colonel Cowhey must have appealed to General Patton, who liked no-nonsense decisions. The commitment had to be carried out by the next lower echelon, however.

Colonel Cowhey came over to where we were standing and asked Major Arrington how many welding machines we had in the entire division. Arrington told him that there were forty-two welding units, including those in the maintenance battalion and all of those in the maintenance units of the various combat companies. Cowhey said he would have Colonel Smith make all the welding units available to us.

The plan was an example of how a project could be carried out under extremely adverse conditions. Several abandoned garage buildings in Saint Jean de Daye were taken over and established as the modification center. Tarps stripped from the tops of trucks were used to plug the holes in the roofs of the buildings and cover the doors during blackouts. Warrant Officer Douglas, an expert certified welder in civilian life, was put in charge of the actual manufacturing operation.

Major Arrington called us aside and gave us our orders. Lieutenant Lincoln was to take a truck group with burning and cutting torches down to Omaha Beach and salvage as much steel as possible from leftover German beach obstacles. Lieutenant Lucas would take another group to Cherbourg, fifty miles away, and secure all the four- to twelve-inch channels and I beams he could handle from a large fabricating shop and steel warehouse on the south side of the city. All this steel was to be brought back to Saint Jean de Daye as quickly as possible. Major Arrington told me to contact Major Johnson, motor officer of the 33d Armored Regiment, and ask him to have the 33d's tanks report to Saint Jean de Daye at 2330. These tanks were to go down the "B" line in the garage building. The 32d Armored Regiment's tanks would start reporting at 2400 and go down the "A" line in an adjacent building.

By the time the first tanks from the 33d arrived at Saint Jean de Daye, things were well organized. Onan portable generators were set up inside to produce electric lights for the welders. The 486th Antiaircraft Battalion had extra vehicles stationed around the area to be on alert against German air attacks in case arc flashes from the welding torches were seen.

Warrant Officer Douglas had no drawings to go by; he simply made field sketches on pieces of scratch paper and gave them to the men. One group cut out the parts and tacked them together. The welders completed the units, then another group installed them on the clevis brackets of the tanks. In the meantime, Douglas and his crew had come up with a design that included plow-type plates on the edges of the outboard cutters, which did an even better job of breaking through the hedgerows.

The men worked all night and by daybreak had actually completed and installed seven hedge choppers and fabricated many other parts and partial assemblies. It was determined that it took forty man-hours to complete one hedge chopper; this meant that forty welders had completed approximately one hedge chopper an hour, allowing for production slowed by the fact that no two hedge choppers were identical.

Fortunately, misty and foggy weather delayed the bombing attack, and the assault was put off for another forty-eight hours. The welding crews continued around the clock with no relief. Some men worked so long, continuously exposed to the welding arc, that they became temporarily blinded and had to be relieved. This blinding effect was due to severe eyestrain and was not permanent.

Planning Operation Cobra and the Saint-Lô Breakout

At a CCB briefing, General Boudinot went over the entire situation involving Operation Cobra. Military intelligence had discovered that an attempt had been made on Hitler's life the day before. Although details were sketchy, the information was that a bomb had exploded but Hitler was thought to have escaped without serious injury.

I was startled that this information had gotten to us so quickly. I had no idea that the British, through Operation Ultra, had broken the German code. General Truman Boudinot said some people thought this attempt on Hitler's life might be the beginning of an uprising in the ranks of the German general staff, but no one could know for sure and we should not count on this possibility.

The initial objective of Operation Cobra, as the plan was known, was to deliver a crushing blow to the German front lines and also to the rear areas to break up the German reserves. Our experiences in Normandy had shown clearly that once an attack started through the hedgerows, it soon became exhausted. This slowed the attack and gave the enemy a chance to counterattack when the troops were stretched out and most vulnerable. To make a successful attack, this capability of the German reserves had to be reduced.

The initial penetration would be made by the VII Corps of the First Army under the command of Maj. Gen. Joseph (Lightning Joe) Collins, an extremely aggressive commander with a brilliant combat record in the Pacific theater. He had also shown extreme aggressiveness in Normandy with the whirlwind capture of Cherbourg. He was assigned the 1st, 4th, 9th, and 30th Infantry Divisions, all crack units, and the 2d and 3d Armored Divisions, the U.S. Army's only two oversized, powerful, "heavy" armored divisions. The VII Corps also included a number of extra corps and army artillery battalions.

The heavy armored division's 390-tank force had the equivalent firepower of thirty artillery battalions. With our own three artillery battalions plus the two attached battalions and the 703d Antitank Battalion, this gave us the firepower of thirty-six artillery battalions. The 2d Armored Division had this same capability, and with the twelve artillery battalions from each of the four infantry divisions and the extra corps- and army-level battalions, VII Corps could concentrate the firepower of ninety artillery battalions into an extremely small area.

The line occupied by the 9th and 30th Divisions concentrated on a narrow area along the northern part of the Périers–Saint-Lô highway. They were backed up by the 1st and 4th Infantry Divisions. The 2d and 3d Armored Divisions concentrated in the Bois du Hommet, a large, densely forested area just north of the Le Mesnil–Saint Jean de Daye highway. This was approximately a mile and a half north of the infantry front line and astride the road running southward from Périers through the infantry line to Saint-Lô. The main attack was to come along the highway from just south of the infantry to Marigny.

An area approximately nine thousand yards long extending south along the highway and a thousand yards wide (five hundred yards on either side of the highway) was selected for the main bombardment. In addition to the artillery, the Eighth and Ninth Air Force would carpet bomb this area and an area from Marigny four miles east to Canisy. It would be the largest aerial bombardment of the war up to this point, and the first time that air attacks together with artillery and infantry fire would be concentrated in such a narrow area.

As if the air force did not have a difficult enough mission concentrating so much firepower in such a small area, it had the additional responsibility of trying to miss the highway from the infantry line south to Marigny. Bomb craters on the road would slow the rapid advance of the tank columns and the wheeled vehicles that followed.

The attack had been delayed three days due to overcast weather. Now a light mist and drizzle hung above the area, but the air force meteorologist assured us it would lift by morning, in time for the attack.

This night the entire division concentrated in an extremely small area in the Bois du Hommet. We had tanks, half-tracks, artillery pieces, and wheeled vehicles jammed bumper to bumper, some 4,400 vehicles in an area approximately one mile square. This was completely contrary to all our training. The fact that the German Luftwaffe showed little strength during daylight, and the fact that we had to concentrate like this for the attack to come off rapidly enough, made the risk worthwhile.

The Danger of Smoking in a Foxhole

B Company under Captain Roquemore transferred to CCR, and C Company under Capt. Sam Oliver transferred to CCB. My driver, Smith, returned to headquarters company's antitank section, and I got a new driver, Vernon, from C Company. Vernon was a tall, lanky boy from Tennessee who took great pride in keeping his vehicle maintained and clean, which greatly appealed to me.

The area where C Company had chosen to bivouac was right in front of the 391st Field Artillery Battalion. Vernon soon located two German foxholes that had been dug side by side; they appeared to be in excellent condition and showed no signs of booby traps. We decided to use these rather than dig new foxholes that evening.

I was a little apprehensive about using a German foxhole, but once I got inside and examined it, I was impressed. It was a one-man foxhole almost seven feet long, about two feet wide, and four feet deep. It was completely covered and had a narrow opening at one end. The floor was flat except for a three-inch-deep trench that extended around the edge of the wall. Any moisture that seeped into the foxhole would accumulate there, so the floor would stay reasonably dry. The German who occupied this foxhole apparently had plenty of time for refinements.

I tossed my bedroll into the foxhole, got inside, and closed my shelter half on the entrance. With my flashlight I could see pretty well. I took off my shoes, pants, combat jacket, and shirt and used the clothing for a pillow. My .45-caliber pistol and shoulder holster went underneath my helmet at the head of the foxhole. I would sleep in my long underwear and socks.

As soon as I stretched out and relaxed, I decided to catch that midnight drag, a habit I had developed when I was a cadet at VMI. We were not allowed to smoke in the room after lights out, so we always felt as though we were getting away with something. One of my two roommates, Jimmy Ellison, smoked. Tommy Opie didn't, but he would join in the conversation and we would lie there in the dark, shooting the breeze. We called this catching the midnight drag. Jimmy wound up in the navy; Tommy died while serving in the air force. Although cadet life at VMI was rugged, it beat the hell out of living here in a foxhole; at least we had clean sheets and a shower once a day.

The 391st Field Artillery, right behind us, fired intermittent interdictory fire practically all night long. Occasionally, the German sound and flash system would pick up the location of the artillery battalion and they would send a few incoming rounds. The 391st would stop firing for a little while, then start again. I soon got used to the noise. I lay back, lit up a cigarette, and was really enjoying myself. I must have dropped off to sleep immediately, because I began to dream about being branded on the chest with a hot iron, a scene I remembered from the movie *The Scarlet Letter*. In my dream I could feel the extreme heat on my chest. I even thought I could smell flesh burning.

I awakened with a start and looked down to a glowing ring about eight inches in diameter smoldering on my chest. The cigarette had apparently fallen out of my hand and set the kapok of my sleeping bag afire. I threw back the sleeping bag, jumped out of my foxhole, and made a mad rush to a nearby kitchen truck to find water. I grabbed the first can I found in the dark and headed back to douse the smoldering sleeping bag. Just as I reached the edge of the foxhole, I put my hand on the cap and realized that the can held gasoline rather than water. The two cans were identical except for the caps.

Not only would the gasoline have caused an explosion that would have killed me instantly and set the whole woods on fire, the Germans would have started counterbattery fire that would have resulted in horrendous casualties. I rushed back to the kitchen truck and grabbed a water can, making sure about the top this time, then ran back to the foxhole and flooded it. I got back in the soaking wet sleeping bag, so grateful to have been saved from a ghastly inferno that I just lay back thankfully and went to sleep.

Although the hedge-chopper crews continued to work around the clock, by dawn of July 26 they had installed less than half of the planned fifty-seven units. The remaining tanks had been returned to the assembly area the previous evening, but the welding crews continued to work on them anyway. After the attack started, the crews took the remaining parts of the partially completed hedge choppers with them to install on the designated tanks later.

The operating hedge choppers proved effective and helped keep our tank casualties low because the Germans did not anticipate the next hedgerow breakthrough. The devices were mounted so low on the tank transmissions that the German tank crews could not tell by looking over the hedgerows which tanks had the choppers and which did not. The entire project showed the ingenuity of the American soldier and his ability to improvise.

At dawn on July 26, there was still a slight haze in the air, but the sun soon burned it off and we knew the day would be clear. Green luminescent panels had been issued to the infantry and the armored units to mark the front lines and to identify the tanks. These replaced our original red luminescent panels, which could have been confused with the red Nazi flag sometimes carried by German tanks.

The ammunition supply company had been working night and day to get ammunition to the artillery and tank units. The tanks and the M7 gun carriers filled their ready racks first so they would have a complete combat load of ammunition when they moved out. They stored excess ammunition on the ground and used this in the initial barrage. The interdictory fire that had started the night before continued at a fairly low level.

The Bombardment

The initial barrage started at about 1000, some thirty minutes prior to the air attack. The ground fog had completely dissipated. Because bombing in a heavily wooded area is difficult under ideal conditions, the bombardiers needed every possible advantage.

The L5 Cubs cruised over the lines approximately a thousand feet back and up. I'm sure the observers and pilots felt a lot better with their armor-plated seats. The first targets were enemy artillery and antitank guns. The German dual-purpose 88mm guns became a particularly high-priority target.

The first flight, B26 attack bombers, came over in a column of squadrons in tight formation at approximately eleven thousand feet. There appeared to be one-half to three-quarters of a mile between the squadrons. Once they started, they formed a long gray continuum across the sky and over the horizon. I was reminded of Leonidas in the battle of Thermopylae; told that the Persian arrows were so numerous that they would darken the sky, Leonidas said, "Good, so much the better, we can fight in the shade."

The constant drone of the motors was interrupted only by the artillery and the terrible bomb blasts when yet another salvo struck the ground. A few of the 88s that survived the initial barrage opened fire on the first flight as they came over the target area. Three of the planes in the first squadron were hit and appeared to disintegrate in midair.

This victory was short lived for the Germans. The L5 observers saw the blasts of the antiaircraft guns and immediately called down on them the full power of ninety battalions of field artillery. The guns were eliminated within seconds. It appeared thereafter that every time an antitank or antiaircraft gun opened up, it was immediately destroyed.

In spite of all the precautions, some mistakes were made. The Bois du Hommet–Pont Hébert highway was mistaken for the Périers–Saint-Lô highway. The latter was the real bomb line, but the constantly churning dust and debris from the bomb blasts apparently hid some of the marker panels. As a result, some of the bombs dropped short on our side of the line. There were about six hundred casualties in the 9th Infantry Division. One bomb actually dropped in our 3d Armored Division area, but we sustained no severe casualties from it. Lieutenant General Leslie McNair, chief of the army ground forces in Washington who had come to Normandy to observe the operation, was in a foxhole in the Vents Heights area when a bomb dropped short and killed him. McNair was the highest-ranking American officer killed in combat in World War II.

It took an hour for the more than nine hundred B26 medium bombers in the first flight to pass over the target. If we thought that the B26 attack was something, we hadn't seen anything yet. Immediately following the B26 attack, seventeen hundred B17 and B24 high-level bombers from the Eighth Air Force flew over at approximately twenty thousand feet. By this time, the German antiaircraft fire had been pretty well eliminated, and there was little evidence of flak. Because the planes had to fly only a few hundred miles from England to the target, they could carry a relatively light load of gasoline and a full armament of six to eight tons of bombs.

The bomb load of each plane included 500-pound demolition bombs and 150-pound antipersonnel bombs. The demolition bomb would produce a crater forty-five to fifty feet in diameter and fifteen to twenty feet deep. It didn't take many of these bombs to produce overlapping craters in a small field. A direct hit on a tank would demolish it completely; at a distance of five to ten feet, it would break the tracks and turn the tank on its back. In a small town such as Marigny, one of these bombs would take out an entire block. Marigny was so completely devastated that only rubble remained. When American troops finally assaulted the town, it was difficult for them to tell where the streets had been.

The 150-pound antipersonnel bomb had a heavy steel case with grooved segments, similar to a hand grenade; when it exploded, it fragmented into many small, deadly missiles. In the two hours it took the B17s to make their bomb run, the combination of these two types of bombs obliterated everything in the target area. In our assembly area in the Bois du Hommet, approximately a mile from the bomb line, we could feel the ground shake whenever a bomb load struck.

Next came 700 P-47 fighters, whose mission was to patrol the exposed flanks of the armored divisions, as they expanded the breakthrough, until the infantry divisions could come forward and occupy this ground.

This made a total of 3,300 planes dropping some 14,000 tons of bombs in three hours. This was the largest single bombardment of the war until Hiroshima.

New Mission for Air Support

The effect of the bombing was totally and completely devastating. The air force and the artillery obliterated the area on both sides of the road south of the Bois du Hommet to Marigny. In a few instances the highway was hit, but in most areas the road was still passable by wheeled vehicles.

As soon as the bombing and artillery ceased, the infantry moved out. The 9th Infantry on the right and 30th Infantry on the left moved about nine hundred yards in the first forty-five minutes; in conventional hedgerow fighting, this could have taken several days. Immediately after the infantry's initial penetration, the two armored divisions with their supporting infantry moved through the gap. In addition to their ground support role, the P47 fighter-bombers of the Ninth Air Force had the unique mission of holding and securing ground on the flanks of the armored divisions.

The 3d Armored Division and the 1st Infantry Division were on the right and the 2d Armored Division and the 4th Infantry Division were on the left. Our division's objective was to capture Marigny and swing to the right to secure the high ground north of Coutances, approximately seventeen miles away at the base of the Cotentin Peninsula. This rapid thrust would completely envelop the left flank of the German army, which was pinned to the coast eight to ten miles north of Coutances, and complete the first phase of the breakthrough.

As soon as the CCB task forces passed through the penetration area, C Company of the maintenance battalion followed. The area beyond the northern boundary of the bomb line looked like the surface of the moon. The bomb craters had overlapped in many areas, and in some cases entire hedgerows were taken out. About a mile inside the bombing area, we encountered a Mark IV German tank, which had apparently been dug in on the side of the road as an antitank roadblock. A near miss of a 500 pound demolition bomb had turned the tank completely on its top.

A little bit farther down, we pulled off to the right and moved the company into its first bivouac inside the bomb line. The first field that had reasonably clear spaces happened to be right in front of one of the batteries of the 391st Field Artillery, which was firing a mission on Marigny. The vehicles moved around the edge of the field next to the hedgerows, and we immediately started to set up our defenses and install the green identification panels.

As we were moving into our bivouac, we were apparently spotted by a German battle group of tanks and infantry that had been outside the bombing area and was moving in toward our flank. We were busy digging our foxholes and setting up our 57mm antitank gun when we spotted the German group in the next field. The 57mm would not have a chance against a Panther. In addition to the 57mm, we had an armored scout car with a .50-caliber machine gun plus half a dozen .50-caliber machine guns on ring mounts on GMC

trucks. The men themselves had .30-caliber M1 carbine rifles and
were prepared to put up a hell of a fight.

At this point, the artillery battery commander realized that our
57mm antitank gun and his howitzers would have little effect against
the Panther tank. He called his air force liaison officer and ordered
an air strike. Within less than forty-five seconds, two P47s appeared
right over the treetops, traveling at an altitude of three hundred to
five hundred feet. Because their approach was from the east, they
had to let their bombs go long before they reached our area. The
bombs passed directly over our maintenance company and struck
the target on the other side of the hedgerow. It seemed as though
the bombs were going to land squarely in the middle of our area,
and we took cover in our foxholes, shallow as they still were.

As the two P47s came screaming in, with their four 500 pound
bombs arcing overhead, they let go with their eight .50-caliber machine guns. The Germans were apparently just about to breach the
hedgerow with an explosive charge when the bombs struck. The blast
was awesome; flames and debris shot five hundred feet into the air.
There were bogey wheels, tank tracks, helmets, backpacks, and rifles flying in all directions. The hedgerow between us and the German tanks protected us from the direct effect of the blast, but the
tops of the trees were sheared off.

With the exception of perhaps some broken bows in the tops of
the trucks, we didn't sustain any damage but I kept digging my foxhole in fear that German stragglers would still try to come in on us.
If there were any survivors left in this group, they were soon taken
care of by the 9th Infantry, who moved up, shored up our flank, and
consolidated the area.

I remembered back to when we were in England, before the invasion started, that we would tease the air corps about the fuzz-faced
flyboys who flew the fighter planes. By this time, the air corps had
lowered the age limit for commissioned officers to eighteen, figur-
ing that these young men were full of piss and vinegar and had
enough hot-rod instincts to make excellent fighter pilots. Men beyond their midtwenties were supposedly no longer foolhardy enough
to make good fighter pilots. I realized the truth of this on that day.
Because of the Ninth Air Force, the men of C Company of the main-

tenance battalion and one battery of the 391st Field Artillery became *survivors.*

Operation Spark Plug

I received word from Maj. Dick Johnson that a number of tanks from CCB were shut down about halfway between Marigny and Coutances due to spark-plug fouling. Idling while waiting to cross the bomb line was taking its toll on our tank engines. I immediately got two empty ration boxes and filled them with every spark plug we could spare. Although I didn't know where the tanks were, I knew the route they were supposed to take.

My driver, Vernon, and I took the bypass route around Marigny that CCB had taken, because fighting was still going on in the town. One of the things I had learned is not to go looking for trouble, because there is enough out there to go around for everybody. As we started down the main highway, we soon became accustomed to what we later referred to as the debris of combat: spent tank shells, paper, shot-up German vehicles, and sometimes a few German dead. It made me feel certain that we were on the right road.

About halfway to Coutances, we came down a hill toward the little town of Camprond. According to the map coordinates, the CCB column took a right turn here and should be somewhere on the north road right outside of town. As we approached the town, I could hear sporadic rifle fire. Just as we were about to enter the town, I heard a loud blast that sounded like a tank firing right at us. Vernon hit the brakes and the Jeep skidded sideways. I yelled, "Let's get the hell out of here." We turned and headed back up the hill at top speed, then moved into a defiladed position behind the brow of the hill. I looked through my field glasses to see what was going on.

Apparently, a German Mark IV tank had backed into a building and was firing across the street at some of our infantry. I decided to wait and see what happened. The tank firing soon ceased, so I assumed that the tank had been knocked out. But considerable small-arms fire continued. I would wait until it subsided. While I was lying there with my field glasses aimed at the town, another Jeep approached from the rear and parked beside us. Out stepped a soldier in a trench coat. I thought at first he was an officer but soon realized by the patch on his shoulder that he was a member of the press corps.

"What's going on down there?" he asked as he came up beside me.

"Damned if I know," I replied.

"But I just saw you come up the hill a few minutes ago from the town."

"I didn't stay around long enough to find out what was happening."

I explained that I had a bunch of spark plugs to deliver to our tanks on the other side of the town, where I'd be going as soon as the firing subsided. He asked if he could follow me. "Be my guest," I replied.

Shortly thereafter, the firing seemed to subside considerably, and I figured it was time to go. Just then a 36th Armored Infantry half-track came down the road. We decided to follow it.

Suddenly, the reporter became apprehensive. After much cogitation, he turned to me. "Lieutenant, you go on down there and deliver those spark plugs. I think I'll go back to battalion, look at the map, and get the 'big picture'." This was the first time I'd heard the expression "big picture."

As we followed the half-track down the hill into Camprond, the firing continued to subside. We passed through the village and found the road to the right on the map and started back up the hill. About half a mile out of town, we came upon the tank column, which had just been engaged in a heavy firefight. There were German vehicles and litter on the road. The body of a young German soldier, stripped to his waist, lay on a stretcher beside the road where he had evidently been left by his own medics. Some soldiers in their final agony develop a waxlike hue, then later turn whitish gray, particularly if there had been a great loss of blood. This man, with his blond hair and ivory skin, looked like a wax figure.

The 33d Maintenance people were glad to see me coming with their spark plugs, and they wasted no time in placing them in their engines. They gave me the old plugs so I could have them sand-blasted, then the tank column continued to the high ground north of Coutances. From this position they could dominate the road net into the city in all directions while the infantry secured the city itself. This opened the road for Patton to move his divisions south toward Avranches and the Brest peninsula.

Lessons from Operation Cobra

The first phase of Operation Cobra ended with the complete destruction of the left flank of the German army. This enabled First Army to move south to widen the gap and outflank the Germans south of Saint-Lô.

The comparison between this operation and the operations in the *bocage* country, south of Airel, was astonishing. Previously, it had taken twelve days to penetrate eight miles. Including the operation around Villiers-Fossard, our total tank losses had been eighty-seven. In the first phase of Operation Cobra, from the morning of July 26 through July 28, the division moved forward seventeen miles to Coutances with a loss of only two tanks.

The lessons were straightforward. The hedge choppers, although we had fewer than half of those ordered, allowed the tanks to break through the hedgerows at a number of points simultaneously without forewarning the Germans. Next, we had the almost perfect classroom solution of air, armor, infantry, and artillery working in support of one another. The crushing firepower completely destroyed enemy troops in the area and neutralized their reserves. This kept the flanks open long enough for the armor to secure a complete breakthrough.

The armored division is in its ideal element once it is through the main line of resistance and has a more or less open field. Here it can move rapidly, bypass pockets of enemy resistance, and keep casualties at a minimum. Conversely, when it gets bogged down and moves slowly, casualties reach a maximum. Operation Cobra will be remembered as one of the best-planned and best-executed examples of combined-arms warfare in military history.

4

The Falaise Pocket

Breakthrough Becomes Breakout

Operation Cobra now entered its second phase. On August 1, the 12th Army Group, with Gen. Omar Bradley in command, became operational. The army group consisted of the newly activated Third Army under Gen. George Patton and the First Army under Gen. Courtney Hodges. General Montgomery retained command of the 21st Army Group, which consisted of the British Second Army and the Canadian First Army. With the British 21st Army Group maintaining terrific pressure on the Germans in the Bayeux-Caen area facing southward, the American 12th Army Group made the deep penetration through the Saint-Lô breakthrough and now began to swing around to envelop the entire left flank of the German 7th Army.

As the infantry moved into Coutances, CCB was ordered to leave the high ground and to double-back to Camprond. There they helped the 1st Infantry Division reduce a German strongpoint. They then headed south toward Cerisy la Salle. In the meantime, CCA came down on the left flank of CCB and bypassed the town of Montpinchon, a German strongpoint. They put a roadblock north of Montpinchon, and elements of the 2d Armored Division swung to the left and south of CCA and blocked the road south of Roncey. This cut off the retreat of a large German column consisting of fifty tanks and self-propelled guns plus infantry, artillery, and a number of horse-drawn vehicles.

The American armored commanders called for an air strike. A drove of P47s came in, bombing and strafing the entire length of the column. When the Germans tried to abandon their vehicles and run into the fields, they came under the roaring fire of the strafing planes. This, plus the tank, artillery, and automatic weapons fire from both the armored divisions, produced a horrendous debacle for this German column.

Tanks, half-tracks, and self-propelled guns littered the highway. Many were burning; others had been abandoned by the troops in a mad dash to avoid the screaming P47s. The burned bodies of German tankers climbing out of their tanks looked like charcoal mannequins. Dead German soldiers were strewn along the highway and the fields on both sides. Many horses were killed because they could not escape the traces holding them to the burning caissons. Tank dozers had to clear the road in many areas to allow our columns through.

After the air strike, CCB headed south toward its next objective, the high ground just west of Villedieu-les-Poêles. The retreating German army was at a great disadvantage. The units that had survived outside of the initial bombardment area and then were overrun during the first phase of the breakthrough broke up into smaller columns and headed south and east as rapidly as possible to escape the oncoming Allied juggernaut. With complete air superiority in daylight, the P47s ranged ahead of the columns and notified the ground troops of the Germans' positions and movement. This enabled the armored columns, with infantry riding on the backs of the tanks, to intercept the retreating enemy columns. Nothing is more devastating to an infantry column than to be caught in the open by tanks. The tanks would fire rounds of high explosive (HE) aimed to hit the road in the middle of the column, then glance up about three feet before exploding. Where the two columns ran into each other, the armored column's overwhelming firepower was immediately apparent. In many cases our armored columns would race ahead of the Germans, block the road in front of them, then call for an air strike. This ideal situation for an armored division demonstrated time and again the catastrophic results on the enemy of mobility, firepower, and shock action.

In addition to the 75mm and 76mm guns on the tanks, we had the awesome firepower of massed automatic weapons. Our .30-caliber machine guns, both air and water cooled, were of World War I vintage. The cyclic rate of fire, some six hundred rounds per minute, was much slower than that of the German counterpart, but they were reliable weapons and easy to maintain. Both the barrel and the bolt mechanism could be interchanged in a few minutes. The German standard .30 caliber was an MG42 of much more recent design and with a higher cyclic rate—twelve hundred rounds per minute. This was an excellent design, but the tolerances were so close that the barrel and the bolt were not interchangeable. For that reason, the German spare parts situation was much more critical than ours; in many cases it was easier for them to replace the entire gun if the barrel went bad. The Germans had no weapon comparable to our .50-caliber M1 machine gun. If this massive slug penetrated the torso, the hydraulic shock would generate a virtual explosion inside the body. If an arm or a leg was struck, the entire limb might be severed. The Germans were terrified of it.

Lightning Joe Collins, our corps commander, utilized his divisions with maximum efficiency. It was as if a chess master was maneuvering his key men in various combinations to trap the enemy pawns.

Combat Command B with elements of the 4th Infantry Division secured the high ground west of Villedieu-les-Poêles, bypassed the main city across the Sienne River, and headed south toward Saint Croix. Combat Command A with elements of the 1st Infantry Division secured Mortain, turned it over to the 1st Division, and headed southward in a wide end swing. After securing Saint Croix, CCB went to Reffuveille for a twenty-four-hour rest and maintenance period.

This was the first time that the entire combat command had been out of the line since July 8. From a maintenance point of view, the M4 Sherman's engine was supposed to be pulled after a hundred hours of operation. Many tanks were due this hundred-hour check; the number would have been higher had medium tank losses not been so great that many tanks were brand new. In spite of easier going during the offensive, tank losses had been high whenever we encountered German tanks. The hundred-hour check is normally time-consuming, requiring six to eight hours under the best conditions in garrison. In the field with rough ground and limited wrecker facilities, it required more time.

• • •

On the afternoon of August 5, C Company of the maintenance battalion bivouacked about half a mile east of Reffuveille. Juvigny and Reffuveille, two small villages about three miles apart, had been the site of a heavy firefight two days before. Because we expected a twenty-four-hour or longer maintenance period, my driver, Vernon, bivouacked our Jeep next to a hedgerow, then chose a site for a two-man foxhole.

Even in the soft ground, the foxhole, roughly seven feet long by five feet wide by two feet deep, took us more than an hour to complete. Vernon went over to the kitchen truck and drew us a box of 10-N-1 rations, which would feed two men for five days. In addition, we had a whole box of K rations, which would last us for some time. Vernon always kept us well supplied with food.

The 10-N-1 contained two types of canned meat—Spam and corned beef. Most GIs ate more Spam than they care to remember. I suppose that's why most GIs hated it when the war was over. The rations also contained canned green vegetables, canned fruit, crackers, coffee, toilet paper, and cigarettes. This was supplemented occasionally by a stray French chicken or some eggs, which was the next best thing to actually getting back to the headquarters company main chow line.

The next morning, just as we were packing the Jeep to move out, an MP Jeep arrived in the bivouac area with an MP officer, a driver, and a French farmer and his young daughter. The officer told Sergeant Fox that he would like to see the company commander. When Captain Oliver appeared, the MP officer told him that the French farmer's daughter had been raped the night before by soldiers, perhaps from this company. The Frenchman's farm was in the next field, just over the hedgerow. The mademoiselle claimed that when she had gone out to the barn to check her livestock, she'd been accosted by several American GIs. She claimed they held her down in the hay and gang-raped her.

Captain Oliver told Sergeant Fox to line up the company in formation. Seated in the Jeep, the MP captain, the driver, the farmer, and the young lady passed slowly in review in front of the men, stopping from time to time to look at individuals. She was trying to identify the men who had raped her. Everyone was extremely nervous, because rape was a serious offense in the U.S. Army and was punishable by death.

At the end of the inspection, the Jeep went back to the head of the column and the farmer and daughter had a powwow with Captain Oliver. Apparently, the mademoiselle was unable to identify her attackers, which relieved everyone. Some of the men later said that the French girl had voluntarily taken on several GIs in exchange for cigarettes and chocolate candy and had yelled rape when her father caught them.

The Battle of Mortain

The 33d Armored Regiment and its maintenance company were bivouacked nearby in Reffuveille. They had been working on the tanks; by daybreak they had removed the armor plate from the back of many tanks and placed the engines on the ground. The tank crews helped with the heavy work, then enjoyed a short but well-deserved rest while the maintenance crews took over.

I was with Maj. Dick Johnson at about 1000 when word came to cut short the maintenance effort and get the tanks back together as quickly as possible. It seemed that no sooner had the 1st Division turned over Mortain to the 30th Division than the Germans launched a massive counterattack. A 30th Division regimental combat team had been completely cut off, and CCB was to attack immediately and relieve them.

Everyone scrambled to get everything back together. Tank engines that had their maintenance check only partially completed were hurriedly reassembled and put back into the engine compartments. The armored decks were put back and bolted down. The battle-weary tank crews got back into their tanks. Although grumpy and teed off, they realized they had to rescue their fellow GIs. By noon the tanks were buttoned up and ready to go. This was an all-time record for getting an engine back in a tank and doing whatever was necessary to prepare it for battle.

A breakthrough as massive as that at Saint-Lô required a certain amount of calculated risk. Sooner or later the enemy would make a stand and counterattack. Just exactly when and where the counter-attack would come, no one knew.

On August 6, the die was cast. The Germans massed their armor and motorized infantry at Mortain and attacked due west, driving toward Juvigny and Reffuveille to Avranches. The objective was to separate the First and Third Armies and cut the Third Army's supply routes. General Bradley ordered an all-out effort to recapture and hold Mortain.

Combat Command B's immediate objective was to relieve the isolated elements of the 30th Division. To do so required crossing an open valley between two hills and seizing the German-occupied high ground on the other side. Together with elements of the 2d Armored Division and the infantry divisions, CCB began the assault. The units were met by murderous artillery and direct tank fire from two German panzer divisions and supporting infantry. One M4 tank received a direct hit from a 155mm HE shell on the glacis plate about five inches above the bolted seam where the final drive casting (a heavy, contoured casting containing the control differential, drive axles, sprockets, and transmission) was bolted to the glacis plate. The armor was about four inches thick at the point of the radius and tapered to about two and a half inches where it bolted to the glacis plate. The bolts in this armored seam were ripped out for a span of twelve to fourteen inches, and the glacis plate was dented inward about one and a half inches. This allowed the blast to come directly into the body compartment of the tank and neutralize the crew.

Our tanks on open ground such as this were no match for the superior firepower and heavy armor protection of the German tanks. As our tank casualties began to mount, our troops called for an air strike. The Ninth Air Force was already overextended, so the Royal Air Force (RAF) was called to help.

A group of low-flying Hawker Typhoons came screaming in at low altitude, firing rockets at the German armor and infantry on top of the hill. This, combined with our heavy artillery, infantry, and tank fire, eventually brought the German counterattack to a slow, grinding halt. Combat Command B with supporting infantry finally broke through to the isolated 30th Division regiment.

The entire valley was littered with burned-out tanks and half-tracks. When we finally got our recovery vehicles into the area, the maintenance crews worked around the clock.

During this operation, the crew came upon the crashed wreck of one of the British fighters lying next to one of our tanks. It apparently had been shot down by German ground fire. The pilot had been able to crash-land the plane, but it was upside down with the tail section dug into the ground. One of the maintenance mechanics notified the sergeant that a body was hanging upside down inside, still secured by his seat belt.

There was a strong odor from the gasoline leaking from the plane's tanks as the graves registration people removed the young British flight lieutenant's body and put it on a stretcher. But suddenly they realized that the lieutenant was still alive. He had been hanging upside down for a number of hours; it was a miracle that he survived. A fuel line in the engine compartment had broken and fuel was leaking inside the cockpit and running down his seat, down his back, into his hair, and onto the ground. He was soaked with gasoline from head to foot and was beginning to develop red burns on his neck and hands from the high-octane fuel.

The medics brought some blankets, rolled him on his stomach, and stripped off his gasoline-soaked clothing. His entire back, buttocks, and the back of his legs were burned raw from the gasoline. As he slowly regained consciousness, he was obviously in severe pain. As soon as the medics had moved him a safe distance from the plane, he asked for a cigarette. One of the men remarked, "Damn, I knew those Limeys had guts, but this beats the hell out of anything I've ever seen!"

This young pilot had risked his life to help save our tankers, and our men felt deeply indebted to him, particularly because he was not an American. This type of bonding was common among Allied soldiers.

A frail, gaunt-looking member of the press corps had come over with the medics when they removed the pilot. I don't think anyone recognized him at the time; years later when I read his book *Brave Men*, I realized that this was Ernie Pyle. He described this incident in such detail that he must have gotten his information firsthand.

• • •

While the work was going full blast on recovered tanks, we secured a list of the "W" numbers as well as the extent of damage and map coordinates on all the tanks and other vehicles that had been damaged beyond repair and left on the battlefield. We turned this list over to Division Ordnance in order to secure replacements as quickly as possible. In the meantime, the mad rush was on to repair those vehicles we had in the best and most expeditious manner. If the tank had not been set on fire completely, we could usually repair it.

When a projectile penetrated a tank, a series of incandescent particles usually showered the inside of the fighting compartment. Any crew member in the way would be killed instantly; if not, the ricochet effect inside the tank would utterly destroy him. In some cases, at close range, a projectile would strike the side of the tank and go all the way through, exiting on the other side. In this case the crew would be lucky because they would avoid the terrible ricocheting effect.

The incandescent particles would also generate many small slivers, which embed themselves in the electrical cables, causing them to short out. Often the sparks from this would set the tank on fire. There were manual fire extinguishers inside the tank and also a master lever, which the crew could pull to engulf the fighting compartment with CO_2. A penetration in this compartment would often kill or severely wound several crew members, and those abandoning the tank would not have time to set off the fire extinguishers. The oil and gasoline vapors inside the tank plus the paint, seats, insulation, and other flammable materials made any fire difficult to put out once it started.

Penetration of the gas tanks or the engine would also cause fires. Once the gasoline and the ammunition went up, the tank would explode. The open cupola acted like a smoke stack, and the fire would generate such great heat it would anneal the hardness of the armor plate leaving the tank beyond repair.

If the tank struck a mine, the bottom plate would sometimes be warped to the extent that the hull could not be repaired. In this case, if the turret was not severely damaged, it could be removed and replaced on a good hull. If the turret was struck in the trunnion mount, jamming the gun elevating mechanism, it could not be repaired but could be removed and replaced with a good turret. If the tank was penetrated in the ring mount (the junction between the turret and hull), it would warp and damage the ball bearing races on the bottom of the turret and the entire tank would have to be replaced.

One of our maintenance welders found a spent projectile inside a hull. He took a carbon arc and cut the tip off, using this cone to make a plug to weld up the hole the projectile had made. After he ground the surfaces smooth on both sides and we painted the tank inside and outside, it was difficult to find the patch. I always thought this technique was one of the true ironies of warfare, that the projectile also served as the patch. It took considerable skill on the part of the welder to grind and thus camouflage these patches, because a tank crew did not like to get a replacement tank that had been penetrated, particulary if they felt there had been casualties in the tank. In spite of this, tank crews liked to get their old tank back because of sentimental attachments. After a reasonably short time, all the damaged vehicles had either been repaired or replaced, and C Company of the Maintenance Battalion headed south to join CCB near Gorron and Mayenne.

Northeast Toward Falaise

Once the German penetration at Mortain had been sealed off, it became our turn again. The Germans had committed all their available reserves to make the breakthrough at Mortain, and they had overextended themselves. SHAEF immediately recognized this opportunity, and General Eisenhower ordered Bradley's 12th Army Group to make a wide end run deep into enemy territory. In the meantime, Montgomery's 21st Army Group was to mount a major offensive in the Caumont-Falaise area and drive south to meet the 12th Army Group, which would trap the bulk of the German 7th and 5th Panzer Armies.

I left the VCP in the afternoon of August 11 and headed south in my Jeep to try to catch up with CCB. I knew that their route was down through Saint Hilaire-du-Harcouët to Gorron and on to Mayenne, but I did not know exactly how far they had gotten. Gorron and Mayenne, heavily damaged by air strikes and artillery and tank fire, were important road junctions, and wherever the Germans held out there was a firefight.

The 3d Armored Division would lead the VII Corps attack and would move rapidly. The corps was getting stretched out, and I realized that the supply routes would be vulnerable. Occasionally, I would pass infantry, artillery, and other motorized units, but a great deal of the time my driver and I would find ourselves alone on a highway in our Jeep going as fast as we could. As we entered Gorron, we had to slow down and pick our way through the heavy debris, then check which route the combat command had taken.

Many of the houses had been damaged and burned. As we drove slowly around the ruins, Vernon suddenly whistled and hollered, "Here, here!" A small gray object emerged from beneath the charred timbers of a smoldering house, ran toward our Jeep, jumped into Vernon's lap, and started licking his face. The wire-haired terrier puppy, about twelve inches high and probably about three months old, had no collar and apparently had been wandering in the rubble for some time.

Vernon wanted to keep the puppy as a mascot. I told him that the last thing we needed was a puppy to take care of when we were trying to catch up with CCB. We decided that the French would return to the village soon because the Germans had been gone for at least six hours. Civilians normally hid in the woods until the fighting was over, then returned to their homes to see what they could recover. With a look of disappointment, Vernon put the puppy on the ground and gave him a pat, and we took off in a cloud of dust.

Looking closely at the rubble in the streets for signs of tank tracks and examining the map, I finally was able to determine which road CCB had taken. We got on the highway, and Vernon accelerated the Jeep to top speed and drove in stony silence.

About a quarter mile out of town, I happened to look in the rearview mirror and saw a small object bounding down the middle of the road behind us. My resistance melted. "Vernon, stop the damn Jeep!" I yelled. The puppy, which had gathered considerable momentum, got a few feet from the Jeep, then cleared the back end in

a single leap. Vernon reached into the air and snagged it like a forward pass.

"Well, I guess we do need a mascot," I replied as Vernon cuddled
the puppy, "but he'll be your responsibility."

"Don't worry, Lieutenant. I'll take good care of him."

The "he" turned out to be a "she," and Vernon named her Bitch.
He put her in the backseat on the cushion next to my map box, and
we took off again.

We encountered no more Americans on the road toward
Mayenne. I realized that we were in the area known as "the void,"
somewhere between the combat command and the following mop-
up elements. I knew that CCB was moving fast, and the faster it
moved the greater this void became. I did not know whether
Mayenne was in our hands or whether CCB had bypassed it and gone
ahead; in any event, I did not want to go into Mayenne after dark.

It was beginning to get dark, and I thought it best to find a place
to bivouac for the night. We saw a small field on the left of the road
with a dry creek running through it. Poplar trees and heavy hedges
flanked both sides of the creek. We decided this would be a good
place to stop.

Vernon found an opening in the hedges where wagons had
crossed the little stream, and he drove the Jeep through the opening into the creek bed. It was flat and sandy, about ten feet wide and
four feet below the level of the field. This made for perfect camouflage; the entire Jeep and all our equipment were below ground level.
Someone walking past would not be able to see us.

I laid out our bedrolls and put an M1 rifle on each side. We decided to eat K rations; it was late and we were both too tired to deal
with our mess kits. The K rations came in a small waterproof box and
were of three types: breakfast, lunch, and supper. The breakfast box
contained a small can of scrambled eggs and bacon bits pressed into
a patty, which was tasty once you got used to it. Lunch consisted of a
can of Cheddar cheese, and supper was a can of potted meat. All the
meals contained Waverley crackers, which had lots of protein. There
was also coffee, powdered milk, sugar, cigarettes, and toilet paper.

Vernon gave Bitch a can of potted meat. She was ravenous and consumed it in no time. We decided not to build a fire, because it was

getting late. We drank water instead of coffee. One thing I wasn't going to do was light up a cigarette and get in the bedroll; I had learned my lesson in the Bois du Hommet.

I suppose all soldiers develop certain hang-ups after they've been in combat for a while; I've had my share of them. Vernon's main hang-up was that the Germans might sneak up on us at night and throw a hand grenade into the foxhole. It was easy enough to assure him that this was highly improbable when we were with the combat command inside the security line, but when we were in the open and on our own, the situation was different.

Suddenly, I began to appreciate the dog. Bitch seemed to be extremely intelligent and would do what we told her. She had an almost instinctive understanding of the situation, and she fitted in perfectly with our sleeping arrangements. Vernon placed her between our bedrolls; she snuggled against him and we all dozed off.

I woke with a nudge from Vernon.

"Lieutenant, somebody's in those bushes on the other side of the bank."

Bitch had apparently heard the noise first, but instead of barking she nuzzled Vernon to wake him.

I strained my ears, listening intently; suddenly, I heard a crackling noise as if someone took a step in dry grass. I reached under my combat jacket, which I was using for a pillow, and took out my .45 pistol. I slowly pulled back the bolt and engaged the cartridge in the chamber. Vernon took the safety off his M1 carbine.

There was another crackling noise. If it was a German patrol, there would probably be several of them and they would be making more noise than this. If it was two or three stragglers who had seen us come into the field earlier, they could be trying to bushwhack us. On the other hand, it was dark and they probably couldn't see us as well as we could see them.

After waiting some time with bated breath, we heard no further noises. I was beginning to think it was just a rotten limb falling. I whispered to Vernon that I didn't think the noise was anything unusual, trying to convince him and myself at the same time. I lay back down with my pistol at my side and was just beginning to doze off when Vernon nudged me again. As I emerged out of a semisleep, I could definitely hear a crackling noise. But then the noises came further and further apart, then ceased altogether. Exhausted, we both finally drifted off to sleep.

When I awakened it was barely daylight. Bitch was snuggled against Vernon; her muzzle rested on his shoulder blade, and he had his right arm around her. Lying there in the early morning light, Vernon looked like a little boy snuggling his teddy bear. I was glad we had kept the dog. What a terrible thing war does; it takes young men in the flower of their youth, it demeans them, it humiliates them, it destroys the last vestige of dignity. It sometimes kills or horribly maims them. Those who survive are never quite the same.

I had gotten out the K rations and loaded my bedroll and the two rifles back into the Jeep when Vernon awakened. "Lieutenant, did you ever figure out what was making that noise?"

"No, Vernon, I didn't hear a thing after I finally dozed off the last time."

Vernon got up and stretched, then walked about fifty feet downstream in the dry creek bed to take a leak. He suddenly called out, "Lieutenant, I found it."

A large goose and her goslings had a nest in the high weeds on the embankment. Apparently, every time she ruffled her wings, they made a crackling noise. She appeared to be asleep and we did not disturb her.

We took off down the road and soon found CCB maintenance company just west of Pré en Pail.

General Rose Assumes Command

All of the division's units reverted back to division control on August 12 under our new division commander, Gen. Maurice Rose. General Rose had led a combat command in the 2d Armored Division and had an outstanding record in North Africa as well as in Normandy.

Combat Command B had taken the brunt of the heavy fighting in Mortain and suffered severe casualties. The command's four task forces, plus elements of the 2d Armored Division and additional infantry, engaged three German panzer divisions and one German infantry division in a bitter battle around Mortain. With the timely assistance of the Ninth Air Force and the RAF, they finally brought the

Germans to a halt and turned them back, though not without severe losses. Task Force Hogan alone lost twenty-three tanks plus a number of personnel. The Germans also suffered severe losses. The 116th Panzer Division lost approximately half its strength. The 85th Division was severely depleted, as were the 2d Panzer and 17th SS Panzergrenadier Divisions. The objective of preventing the Germans from breaking through to Avranches and splitting the First and Third Armies in two had been accomplished.

As the division regrouped west of Pré en Pail, new personnel replacements arrived, and the maintenance, ordnance maintenance, and ordnance supply units once again worked around the clock to repair and replace all the damaged tanks and other vehicles. By August 12 the personnel strength had been rebuilt to about 91 percent officers and 96 percent enlisted men. The artillery was up to 100 percent strength, tanks to 94 percent, and the other vehicles to approximately 98 percent. The remarkable American supply and maintenance system had shown its worth again. The division had been thoroughly bloodied and tested. In spite of our heavy casualties, we had learned invaluable lessons.

When we first started in Normandy, the officers rode the column's lead tank, but most of the time the lead tank was knocked out. If the officer was killed and his tank was knocked out, the platoon lost its command center as well as any radio contact with the company.

The platoon commander started taking the third tank in the column, which gave him a better chance to coordinate the platoon and maintain contact with the company commander. If the lead tank survived the day, it would rotate back to the rear of the column and the next tank would take its turn.

The platoon commanders also learned that they should not frontally assault German positions fortified with tanks and antitank guns. Instead, they should lie back and call for artillery support, then try to outflank the target. This was strictly according to Armored Force Tactical Doctrine, but it took many bitter losses for some men to learn it.

In other cases, the tank column would unknowingly run up on a German roadblock and come under withering high-velocity antitank fire. Sometimes, the Germans would let a column pass and catch them on the flank, exposing the tanks' vulnerable side armor. Time and again it was thrown up to us that we simply did not have a heavy tank to match that of the Germans. As a result, many Americans were bleeding and dying needlessly.

Closing the Falaise Pocket

On August 12, the Saint-Lô breakthrough entered its third and final stage. The left flank of the German army had been shattered, and General Patton's Third Army was now ranging deep into enemy territory with little resistance. The First Army had driven far to the south, then swung east to roll up the shattered flank of the German army. The German 7th Army tried to retreat as rapidly as possible using the roads between Condé-sur-Noireau and Argentan. The American First Army was then ordered to swing north and the British Second Army and Canadian First Army to drive south in an attempt to meet and cut off the German retreat.

In the early morning hours of August 13, the VII Corps, now back up to strength, launched an attack toward the north, led by the 3d Armored Division. It was to meet British units driving south from Thury-Harcourt and the Caen area. Combat Command A advanced along the right flank and CCB to the left. The task forces of the two combat commands would sometimes cross over one another.

By this time, we had driven so deep into enemy territory from the beachhead (approximately a hundred miles) that we were through the dense part of the *bocage*. The entire corps was moving rapidly in fairly open tank country. The 2d Armored Division with its accompanying infantry secured the left flank. The motorized infantry divisions leapfrogged over one another and secured the strongpoints that the armored divisions had bypassed.

This was classic armored warfare. The situation was highly fluid, and it was extremely difficult to know where the friendly and enemy units were at any one time. We did have the tremendous advantage of our airpower dominating the skies in the daylight hours. The Germans could not spot our positions by air, whereas we had a fairly good idea of theirs. Although resistance may have started out much lighter, as we advanced north it became stronger and stronger; the Germans were determined to prevent the encirclement of their 7th Army.

After passing through Carrouges and Rânes, we found much heavier resistance and had to contend with an unanticipated situation. Political rather than military, it came as a complete surprise to the troops in the field. General de Gaulle had insisted that French troops be involved in the battle of France. On the surface, this appeared to be a good idea, because the Poles and other Europeans had been involved with both British and American troops for some time. However, bringing in an entire division that had not been training with British and American units was a different matter than working with small continental European units attached to either British or American units.

The French 2d Armored Division, which did not participate in the Normandy landings, suddenly appeared on the road between Pré en Pail and Rânes. Although the higher commanders must have known about this, the troops in the field were generally uninformed and were much surprised to see the French. With extremely poor march discipline, the French got their half-tracks scattered up and down the highway, then stopped without pulling off the highway, which blocked the roads for our follow-up infantry reinforcements and maintenance and supply units. This impeded both CCA and CCB, which were trying to get forward before the Germans could set up strong roadblock positions.

Finally, General Collins ordered the French division commander to get his troops completely off the road and clear the way. This was not intended to disparage the French troops, who I'm sure were dedicated brave soldiers trying to help liberate their homeland. It merely demonstrated that an extremely poor decision had been made at a higher level. The French 2d Armored Division later performed extremely well when they were attached to the French First Army under a French army commander with their own communications.

The fighting between Rânes and Fromentel became much heavier as the Germans brought down crack units to prevent our trapping the 7th Army. As CCA advanced along the main highway toward Rânes, CCB traveled a parallel route toward the high ground just

southwest of Fromentel. Both CCA and CCB task forces bypassed all
heavy opposition where possible. At night they would coil off the
road and set up their perimeter defenses with tanks and infantry in
order for the maintenance, supply, and medics to work all night. The
Germans, in the meantime, would completely surround the task
forces, forcing them to break out again the next day in order to advance. After the fall of Rânes, both CCA and CCB continued northward.

The road between Rânes and Fromentel was a typical French
country road, fairly straight with lines of poplar trees on both sides.
The Germans cut down alternate trees on either side of the road to
form roadblocks, in some instances more than a hundred yards deep.
They sewed Teller mines on both sides of the road and covered the
roadblocks with heavy antitank and automatic weapons fire. Bands
of Panther tanks roamed the countryside and covered the flanks. In
one incident, the tanks hid in a cave; they would come out to fire
and then go back into the cave, making them difficult to find.

The Germans were desperate by this time, and some of their SS
troops began to resort to brutality. One SS unit infiltrated one of our
703d Antitank Battalion positions and captured the platoon commander and four soldiers. One of the soldiers, a combat engineer,
managed to escape. Shortly thereafter, the young officer and the
three men were discovered; they had all been shot in cold blood.
This enraged our men and undoubtedly resulted in severe retalia-
tion later against other SS troopers.

The battle for Fromentel became a series of intensive separate actions, completely isolated and highly fluid. The fighting in some instances was at extremely close range. One of our tank destroyers
knocked out two Panther tanks at a range of twenty-five yards. The
tank destroyer commander dismounted to try to rescue the crew
from one of the burning tanks, but he was killed by exploding ammunition in the German tank. Even under the severe strain of combat, the quality of mercy was always present.

The Germans were putting up a desperate, courageous fight, and
in some cases fanatics refused to surrender. Our tanks came upon
an isolated group of young Hitler *Jugend* who had been drafted into
the 1st SS Adolf Hitler Panzer Division, which at one time had been

Hitler's personal bodyguard. One tank commander reported that the young German soldiers would not surrender. In their fanatical, desperate last efforts, they had to be gunned down by the tanks and finally physically run over and crushed in their foxholes. The carnage sickened the tank crew.

The situation in Fromentel became so fluid that it was extremely difficult to tell which part of the town the Germans occupied and which part the Americans occupied. This confused the air force, and on two occasions CCA had to abandon positions when they were mistakenly bombed by P38s. Finally, after seesawing back and forth, CCA occupied the town. Although we had expected to meet 21st Army Group units before this time, the Canadian First Army, which was leading the group, was having a hard time and was still north of us.

On August 17, CCB moved north and west of Fromentel and secured hill 214 just south of Putanges. On the same day, twelve hundred German armored vehicles plus several thousand other vehicles streamed across our front and came under heavy bombardment by both British and American artillery and airpower.

On the morning of the eighteenth, elements of CCB made contact with Canadian armored units south of Putanges. Although the VII Corps captured approximately five thousand German prisoners, and other units captured many more, a number of German units escaped. Field Marshal Kluge, apparently anticipating our action, had moved his major gasoline dumps forty miles to the east, which gave the Germans sufficient fuel to head east across northern France. German units that escaped were badly mauled and suffered a crushing defeat.

On August 19, the infantry continued to mop up the smaller, isolated pockets of resistance. On August 20 and 21, the 3d Armored Division reassembled for a two-day maintenance and supply period in an area just south of Rânes. The 23d Engineers set up a shower area in a nearby stream. I didn't give it much thought at the time, but later I realized that my last shower had been on July 1, just before we left Codford, England. It had been fifty days since I'd had a shower! For some of the fellows in CCA who came over before us, it had been more than sixty-five days. Even after we had moved out into the field at Codford, about a month before D day, we still en-

joyed the luxury of a shower each night at the nearby Quonset hut
lavatory.

Personal sanitation in the field is difficult at best. I was able to
brush my teeth and wash my face almost daily and shave with cold
water every third or fourth day, but I had no change of clothing except clean socks. When my turn for a shower finally came, I took off
my helmet, pistol, combat jacket, money belt, regular belt, and combat boots and put them in one pile along with the contents of my
pockets. I stripped off my wool shirt, wool trousers, long underwear
tops and bottoms, and socks and made a dirty clothes pile next to
the shower area. Having worn the same shirt, trousers, and long underwear for fifty-one days, I felt that they were raunchy enough to
walk to the pile by themselves.

The quartermaster gave us fresh cakes of soap, and I indulged myself even though the water was ice cold. When we came out of the
shower, we were each given a clean olive-drab towel and a new wool
shirt, wool pants, socks, and long underwear. We never wore khaki
uniforms and always wore long underwear, because in northern Europe the evenings were cool even in summertime.

Regrouping After Falaise

On the road between Rânes and Fromentel, the division had been
severely bloodied, and our losses in personnel and combat vehicles
were high. On one roadblock alone where the Germans had laced
the highway with felled trees for a hundred yards or so, we lost eighteen tanks. Few of these were recovered, because most of them had
been fired at until they burned. The tanks that could be recovered
from that spot and other areas were dragged back to the VCP south
of Rânes, where the maintenance and ordnance troops worked
feverishly to repair them.

Replacement tank crews, infantry, and other troops were also
brought in and integrated into their units. The combat troops and
the ordnance, maintenance, and supply troops had developed a
healthy respect for one another. The combat troops laid their lives
on the line constantly, and we were determined to do everything possible to supply them with the best and most efficiently repaired com-
bat-ready equipment. We did this knowing that our new M4A1 tank,

even with the 76mm gun, was hopelessly outmatched by the heavier German tanks.

The M4 tank had two types of power traverse on the turret—hydraulic and electric. The hydraulic drive was smoother and easier to maintain. We went to great pains in England when we were drawing our initial tanks to select only those with hydraulic traverse. Although many of these tanks had now been replaced, we tried to continue using the hydraulic traverse.

The Ford Motor Company, under the direction of the ordnance department, had taken the British Rolls Royce Merlin engine and cut it down to eight cylinders. This made an excellent 550-horsepower tank engine, about 25 percent more powerful than the radial engine. The V-8 design made the engine easier to maintain, and it had fewer problems with spark-plug fouling. Because of this, we selected Ford engine tanks for replacements when we could get them.

When tank crews came to pick up their tanks, the new replacement crewmen had no idea of what the tank was like. Whenever a tank was knocked out, one to three men were usually killed or wounded, so it was not long before the new recruits outnumbered the veterans. If the recruits survived their first engagement, they became veterans themselves.

The ordnance maintenance crews did everything they could to familiarize the new crews with the tanks, particularly any new equipment. This participation became more prevalent as the number of veteran tankers continued to decline. It became more and more apparent that the ability of the division to revive after heavy combat operations depended largely on the ability of maintenance crews to train the new people and get the tanks and crews ready to go again.

Major Dick Johnson, as the ranking maintenance officer in the combat command, had the responsibility of recovering vehicles from combat areas. He insisted on every precaution while recovering vehicles under combat conditions. Most maintenance men had eighteen months to three years of training and were deemed irreplaceable. It was unwise to risk their lives to try to recover burned-up tanks that could not be repaired.

Tank Recovery in Combat

When a firefight broke out, several tanks and other vehicles would be knocked out. The maintenance crews from the regiment would go forward with T2 recovery vehicles to evacuate the shot-up equipment. If there were mines, the engineers would clear a path for the recovery vehicles. If the area was still under direct fire, we would wait, because a T2 recovery vehicle and maintenance crew would be a far greater loss to the division than a few shot-up tanks.

Even after the recovery operation had started, the enemy fire would often start again and the recovery crews would take cover. Sometimes, the Germans would use an abandoned vehicle as a decoy in hopes that a maintenance crew would come to recover it and they could catch them in the open.

One day I approached a knocked-out tank on the forward slope of a hill. I came up from the rear to study the damage and also get the "W" number. When I stepped in front of the tank to determine the extent of the penetration in the faceplate, I heard a dull thud like the popping of a champagne cork. I immediately recognized it as the muzzle blast of a mortar. I jumped behind the tank just before the round landed on the other side, and the tank took the blast. I got out of there as fast as I could and we recovered the tank later.

A New Commanding Officer

By August 20, we had gotten the division in good shape. We were ordered to move out the next morning toward Chartres and to Paris in a routine road march, which meant that the roads had already been traveled by friendly troops and we would probably not encounter anything but sporadic enemy resistance.

I headed over to the maintenance battalion headquarters for the night. Even though it was late and getting dark by the time I left C Company, I knew there was a good chance of getting a hot meal there.

As I approached the mess tent, I passed a three-quarter-ton weapons carrier and heard the tune of the old Negro spiritual "Dry Bones." I could tell by the sound of the voices that the singers were feeling no pain. I caught some of the words.

Oh the wheel bone's connected to the axle bones,
the axle bone's connected to the differential,
the differential's connected to the propeller shaft,
here we go round and round.
   Oh the propeller shaft's connected to the transmission,
the transmission's connected to the flywheel,
the flywheel's connected to the crankshaft,
here we go round and round.
   Them bones, them bones, them dry bones,
them bones, them bones, them dry bones,
here we go round and round.

I thought I recognized the voices, and when I looked under the tailgate I saw four of my old lieutenant buddies, Nibbelink, Lincoln, Binckley, and Lucas. They had managed to stash away several bottles of Eau de Vie, a powerful Norman Cognac, and had gotten loaded to the gills.

"Cooper, where in the hell have you been? We've been waiting on you. We got some big news!"

"I've been over at C Company working my damn butt off. I haven't had time to get drunk like you fellows, but I'm ready now. Lay it on me."

Lincoln passed me the bottle and I took a big swig. I thought it was the worst liquor I had ever tasted, worse than the white lightning corn whiskey I had sampled as a teenager back in Huntsville.

Ernie tossed back his head and broke out in a broad, boyish grin. "Cooper, listen to this. Would you believe that Colonel Cowhey is no longer commanding the maintenance battalion? Colonel McCarthy is our new CO."

Cowhey had been transferred to the XX Armored Corps to serve as ordnance officer under General Walker, who had been commander of the 3d Armored Division back at Camp Polk. Walker thought highly of Colonel Cowhey.

I felt immense relief. Was it really possible that we no longer would have to live under the constant threat of Cowhey's distorted ideas about having the most battlefield-decorated maintenance battalion in the entire U.S. Army? If this transfer was true, our chances of survival had increased immeasurably. Cowhey had many fine characteristics, but his deep frustration affected his judgment. Apparently, this went back to his early days, when he graduated near the top of his class at West Point.

It was a custom in the regular army during the 1930s for the top 10 percent of the West Point graduating class to be chosen to go to Fort Belvoir for engineering training. After two years at Belvoir, the top 10 percent of that group was given an opportunity to go to the Massachusetts Institute of Technology (MIT) for another two years and be trained as ordnance officers. These young officers belonged to an elite group during the mid-1930s in the peacetime army; there were only six hundred of them when the war started. The remaining ordnance officers had to be drawn from the nine universities that taught ordnance ROTC.

When World War II started, the situation began to reverse itself. As the army quadrupled in size, the vacancies in the combat units were many times greater than those in ordnance. Thus, many of Cowhey's former classmates in infantry, artillery, or cavalry, all of whom he had outranked, advanced much more rapidly than he did.

Cowhey's combat military career ended tragically. He was approaching a roadblock near Trier when he was stopped by an infantry captain and warned that a German roadblock was right around the corner. Cowhey ignored the warning and proceeded down the road. The Jeep had barely gotten a hundred yards when the captain heard a wild burst of machine-gun fire. He crawled around the bend and saw Cowhey's Jeep on the shoulder of the road. The driver was dead and Cowhey was severely wounded, with many machine-gun penetrations in his stomach and torso. This captain, at great risk, dragged Cowhey to safety. He was evacuated back to the States, where he eventually recovered after a long hospitalization.

I met Cowhey, who was then a captain, when I first arrived at Camp Polk in June 1941. For the first couple of days he was as nice as he could be; he took me around the post and introduced me to my company commander, then took me to the ordnance office and described the procedures used there. I remember being warned by another second lieutenant, who had been there several months longer, about Cowhey's vicious temper.

"You've really got this guy all wrong," I said. "He's all right once you get to know him."

"You just wait and see," the lieutenant said.

I didn't have to wait long. I was assigned to A Company as shop officer but had no knowledge of tanks and other armored vehicles. I was fortunate to have Gus Snikers as my shop master sergeant. An enlisted man in World War I, Snikers was probably the most experienced and best master sergeant in the entire ordnance department.

A Company was assigned to remove a 75mm M2 tank gun and its mount from an M3 tank and set it on a wooden platform for instruction purposes. These tanks were new to us, and no one in the division had ever tried to remove one of the guns. It was Sergeant Snikers who finally figured out how to do it.

While the crews worked on the gun, I designed a wooden mount. I knew that it had to be extremely rigid and heavy to support the gun while the men practiced on it, and I was having difficulty getting the right size timbers. The whole project took longer than we had anticipated.

The next morning in the officers' mess, Captain Cowhey was seated at his table drinking his after-breakfast coffee surrounded by a group of the higher-ranking officers in the battalion. I had discovered that this was a customary practice; the officers were trying to get their points in and at the same time do a little brownnosing. I was seated at another table with some of my lieutenant buddies when the captain called out, "Lieutenant Cooper."

"Yes, sir," I replied as I picked up my cup of coffee and headed toward his table, overjoyed that I had been invited to the inner sanctum. Little did I realize what was about to take place.

"Lieutenant, I've been telling the other officers about the gun mount you've been making," said Cowhey. "Is it ready for testing this morning?"

"No, sir," I replied. "We encountered some difficulty in obtaining the right size timbers. I think it will be ready this afternoon."

Immediately Cowhey's expression changed. The veins on his neck bulged as a red flush rose in his cheeks. His dark, piercing eyes fluttered as he looked at me, and he appeared to be momentarily speechless. In the next instant, however, he exploded.

"Lieutenant Cooper, when I ask you a question, I expect an answer and no damn excuses. It's either, 'Yes, sir' or 'No, sir.' Do you understand?"

I was caught so completely by surprise that I could not answer. Before I could collect my thoughts, he started out again. "Another thing, you are an officer in the United States Army and you are supposed to know, not think. Don't you ever tell me that you think something. You either know it or you don't know it. Do you understand?"

It took me a few moments to regain my composure, and I replied rather weakly, "Yes, sir, I understand."

Like a puppy with his tail between his legs, I went back to the table where my lieutenant buddies were sitting. They couldn't help but hear what had transpired, and as I sat down I felt completely humiliated. The silence was deafening. Finally, it was broken by Bissell Travis, the lieutenant who had cautioned me about Cowhey in the first place. He could have easily said, "I told you so," but instead he said, "Don't worry, Cooper, he treats all new officers that way, and this just happened to be your turn. It's his way of indoctrinating a new officer into his way of thinking."

I knew that Cowhey had violated one of the basic principles of conduct: Never reprimand a subordinate in front of others. If a reprimand is due, it should be done privately and on an individual basis, between the superior and the subordinate.

I had been through a military cadet hazing system at VMI that was probably equal to or more severe than what Cowhey had gone through at West Point. The cadet hazing system is designed specifically to humiliate a person and convey the lesson that until you learn how to take it, you shouldn't dish it out. If you are going to be an officer and give orders, you have to learn how to receive them, regardless of the conditions.

In spite of his shortcomings, Cowhey exerted many positive influences. His tremendous drive and determination to get the job done as quickly as possible, come hell or high water, was the type of thinking that an officer must develop in combat. Although I have ambivalent feelings about Cowhey, his total influence on me was positive, and I have always been thankful for it.

To Paris and Across the Seine

The next morning, we proceeded south to Carrouges and on toward Alençon. The 7th Armored Division, which we considered our sister division because it was activated at Camp Polk and drew its initial cadre from our division, was traveling on another road somewhat south of us.

As their forward recon elements approached a small French village, they were reportedly met by a German officer with a white flag who, after surrendering, said he'd left a small contingent of men in the village to protect a large poison gas depot. He was afraid that if the men abandoned the depot and went back to Germany, French civilians might release the gas and blame it on the Germans. The recon officer sent word back, took all the Germans prisoner, and impounded the gas dump. Our intelligence was evidently correct that the Germans had poison gas in northern France.

During the day, I had to drop back several times to see if I could assist any broken-down vehicles. The tail end of each column was always followed by an ordnance maintenance wrecker and a three-quarter-ton weapons carrier with several tank mechanics. With breakdowns strung out over fifty miles of road, it was important to keep the ordnance company commander informed.

During a routine road march of this type, one could appreciate the magnitude of maintaining an armored division on the move. The 3d Armored Division reinforced had about 17,000 men and 4,200 vehicles. All of this equipment was of a relatively new design, and there had been little field testing prior to issuing the equipment to the troops. As a young engineer, I could only partially appreciate the tremendous genius and effort that provided our military with great quantities of good equipment. All of our wheeled vehicles, artillery, ammunition systems, and firepower control equipment was excellent. The weakness was the gross inferiority of our tanks and anti-tank weapons.

As we entered Chartres near sunset on August 24, we encountered elements of the French 2d Armored Division. In the main plaza in front of the cathedral, there was a great celebration going on. Young French soldiers were being plied with Cognac, flowers, and young French mademoiselles from every direction.

Of course we were jealous, but we were also resentful that while we were pressing on, these men stayed back and had a ball. We found out later that they were waiting for General de Gaulle to come from London so that the French division commander could parade his troops through the Arc de Triomphe in Paris the next day with General de Gaulle while all the newsreel cameras were rolling. Thus, French history books could tell French children in generations to come that French troops had liberated Paris, with little emphasis on the contribution of the U.S. Army.

It was after dark when Vernon and I arrived at a little French village near Corbeil, just south of Paris. We decided to bivouac in a village green surrounded by houses in the middle of town. Seeing a couple of half-tracks and a scout car parked nearby, we felt that this must be a relatively safe place and for the first time decided not to dig a foxhole. We laid our sleeping bags and bedrolls on the village green and soon were sound asleep.

I was awakened early the next morning by a beautiful young voice. *"Voulez-vous du café?"*

I looked up and saw a lovely little French girl about ten years old standing beside the bedroll. *"Voulez-vous du café?"* she repeated.

"Oui," I replied in my best French. We stashed our bedrolls, followed her across the street, and entered the kitchen of a small house, where her mother and father were seated around a wooden table. They both looked worn and haggard, evidently from having stayed up all night for fear the Germans might return to the village before the Americans arrived. Upon seeing us, they broke into broad grins. We shook hands and sat down at the table. The mother got up and poured a steaming hot brown mixture into a cup.

"Ersatz café," she said. The imitation coffee was made from roasted crushed barley grains. It took a great deal of imagination to think that it resembled coffee, but it was hot and tasted good.

Our conversation consisted of my marginal French and the little girl's English, which she had picked up in school. I was soon to learn that many French, Belgian, and German children had a much better knowledge of English and other foreign languages than American children of the same age. As our limited conversation continued, I began to get the feeling that this little French family was typical of the urban French people who had suffered a great deal under the Germans for the last four years. Hardly any French family had been spared the consequences of the war.

The family seemed genuinely appreciative of our efforts and showed us as much hospitality as possible with their limited resources. In turn we gave them several packages of Nestle powdered coffee and sweetener. As we left their home and walked across the street to our Jeep, we heard *"Vive l'Amérique"* and *"Vive la France"* all the way.

The division's forward elements had already crossed the Seine on pontoon bridges. We crossed on the morning of August 26 and rapidly followed the fast-moving tank columns. The advance columns proceeded to the little village of Saint-Denis-le-Gast, just east of Paris, where they met with other American armored columns that had crossed the river north of Paris. This sealed off the escape of those Germans who had not been captured in the city itself. The battle of western France and the liberation of Paris had ended.

5
From Paris to Soissons

Logistic Innovations

By this time, the success of the invasion and breakout had become obvious. When the breakthrough occurred west of Saint-Lô on the morning of July 26, the total combined Allied forces included approximately thirty divisions. Opposing them were seventy-two German divisions, concentrated in areas where the Germans thought the landings were most likely to occur.

The round-the-clock bombing of the bridges over the Seine and Loire Rivers, which had started four to five months before the invasion, should have tipped off the Germans that Normandy was being isolated. Because the heaviest bombing was in the Pas de Calais area directly across the English Channel from Dover, the Germans were confused. Not until July 25, the night before the Saint-Lô breakthrough, was Rommel able to secure the release of the panzer divisions in reserve in the Pas de Calais area. But by then it was too late to stop the Allied juggernaut.

The Allies had worries of their own. They were busy solving massive logistic problems moving, arming, and feeding their armies. Despite the military bureaucracy, British and American troops showed great ability to generate innovative ideas. Even more surprising, those in authority listened. For example, even with the largest invasion armada ever assembled—more than four thousand ships—we had the landing craft capacity to handle only parts of seven divisions. By careful coordination and quick turnaround time at the English ports, our forces unloaded an average of thirty thousand troops a day and vast amounts of cargo. Precast concrete caissons sunk along the beaches with pontoon bridges between them, known as Mulberrys, were of tremendous help in unloading the cargo on rough days.

One of the major logistic problems of the invasion was the gasoline supply. A full combat load for our division alone was more than 300,000 gallons, which amounted to three hundred GMC trucks each carrying 1,000 gallons in 5-gallon cans. In the initial planning, it had been recognized that the Germans would attempt to hold the Channel ports. Without places for tankers to dock, some other means of handling large volumes of fuel would have to be used until the Channel ports could be opened.

The British built large steel spools approximately a hundred feet in diameter. Around these spools they wrapped quarter-mile lengths of four-inch steel pipe that had been prewelded and had quick-coupling flanges on the ends of each section. Attached to the bridle of each drum was a large hydraulic gear reducer, which converted the drum into a giant winch. The bridle was in turn hooked to the stern of a powerful oceangoing tug. With one end of the pipe fastened to a shoreline pressure pumping station, the tug proceeded to cross the Channel with the pipe unrolling. Drums of this size could contain many miles of pipe.

On the other end of the line, the U.S. Army Corps of Engineers used lightweight four-inch pipe with quick-disconnect couplings that would fit into a GMC truck. As the truck moved slowly down the road without stopping, a crew inside the truck would throw the pipe out on the ground. A pipe crew following behind them on foot would fasten the joints together. Every few miles, a pumping station would be installed to boost the pressure. This fuel supply system depended upon thousands of GMC trucks operating continuously.

Ordnance Innovations

Many innovative ideas, such as the American hedge chopper, came from the field. The British produced the "flail" tank as an answer to the severe mine problem. When a tank struck a mine, the explosion would break the track and sometimes tear off a bogey wheel assembly. In some cases the Germans would stack mines on top of one another, which generated sufficient force to blow through the one-inch armor plate in the bottom of a tank and kill the crew.

The British flail tank had a large cylindrical drum mounted on heavy, adjustable brackets stretched across the front of the tank. Welded to the drum at various points were six-foot lengths of heavy chain. As the tank moved forward, the drum would rotate, and centrifugal force would cause the chains to flail against the ground. If they hit a mine, it would usually detonate without damaging the tank. Normally, these flail tanks were effective in a minefield; however, the horsepower required to drive the flail limited the mobility of the tank in extremely rugged terrain or in muddy fields.

Some tank crews mounted sandbags and even spare track blocks and wooden timbers on the faceplate of the tank for added protection against the murderous German antitank guns. The will to survive increased the innovative spirit.

Soldiers sometimes put sandbags on the floor of a Jeep to protect against mine blasts, which could blow the quarter-ton Jeeps to pieces. Although this might have been effective against small antipersonnel mines, I never felt it would do much good against an antitank mine. We never used sandbags in our Jeep, because I decided that they were too heavy and would slow us down. In running the gauntlet at night, speed was our best protection.

In spite of the American tanks' inferior guns and armor compared to German tanks, they were faster and more mobile on paved highways. Tracks of American tanks lasted longer and achieved greater highway speeds than those on German tanks. The key was in the design of the track block itself. The track would arc upward when it went over the final drive sprocket and would conform to the sprocket contour. As the track went down to the first bogey wheel, it was straightened out, and the tank bogeys rolled along the track. When the track reached the last bogey, the torsional energy stored in the rubber doughnuts within the track caused the track to pick itself up slightly and thus go over the rear outer sprocket more easily.

This made the entire track an energy accumulator. Part of the energy put into the track as it bent around the final drive sprocket was recovered when the track returned over the rear-idler sprocket. Thus, the tank could move with less horsepower, leaving more power available for speed and mobility. In addition, the rubber covering on the track shielded the tank from road shock. This, along with the rubber-tired bogey wheels, gave the track a much longer useful life. The rubber coating on the inside of the track allowed it to be turned over and reversed after the outside had been sufficiently worn. A set of tracks for an M4 medium tank would last for approximately 2,500 miles on the highway, including one reversal. This was far superior to the German tracks, which were thought to last about 500 miles per set, after which the metal pins on the track began to break excessively.

The only problem with the American track was that it was too narrow and got stuck in muddy terrain. German tanks were designed with much wider tracks that could operate over rough, muddy ground. Because most major tank engagements took place off the road, the overall effect favored the Germans.

In addition to our tanks' greater speed and mobility on the highway, all of our other armored vehicles were faster and more mobile than those of the Germans. Our self-propelled guns were mounted on tank chassis, and our half-tracks had rubber tread tracks for greater speed and longer life. The armored cars were fast and had four-wheel drive, which could be disengaged on the front wheels when driving on a paved highway. (All of our wheeled vehicles had four-wheel and six-wheel drive, which could be disengaged on the front wheels when necessary.) This kept the front and rear wheels from fighting one another and increased the life of the vehicle power trains.

Advance from Paris to the Northeast

The excellent Allied intelligence no doubt contributed greatly to our success to this point. Unknown to us, the British had secured a model of the German Enigma decoding machine and were using it to decode German messages. In addition, they had captured a German field order describing the German retreat routes from Normandy back into Germany. A retreat is always difficult, and with our air superiority it was hard for the Germans to move during daylight. Even though a large part of the German 7th Army managed to escape the Falaise Pocket, they now had a new danger ahead. With our speed and mobility, we plunged deep into France and swung around Paris to try to intercept the German columns.

After meeting other American armored units at Saint-Denis-le-Gast and isolating Paris, we headed toward Meaux, on the Marne River fifty miles east of Paris. This was where the French army had stopped the German advance in World War I. We were soon to pass through many sites of the most bitter fighting of that war.

That evening I had to take the combat loss report back to division trains, across the river at Corbeil. As I passed through a small French village, I had an eerie feeling. The village square was completely deserted, and roadblocks made of wagons, furniture, and automobiles blocked the entrances to the town. All of a sudden, the doors of shops and houses flew open and out rushed mobs of people with hoes, rakes, and German rifles screaming, *"Vive l'Amérique! Vive l'Amérique!"* Next they screamed in broken English that the *"marchal"* were coming. I didn't know who the *marchal* were.

Bitch, our adopted mascot, stood on the hood of the Jeep taking it all in. The French children came out and kissed the dog and hung garlands of flowers around her neck. They plied us with champagne and Cognac as though we were great heroes. I was a little nonplussed. I soon learned that they wanted us to take command of the French garrison and fight the *marchal,* who were just a few miles down the road. One Frenchman, who I assumed was the mayor, spoke good English. He explained that the *marchal* was a splinter group of Frenchmen who had collaborated with the Germans. Apparently, the German troops had given them guns.

I tried to explain to the mayor that I had to get back across the river to deliver my combat loss report. I also told him that there was an engineer bridge company about a mile down the road at the river crossing, and if they needed further assistance they could go there. He seemed to understand, and I departed among many *"Vive l'Amériques"* and *"Vive la Libérations."* On my return trip the next morning, I passed through the same village and saw that the roadblocks had been removed. There were no signs of fighting, so I assumed that the *marchal* never came.

I joined Combat Command B at Meaux, and the division immediately moved forward toward Soissons in multiple columns, CCA on the right, CCB on the left. We were well into the German communication zone, and German communications were completely disrupted, with German combat troops trying to retreat behind the Siegfried line. Whenever we came upon a German unit, whether it was a combat unit or communication zone troops, they fought hard. Even though we were moving rapidly, we still had considerable casualties in these engagements.

Soissons appeared to be the next point the Germans would pass through, and the division pushed rapidly in order to get there first. The task force I was following chose a secondary paved road through a wooded area to the left of the main highway. The pavement soon yielded to dirt, and we found ourselves on a logging road. As we penetrated further into the woods, we began to encounter sniper fire. It got heavier as we approached Villers-Cotterêts, a small village about two-thirds of the way to Soissons. I tried to stay as close as possible to the half-tracks. The tanks and half-tracks constantly blasted any suspicious clumps of bushes. Finally, we emerged from the woods into the village. From then on we followed a paved road.

On the morning of August 28, the division advanced rapidly toward Soissons, although we encountered numerous firefights along the way. At Braine, elements of the 486th Antiaircraft Battalion entered the town and saw a train pulling out of the station. It carried a German tank, several armored cars, and a company of infantry with supplies. The battalion opened fire and exploded the locomotive's boiler. As the German soldiers rushed out to man the tank and the armored cars, they were gunned down by automatic weapons fire. Although the 37mm ammunition bounced harmlessly off the tank like Ping-Pong balls, it kept the Germans from manning the tank.

At about the same time, elements of the 32d Armored Regiment and 54th Armored Field Artillery encountered another train in the same area. It had four Mark VI King Tiger tanks aboard and a number of other vehicles, plus many soldiers and supply cars. The Americans raked this column from stem to stern and prevented the Germans from manning the tanks. This turned out to be a real debacle for the Germans; many soldiers were killed and wounded. The few who escaped into the woods were soon rounded up.

As our soldiers surveyed the wreckage in the trains, they were surprised to find that much valuable space was taken up with women's lingerie, lipstick, and perfume instead of sorely needed ammunition and food. The Germans apparently had done a good job of looting all the Paris boutiques before they pulled out. Lingerie, lipstick, and perfume made excellent trading items with young French mademoiselles. The great tragedy at Braine was that, had the Germans not taken the time for last-minute looting, the train might have left before our columns arrived, thereby sparing many German lives.

The advance to Soissons pressed on. It was known that there were a number of French pillboxes north of the city dating from World War I. The French had rebuilt and hardened them with reinforced concrete. There was concern that the Germans might use these fortifications. At the same time, General Collins requested that a detachment be sent to Château-Thierry, the site of a famous World War I battle and now occupied by elements of both the 3d and the 7th Armored Divisions.

As the division approached Soissons, they found that the main highway bridge to the north had been destroyed but that several other bridges that were damaged were still intact. General Rose was riding with a column that approached one of the bridges. Although some mines on the bridge approach had been removed, it was not known whether the bridge was safe for the armored column to cross. Without a moment's hesitation, General Rose crossed the bridge and returned safely. For this act of heroism, along with similar actions in the past, General Rose received the Distinguished Service Cross. The division crossed the river, both at Soissons and to the east, and entered the city. Finding numerous firefights, they set up the artillery to cover the road junctions that the Germans were attempting to use north of the city.

Early the next morning, I started back to the maintenance battalion headquarters, located in Meaux, to deliver my combat loss report. As I approached Villers-Cotterêts, I could not decide which road to take. According to my map, there were three possible routes: the main paved highway to the left, the central road running through the woods, which we had taken the day before, and another main highway to the right.

I wasn't about to take the road through the woods that we had been on the day before. It would have been foolish for two men in a Jeep to take a chance with all those snipers. My choice was one of the other two roads.

Suddenly, we were surrounded by a group of French civilians screaming, *"Vive l'Amérique"* and *"Vive la Libération."* Then a GMC truck appeared with a hundred German prisoners aboard. An MP sergeant riding a motorbike was in charge, and two MPs were in the cab.

The sergeant came up to my Jeep. "Lieutenant, I have a hundred prisoners here that I'm supposed to take back to Meaux. I don't know where in the hell I am. You're the ranking man; you'll have to take charge."

The last thing I needed was to be slowed down with a truckload of prisoners when I was trying to get back with my combat loss report as quickly as possible. But I knew that the sergeant was right. A cardinal principle in the army is that vital decisions must be made by the ranking man.

"Okay, let me find out what's going on," I said. "I have to go back to Meaux, too, so you can follow me."

There they were, a hundred German POWs packed in the back of an open-top truck like sardines in a can. There was just enough room for them to stand up. Some had been there so long that they had wet their pants, but the sergeant knew that if he let them out, he would never get them back. I felt little compassion for them, because I'd heard many stories of what American prisoners were made to suffer.

Vernon had taken the map out of its case and spread it on the hood of the Jeep. I assumed that the elderly Frenchman who was the most verbal in the group was the mayor of the village.

"Parlez-vous Anglais?" I asked.

"Non," he replied.

I explained in my best French that I was trying to find out which of the two roads might be clear. I knew that the Germans often closed in and blocked the roads after an armored column passed through.

The mayor kept saying, *"Non compris, non compris."* I knew he didn't understand a word I was saying. I had studied French for three years in high school and two years in college. "Cooper, if you had not been such a dumb butt and paid more attention to what was going on in class, you would know what these people were talking about."

Suddenly, a young German lieutenant leaned over the side of the truck and said to me in perfect English, "Lieutenant, I speak French, German, and English fluently and will be glad to act as your interpreter if you'll let me out of the truck."

The two MP drivers with their carbines stood behind the truck gate and the sergeant positioned himself there with his tommy gun as the lieutenant got out of the truck and stood beside me. I could tell by his bearing and the way he spoke English that he was well educated and probably from an upper-middle-class background. I also suspected that he was a dedicated Nazi.

He looked at the map. "I do not know about the road on the left; however, I do know that the road on the right would be unsafe for you now."

He pointed to a small, wooded hill about half a mile out of town and told me he had been captured there the previous day after a heavy firefight. He said that even though the Americans had knocked out his roadblock and captured him and some of his men, there were at least two more tanks and a couple of half-tracks filled with infantry that had disappeared into the woods undetected.

I knew that if one of our columns had overrun the roadblock, they would not pursue the Germans into the woods. I also knew that our infantry would not arrive until later that afternoon. If the German was telling the truth, the roadblock could have been reestablished.

Was the man lying or telling the truth? I tried to put myself in his position. If I could get the Americans to go down this road and get shot up, it would give me a chance to get rescued by German troops and free me to fight again for the Führer. There might be some embarrassment for surrendering to the Americans; however, this would be outweighed by the fact that I had misled them in order to get myself free again.

On the other hand, if we went down that road and the Germans spotted us, they would certainly see the high profile of the truck and open fire. They would not immediately know that the truck was full of German prisoners. I would have a good chance of getting my butt shot off and having a lot of my men killed. At the same time, the

American lieutenant in the low-profile Jeep might escape the fire and get away. In addition, I was at least safe as an American POW. If we could get back to the POW enclosure, we had a good chance of surviving the war.

At this moment, my thoughts were interrupted by a French schoolgirl about fourteen years old who stepped forward from the crowd of French villagers. She spoke some English and appeared to understand my poor French. She confirmed what the German lieutenant had said. Some of the villagers who had returned that morning reported that the Germans had blocked the road approximately where the German prisoner had indicated. She didn't know the situation on the left-hand road but thought the Americans had been up the road the day before.

"*Merci beaucoup,*" I said to her many times.

I made my decision and hoped I was right. I told the sergeant we were taking the road to the left. I wanted the truck to follow about sixty yards behind me and I wanted him to ride behind the truck on his motorcycle. I instructed the two MP drivers to watch for any hand signals that I might give. If I encountered a roadblock or any other resistance, I would hit the ditch on the side of the road; the truck driver was to do likewise.

Everybody mounted up and we started toward the road. By this time, the French crowd was screaming and yelling obscenities at the prisoners, giving the well-known single-finger salute.

The road was a main highway, paved and in good condition but somewhat hilly and curving for the first mile or so. As we started up a small hill curving around a high embankment, I saw on the crest of the hill a Panther tank with its gun pointed straight at us. Vernon hit the ditch and we scrambled out of the Jeep, expecting to be blasted at any second. The truck driver saw what was happening and pulled into the ditch to the left.

I grabbed an M1 rifle and a high-explosive grenade from the grenade box. Vernon grabbed his M1 carbine and we started crawling back down the ditch to the bottom of the hill. I had heard no shots from the tank and didn't hear the motor running, so I motioned to Vernon. We circled around the back side of the hill and started up the slope through the woods to a point that I thought would put us above and slightly to the rear of the tank. As we approached the crest of the hill, I could see the top of the tank turret through the woods. The cupola doors were open. I had my hand on the safety and was ready to toss the grenade into the turret when I realized that the back of the tank was completely blackened by fire. The tank was gutted. I felt a tremendous sense of relief.

From the top of the hill we could see no signs of any Germans, so we ran back to the Jeep and motioned the truck crew to move out. We went around the tank and headed down the road at top speed. Seeing the burned-out tank now appeared to be a sign that one of our columns had gone up the road the day before, but I was not sure that the Germans hadn't come back and blocked the road again. Although we proceeded with extreme caution, we felt that speed was our best defense.

About halfway between Villers-Cotterêts and Meaux, we came upon a straight, clear stretch of road about a mile and a half long. Just as we entered one end of this stretch, I saw another vehicle enter the other end headed in our direction. It appeared to be either a Jeep or a Volkswagen. We both seemed to slow down simultaneously. I was holding my rifle and told Vernon to be ready to hit the ditch at any moment.

Finally, both vehicles reached the point where we could recognize each other. I was relieved to find out that it was an American Jeep. A major and his driver were headed north and wanted to know the situation between there and Soissons. I told him that the division had occupied Soissons the night before; I also told him the route I had taken from Soissons to this point. I explained about the German snipers in the woods on the logging road and about the supposed roadblock on the west highway on the other side of Soissons. He thanked me and told me that the road to Meaux was clear as far as he knew.

When we arrived at Meaux, I turned over the sergeant and the truckload of soldiers to the POW enclosure in division trains, went to the maintenance battalion headquarters and turned in my combat loss report, then went to division trains headquarters and told them about the possible roadblock on the west road. I was told that they had already received confirming information on this roadblock and that about forty-five minutes before I came through Villers-Cotterêts, an American ambulance half-track with red crosses painted on the front and both sides and filled with wounded men was ambushed at this same roadblock. All personnel had been killed. I realized what a narrow escape I'd had.

This incident had a profound effect on me, and it is with a deep sense of humility that I recall it. I realized how life takes strange turns and how seemingly unimportant things can become of paramount importance. In all those years I studied French, I felt it was a waste of time, but I realize it was probably the very margin that saved my life and the lives of those with me.

I was reminded of this several years later when I came to Birmingham, Alabama, for an engagement party for me and my fiancée at the home of Frank Dixon, the former governor of Alabama. Dixon was the law partner of my fiancée's father. During the course of the evening, I chanced to step into the den and was immediately drawn to a map on the wall. It was of Villers-Cotterêts. The town didn't seem to have changed much from the way it looked on the map I had used in World War II and still had in my possession.

I told Governor Dixon that I was interested in the map because I'd had an extremely narrow escape in this town during the war. I wondered how he happened to have a copy of it. He told me that he'd also had a narrow escape in this area, and he pointed to an open field about three miles east of the town. This was where he'd been shot down as an observer in the Army Air Corps during World War I. His leg had been shattered, and he lay in a shell hole in no-man's-land for twenty-four hours before the medics could get to him. As a result, gangrene set in and he lost his leg. He said the map had been in his pocket when he was shot down, and he'd kept it ever since.

Soissons and Laon: Battleground of World War I

I arrived back at Soissons about noon that same day and immediately went to CCB headquarters, located in a villa on the west side of town. As I was coming out of the villa from a liaison officers' briefing, I was met by a crescendo of ack-ack fire. There were several M15 and M16 half-tracks from the 486th Antiaircraft Battalion protecting the headquarters, and all of the armored vehicles and some of the GMC trucks had .50-caliber machine guns. They seemed to open up simultaneously.

We had two L5 Cubs aloft observing artillery fire north of Soissons. As I took cover, I looked up and saw what I thought at first were P47s diving in on the area, but I realized as they got closer that they were FW190s. I assumed they were going to strafe CCB headquarters, but instead they went after the two observers flying about a thousand yards to our left at about fifteen hundred feet. They were fighters, and they came in single file one after another.

As the fighters approached our planes, our antiaircraft fire ceased to avoid hitting our own people. One of the L5s was hit and exploded in midair. The flaming wreckage plummeted to the ground. The other pilot immediately put his plane into a steep dive; he barely pulled out and skimmed the treetops before hitting the ground. The FW190 on his tail was going too fast and had to pull out. The second L5 escaped and was covered by the antiaircraft fire that started up again. The German fighters did not stay around long enough to strafe our headquarters.

I finally got out of my cover and went to see if Vernon was okay. One of the other men said that the last time he saw my driver, he was making a beeline for one of the concrete culverts under the road. That's where I found him, about ten feet inside—a much better hiding place than I'd had.

The next morning, with enemy resistance around Soissons neutralized, the division started north to Laon. By that time, C Company Maintenance Battalion Headquarters Platoon had joined Combat Command B, and Captain Sam Oliver asked me to take the company through Soissons and meet him on the other side.

We finally arrived at a straight stretch of road about half a mile outside of town, where I stopped the column. The men were stretched out at normal march interval. I told Sergeant Fox to pass the word for everybody to be on the alert. The column, headed by an armored scout car with a .50-caliber machine gun, was followed by fifty-four vehicles, including thirty GMC trucks. Every ninth truck had a ring mount with a .50-caliber machine gun. This gave us seven .50 calibers, a 57mm antitank gun, and two hundred men equipped with M1 carbines.

I stood on the road beside my Jeep with my map case on the hood and was discussing the route with Vernon and one of the C Company platoon leaders. Bitch was in the backseat next to my maintenance manual box. On our right was a cornfield with a gently rising slope that crested about three hundred yards away. The cornstalks had been harvested and stacked neatly in rows.

Suddenly, our tranquillity was interrupted by a series of sharp cracks, which I knew immediately was sniper fire. I hit the road. The fire became a regular fusillade. We crawled across the road on our hands and knees and dropped into the ditch on the opposite side. Bitch saw us crawling and jumped out of the Jeep, but instead of running at her full twelve-inch height, she got down on her knees and elbows with her little belly dragging on the pavement, crawled across the road, and snuggled underneath my armpit. I wondered if she thought she was a human being.

Sergeant Fox immediately swung the .50 caliber to the right and let go with several short bursts. The fire from the other side stopped immediately. From the field slightly to our rear and to the right came a three-quarter-ton weapons carrier with a 37mm antitank gun mounted on the back. The gun swung toward the top of the hill. The sergeant in charge asked what we were shooting at. I told him we had received some fire from the other side of the hill. Captain Oliver arrived, got in the scout car with Sergeant Fox, and, because the firing had stopped, told me to proceed.

We left C Company and headed toward Laon at top speed. We had gone about half a mile when the road curved to the right and started down a hill. A dozen French underground fighters had congregated at the edge of the road just around the curve and waved me down. As I came to a stop, they pointed toward a World War I–era concrete bunker that had been reinforced and rebuilt. They wanted me to go in the bunker and get a couple of German soldiers who were holed up there.

"*You* go in there and get 'em," I said. "It looks like you've got about a dozen men, and you've all got German rifles."

There was always a language barrier between my poor French and their understanding, and I could hear many statements of "*non compris.*" I could see what was bothering them; they had absolutely no desire to go into that pillbox and face a couple of armed men in the dark. I felt the same way. We had been instructed to move as rapidly to the target as possible and not allow ourselves to be delayed or sidetracked by events that could be easily handled by others. The mission of the infantry, supplemented by the Free French, was to mop up stragglers. In my judgment, this situation was pretty well in hand.

I pulled out a white phosphorus grenade, gave it to one of the men, and explained how to hold the safety, pull the pin, throw it into the bunker, then hit the deck fast. A broad grin broke out on his face. *"Oui compris, oui compris."*

The Frenchman got around the bunker and yelled in French and German for the two German soldiers to come out. When there was no response, he pulled the pin and tossed the grenade down the stairway. There was a muffled explosion, then white smoke began to come out of the bunker. As I started down the highway in my Jeep, two German soldiers came screaming out of the bunker with their hands over their head. I realized that it was the fire from these Free French that had been enfilading our column.

A few miles north of Soissons, we passed through a major World War I battleground. On the right was an American cemetery with a large statue dedicated by the French government to the American war dead. The statue, which stood in the middle of the cemetery, was eighty to ninety feet tall and was made from white Italian marble. It was a Statue of Liberty holding a dead American soldier in her arms; her head was drooped and she was crying. On the base of the statue—a block of granite fifteen to twenty feet square—was an inscription with the names of all Americans killed in that area.

German stragglers were running through the cemetery trying to take cover from the Free French who were following close behind them. There was a considerable firefight in the cemetery before the Germans were rounded up.

I've thought many times of this terrible irony. Here was a beautiful memorial, a symbol of the men who sacrificed their lives in World War I, desecrated by the failure to keep the peace afterward. This profoundly sad moment made me realize that nothing appeared sacred anymore.

• • •

We bivouacked in a large, open cornfield outside of Laon. We were on high ground above the city with only the neatly stacked rows of cornstalks available for camouflage. Each vehicle parked as close as possible to a large stack, then spread a camouflage net over both the stack and the vehicle. Vernon drove the Jeep right into the middle of the stack so that it was almost completely covered. We placed our bedrolls as close to the stack as possible and turned in. It was a clear night with plenty of starlight but fortunately no moon.

Sometime after midnight I was awakened by a heavy drone. Practically overhead appeared a large squadron of German Ju88 twin-engine bombers. Flying in three-column formation, the planes appeared to be spaced only a couple of yards apart. They flew extremely low, perhaps less than a thousand feet, and we expected to be deluged with butterfly bombs at any moment. It was the largest group of German planes—at least fifty—that I had ever seen in combat.

The drone continued overhead for what seemed like an eternity. Finally, the last plane disappeared to the southwest. The planes returned about an hour later, flying northeast; they appeared stretched out and fewer in number. Someone said later that these planes had bombed Paris one last time and had encountered some American night fighters on the way back. In both instances, our antiaircraft people were sharp enough not to fire on them. This large group could have wreaked havoc on our ground forces.

I remembered an incident in Mayenne on the night before we moved toward Chartres and Paris. A lone German reconnaissance bomber flew over our position, and the antiaircraft fire opened up with great intensity. We could tell the difference between the motor of a German aircraft and that of our own. We soon heard a second droning noise, which sounded different. All of a sudden the antiaircraft fire ceased, and we saw a stream of impending tracers make a short burst through the air, then terminate in an explosion as the German plane's flaming wreckage struck the ground. We had heard that the air force had a night fighter equipped with radar, known as the "Black Widow," but this was the first time we had seen it in action. Thereafter, night reconnaissance by German planes decreased.

• • •

The division moved rapidly in multiple columns as it led the VII Corps. Information from captured German field orders apparently was extremely helpful, because the Germans were using Meaux, Soissons, and Laon as main exit points. The other points indicated in the field order were Maubeuge and Mons, to the north of us; the division proceeded rapidly in that direction.

On the morning of September 2, the division crossed the Belgian border and proceeded toward Mons via Maubeuge. The night before, I had gone back to Soissons to division trains to deliver my combat loss report to Major Arrington. He'd told me he had a contingent of replacement tanks to go forward. The convoy was assembled early the next day.

I had seventeen M4 medium tanks, a two-and-a-half-ton GMC truck, and a three-quarter-ton weapons carrier for the maintenance crew. Each tank had a skeleton crew of two men. About a third had been survivors of knocked-out tanks; the rest were ordnance maintenance mechanics. Each repaired or replacement tank was fully loaded and equipped with gasoline, water, rations, and ammunition.

Although the maintenance men had no combat experience, they were skilled in operating the weapons. The tanks were evenly dispersed among the twelve tank platoons of the 1st and 2d Battalion medium tank companies of the 33d Armored Regiment. Only in a couple of incidences did we have two tanks in the same platoon. I mention this because the tanks had radios set to talk only on certain channels. For example, a tank could talk to other tanks in the same platoon and to the platoon commander, but the platoon commander could talk only to the company commander, who in turn could talk only to other company commanders. It was important for the men to understand this in case we ran into a firefight.

I showed the men our route on the map and told them we might meet up with a German column at any time, even though the division had already gone through this area. The turret man in each tank would be the acting tank commander and would man the .50-caliber ring-mount machine gun. Although the tanks might not be able to communicate with one another, the men could use hand signals. As we started up the road to Laon, I realized that although we didn't have full crews, with seventeen tanks we had the equivalent strength of a medium tank company.

The Roadblock at Maubeuge

Whenever I traveled those roads, day or night, I noted potential trouble spots on my map case. Our convoy moved along smoothly through Laon, but the road on the far side of town was new to me, so we proceeded more cautiously.

In the early afternoon, as we approached the crest of a hill about half a mile outside Maubeuge, I stopped the column and went forward to do a little reconnoitering. The main highway crossed a river on a bridge, which I learned might have been damaged. It could be crossed by wheeled vehicles, but a column of thirty-two-ton tanks was another matter.

If there were any Germans in Maubeuge, I didn't think they could see the tank column. At the top of the hill, the highway from Laon to Maubeuge intersected another road that ran between northern France and Belgium. On the lower slope of the hill, about a thousand yards to the west, was a large, heavily wooded area. To our right was an open field with a wooded area about three hundred yards beyond.

Suddenly, a lone man dressed as a typical French farmer emerged from the bushes to our left. I raised my M1 rifle, and Vernon pointed his carbine directly at him. He raised both hands high as he approached our Jeep and yelled in broken English, *"Me no Boche, me Français, me Français!"*

"Parlez-vous Anglais?" I asked.

"Un petit," he replied. He pointed frantically toward the woods down the hill to the left. *"Beaucoup Boche en le bois, beaucoup Boche en le bois."*

I knew he was trying to tell me there were a lot of Germans in those woods. With a better command of English than I had of French, he explained that he was a member of the French underground army and that the woods down the hill to the left hid between one and three thousand German soldiers, perhaps half a dozen tanks, and other equipment.

He also said that an American armored column had gone through

Maubeuge early that morning on the way to Mons. Because I knew
that the division normally traveled in parallel columns, and that
there was another road about two miles to the west, I assumed that
another of our columns came up that road. If the Germans were actually in those woods, they would probably stay there until dark because they were afraid of American airpower.

The Frenchman told me he knew where the French resistance
headquarters was in Maubeuge and we could go there to get more
information. I went back down the hill and told the sergeant about
the situation, then took off for Maubeuge to contact the French resistance headquarters.

As I crossed the bridge into town—it was a modern structural steel
bridge with an arch and a reinforced concrete roadway—I noticed
several pockmarks along the left side of the bridge that had apparently been made by exploding shells. They didn't appear to have
done any damage to the structural steel underneath, so I felt that
the bridge was safe for tanks.

The French resistance headquarters was located downtown in a
cellar next to a restaurant. It was guarded by men with German rifles who stood all around the building and inside. In addition to
German burp guns, which the guards seemed to prize highly, were
a number of American carbines and tommy guns. Many of the
guards wore GI coveralls, which I assumed had been air-dropped to
them.

I was conducted into their situation room. Hanging on the walls
were marked maps with overlays showing the various locations of
known troops in the area, both friendly and enemy. I was particularly impressed with the commander, a tall, good-looking French
mademoiselle with short-cropped blond hair and wearing GI coveralls that looked as though she had been poured into them. In
Camp Polk jargon, she would be considered "some kind of 'licious
chicken." She had an impressive command of the situation and
seemed to know exactly what was going on. Several radios seemed
to be in constant communication with other French resistance
units.

The 3d Armored Division, which had apparently arrived in Mons
the night before, had run into a number of German units that were

making a last, desperate attempt to get through Mons, one of the main junctions on the road to Charleroi and Aachen. The armored division was apparently surrounded and having a hell of a fight.

The commander informed me that, other than bridges over small streams, the only bridge to be crossed was the main one coming into town, and that all of the bridges were intact. I thanked her profusely for the information, returned to my Jeep, and headed out of town.

Sergeant Devers met me at the top of the hill, where he had been in a concealed position observing the woods to the left with his field glasses. Having detected no movement, he felt that the Germans had not seen our tank column. I told him to assemble the acting tank commanders so I could give them a quick briefing.

We would move out, go through Maubeuge, and proceed to Mons. I explained that the division was cut off there and would need these tanks as soon as possible. Because we would be visible to the Germans in the woods as we crossed the top of the ridge, the tank commanders should swing their turrets to the left and be prepared to fire if we noticed any evidence of German movement. Our objective was to get the tanks to the division and not be delayed by a firefight with an isolated group.

Just as we were getting ready to move out, a motorized infantry column led by a one-star general in a Jeep appeared on the crest of the hill to our rear. The column pulled up parallel to ours and stopped. I wasn't happy to think I'd probably have to deal with some high-ranking brass.

Brigadier General Wyman, the assistant division commander leading the 26th Regimental Combat Team of the 1st Infantry Division, immediately demanded to know who was in charge and what we were doing here. I stepped forward, laid a snappy VMI salute on him, and said, "Lieutenant Cooper, ordnance liaison officer, CCB, Third Armored Division, sir."

He wanted to know why a first lieutenant was in charge of an entire task force. I explained that this was not a task force but merely replacement tanks, and we were trying to get to Mons and meet our division as quickly as possible. I told him about my experience with the French underground headquarters in Maubeuge, about the German group reported to be in the forest to our left, and what I knew about our division. I explained that the bridge to Maubeuge was safe, because I had just crossed it.

He asked if I thought I could fight this tank group as an effective combat unit. I explained that the tanks did not have radio communications with one another but could use hand signals, and I felt that we could put up a good fight if we had to.

Wyman told me to set up a perimeter defense around this road junction and await further orders from him. He gave me the name of the commander of an engineer combat battalion in a little village about a mile to the east of us and said he would notify the commander of my position. He explained that this was an important road junction that the Germans might try to cross later and cut the corps supply lines.

He said that although he didn't have time to deal with the Germans in the woods because he had to get to Mons immediately to relieve my division, he would call for an air strike. He turned to his aide, who was sitting in the backseat of the Jeep and already had out the map. Wyman located the position in the woods and gave the coordinates to the air corps liaison officer in the scout car, who in turn got on the radio and called for the strike. Then the column headed down the road.

Six P47s came in at about two thousand feet and circled over the woods to identify the target. They apparently recognized our column and dipped their wings as they circled back over the woods. I knew that the Germans were really in for it. The planes came screaming down single file with their eight .50 calibers blasting wide open. When they reached about a thousand feet, they released their bombs, started to pull out, and gained altitude to get back in line for a second pass.

The woods literally boiled with flame and smoke. Metal started flying through the air. It could have been parts of German vehicles, but at this distance I couldn't be sure. German soldiers started to run out of the woods to the south and west, but none came up the hill toward us. There was no evidence of any German flak. The entire strike consisted of one bomb run for each plane and then one or two strafing runs. The strike was over in less than two minutes, and it was obvious that the Germans had suffered a devastating blow.

I told Sergeant Devers to coil the tank column off the road and circle the perimeter of defense on the back slope of the hill away from the woods. While waiting for the message from General Wyman, we were joined by another American column that came up from the south. It turned out to be Lieutenant Carter, from B Company, and his maintenance platoon, who had been back at the last VCP. They had finished their work and were heading forward to join the division.

Rusty, as Lieutenant Carter was known to his lieutenant buddies, was a down-to-earth good ol' boy from Louisiana and used to be, so he said, a genuine cowpoke. He was the first American officer I ever saw with the audacity to wear cowboy boots with his dress uniform.

There was some question about who received his commission first: Rusty from the CMTC or I through the ROTC. It was generally understood when an officer came on active duty that his date of rank started when he signed up at division headquarters. I signed in on the morning of June 22, 1941; Rusty signed in at about 1400 on the same day. We were both promoted to first lieutenant at the same time by the same order. Thus, Rusty and I had had a friendly ongoing argument about who outranked whom.

Rusty bivouacked his platoon inside our coiled circle of tanks. He had his entire maintenance platoon plus the crews of several repaired vehicles, a total strength of sixty men plus one M15 half-track with twin .50s and a coaxial 37mm antiaircraft gun and two M16 half-tracks with quad .50 antiaircraft guns. These half-tracks had their full regular crews plus a complete load of ammunition, fuel, and rations. Rusty's platoon was indeed a welcome addition.

At about 1500, I received a personal message signed by General Wyman briefly outlining the situation. General Wyman's 26th Regimental Combat Team from the 1st Division was engaged with the 3d Armored Division in heavy fighting in Mons. There was speculation that the Germans might try to bypass Mons to the south. We should be prepared to intercept elements of up to seven German divisions.

The 18th Regimental Combat Team was somewhat south and west of us and should cross this same highway about two miles west of our road junction sometime between midnight and daybreak. I was to prepare a position around the road junction and defend it at all costs. If I did not hear differently from Wyman by 0900, I could assume that the situation had calmed down and I was to proceed to Mons. He sent a similar message to the major who was commanding the engineer battalion about a mile to our east.

I wasn't particularly anxious to assume responsibility of the entire group, but I knew that somebody had to, and I felt that my training and exposure in combat gave me a better background than Rusty had. Our friendly ongoing argument about who outranked whom was to remain friendly, because when I briefed him about the situation, he said without a moment's hesitation, "Cooper, you're in charge. What do you want me to do?"

Combat elements of seven divisions could be as many as 35,000 to 40,000 men. I had heard stories of first lieutenants assuming command of infantry battalions when all the other officers were killed, but I'd never heard of an ordnance officer commanding a task force under these conditions. I began to realize and appreciate the value of the training in armored warfare tactics that I'd had in the Armored Force Tank School in the summer of 1941. German panzer divisions had swept through this same area in May 1940. Small French tank units, we were taught, had held up much larger German units by moving quickly from one dug-in position to another. With this lesson in mind, I made my plan to defend this position.

Rusty and I called up the noncoms and the acting tank commanders and briefed them. With seventeen tanks, three half-tracks, and 120 men armed with rifles and a few bazookas, we had a fairly sizable force. We set up a perimeter defense approximately six hundred yards in diameter centering on the main road junction. On the western flank, facing the enemy, we set up three M4 Sherman tanks staggered in depth. The first tank was behind a hedgerow near the road that ran through the woods where the Germans had been bombed that afternoon. The second tank, also hidden behind a hedgerow, was about thirty yards to the rear and across the road. The third tank was about thirty yards to the rear of the second tank and on the same side of the road as the first tank. The three tanks formed a triangle, so that if one tank was attacked, the attacking force would come under the fire of the other two tanks. This principle had been emphasized strongly at the Armored Force Tank School for an ideal tank defense. We instructed the tank crews to load initially with HE and to fire it directly at any tank in their group that was overrun by infantry. The high explosive would not penetrate the tank but would have a devastating effect on any enemy outside it.

Two men were positioned on top of the hundred-foot-tall water tower that was in the middle of this triangular arrangement. Fifteen men on the ground were well dug in around the tanks. One of the M16 antiaircraft half-tracks trained its quad .50-caliber machine guns down the road. I felt that this firepower could wreak havoc on any approaching enemy force.

We placed a similar force of three tanks, each with fifteen riflemen, dispersed in the same triangular fashion on each of the other three road junctions, facing north, south, and east. We kept five tanks and one half-track in mobile reserve.

We set up our headquarters on the northeast corner of the road junction in a defiladed position away from the woods to the west. We had two tank maintenance sergeants, one acting as sergeant of the guard and the other as his assistant. All the men were informed of the password and parole, which had been established in a previous division order for this phase of the operation. Runners went from headquarters to each roadblock at fifteen-minute intervals. We had no radio contact with any other unit and were strictly on our own for the next eight to ten hours, but I felt we had done reasonably well with what we had.

Rusty and I took turns on watch; I took the first watch, from 2000 until 0200. I spent most of the time at the command post talking to the runners as they came in. Things were pretty quiet until about 0100, when firing suddenly erupted down the road to the west. As I approached the roadblock, I was properly challenged by the sentry and gave him the password and parole.

The sergeant in charge of the roadblock said that the men on the water tower reported some activity about a mile down the road. Sporadic machine-gun fire was coming from the south side of the road across to the woods to the north. We knew that these were American units, because the machine-gun fire was .30 caliber and .50 caliber, but mostly .50 caliber. Apparently, elements of the 1st

Infantry Division had arrived at the road, which was in accordance with what General Wyman had told me to expect. I told the sergeant to look out for any German units diverted up the road toward our roadblock but to be extremely careful not to fire on our own troops. I assumed that General Wyman had notified the 1st Infantry Division of our position.

The sporadic firing continued throughout the night. By daybreak, it completely settled down as the 1st Infantry Division moved north around the western flank of Maubeuge and headed toward Mons. I was considerably relieved that we had not been attacked by the Germans. I was sure they had seen our tanks on the hill and had probably estimated us to be a large force.

Following General Wyman's orders to move out by 0900 if we received no further word from him, I had Rusty line up the column. We headed for Mons, the tank column in front and Rusty's maintenance platoon behind it.

I have often reflected on the significance of our position at this road junction on the outcome of the battle of Mons. The battle cut off the last escape route of German troops in northern France heading for Germany and the Siegfried line. German troops retreating from Paris, Normandy, and the Pas-de-Calais area were gradually squeezed and funneled into a narrow corridor. This road junction, south of Maubeuge, included a major road that would have allowed the Germans to bypass Mons and go directly to Charleroi. This was the reason that General Wyman had said to expect perhaps seven divisions to try to come down this road. The Germans, forced north into Mons, were blocked by the main elements of the 3d Armored Division and the rest of the 1st Infantry Division.

A Meeting Engagement at Mons

The situation at Mons was confusing. The advance elements of the 3d Armored Division as well as some of the German units arrived simultaneously. It was late, and neither side was aware of the other's exact position. In one incident, some of our soldiers moved into a building only to find the upper floors already occupied by the Germans. They met the Germans on the stairway and took them prisoner. In another incident, one of our MPs was directing traffic into a bivouac area with tanks approaching from two directions. In the darkness and noise, the MP became confused and stopped one of our columns to let a German tank pass into the bivouac. When the Americans realized that it was a German tank and saw the commander trying to crawl out, they climbed on the back of the tank and knocked the commander on the head with a monkey wrench. The German tank crew was subdued and taken prisoner.

In the meantime, the 3d Armored Division set out reinforced roadblocks on all the main entrances to the city and awaited the German advance. The Germans came fast and furiously in tanks, half-tracks, armored cars, trucks, horse-drawn artillery, wagons, and all types of miscellaneous vehicles that crowded down the narrow roads. They were making a desperate attempt to get back behind the Siegfried line, because France and Belgium were no longer defensible.

As the Germans approached the roadblocks, the lead tanks were knocked out, which blocked the road. The reinforced roadblocks poured murderous fire into these vehicles, setting many of them on fire. As the Germans abandoned their vehicles and took off into the fields on either side, they came under fire from infantry, automatic weapons, and other tanks dug in on both sides of the road.

Pandemonium broke out among the fleeing Germans. Some units managed to regroup and infiltrate into the city. Other groups brought up some of their heavier Panther tanks and inflicted considerable damage. It was difficult to knock out a Panther tank from the front end with an M4A1 Sherman's 76mm gun, but a hit on the flank could penetrate and set the Panther on fire. At one roadblock, an M4A1 Sherman, with supporting infantry and automatic weapons, was credited with destroying five 170mm heavy artillery guns, one 88mm dual-purpose gun, and some 125 miscellaneous trucks, half-tracks, Volkswagens, and horse-drawn carts.

Even with periscopes in the cupola hatch, it is extremely difficult to see out of a tank when it is buttoned up. Sometimes the tank commander must open the hatch and look out momentarily. When one of my good buddies, a tank platoon leader in the 33d Armored Regiment, stuck his head out of the turret at a roadblock, he was struck by a 75mm antitank projectile and was decapitated instantly. I was horrified to learn of his violent death.

I had often thought about casualties when we were back in England, and I knew that a certain number of our soldiers would be killed or wounded in the upcoming invasion. It was wishful thinking to hope that there would be none with whom I was too personally connected. Combat proved my early thoughts completely out of touch with reality. Our casualties had been much higher than we had been led to believe, and the ranks of our platoon leaders and tank commanders were rapidly decimated. They were difficult to replace; because the army had underestimated the number of tank casualties, it was reported it closed the tank replacement crew training school at Fort Knox. I never knew whether they started the tank training school back up after they began to receive the very high tank casualty figures from Normandy; regardless, it was too little too late.

After General Wyman passed through our position at Maubeuge, he headed north to reach the 3d Armored Division, which had been cut off at Mons. He was immediately followed by the 16th Regimental Combat Team.

The 18th Regimental Combat Team was on a parallel road about four miles west of us. After crossing the road near us, the 18th Regiment continued to Bavay, then headed off across open country to strike the Germans on the flanks as they were coming from Valenciennes toward Mons. The German columns piled up here, in some cases three abreast, and the traffic jam made them ideal targets for air force P47s, which raked them from one end to the other all day long.

The battle of Mons was a classic example of how an armored corps could completely emasculate a much larger force if the column moved rapidly. The German forces probably numbered in excess of 100,000 men, whereas the combined forces of the 3d Armored Division and the 1st Infantry Division totaled less than 30,000 men. Our advantage was that we arrived in considerable strength, whereas the Germans had only their forward recon elements. By overcoming these elements and quickly establishing roadblocks around the perimeter, the 3d Armored was able to block the main highways.

When the Germans found the roads blocked, they flowed around them, so the division was surrounded by the morning of September

3. General Wyman and the 26th Regimental Combat Team broke through and relieved them, then set out flanking protection all around the city.

The combined forces of the P47s constantly raking and bombing the columns, the tenacious roadblocks set up by the 3d Armored tanks, and the flanking protection provided by the 1st Infantry Division proved too much for the Germans. Although we suffered considerable casualties, they lost many times more. They suffered five thousand men killed and wounded, and we took in excess of thirty thousand prisoners.

By noon on September 4, we arrived at Mons and turned over the much-needed replacement tanks to CCB. General Collins, continuing his vigorous and daring pursuit of the Germans, had ordered the 3d Armored Division to turn over its positions to the 1st Infantry and advance rapidly to Charleroi to cut off and isolate more German units. In the meantime, the 9th Infantry Division on the eastern flank had bypassed Mons and was proceeding rapidly south of Charleroi toward Namur. This allowed the VII Corps to continue cutting off and isolating German units and overrunning them. The Germans dropped off units at various points and fought a desperate rear guard action to protect the balance of their forces as they tried to get them behind the Siegfried line.

Attack on Charleroi

We entered Charleroi late in the evening. The Germans put up a desperate, block-by-block fight. As the tank columns moved through the city, protected by infantry and combat engineers, the Germans maintained heavy fire.

Our maintenance unit was riding right behind the tank column; when they stopped for a firefight, we would stop. When they started up again, we would move forward fifty to a hundred yards, then stop while the fight resumed. The firefights would last between fifteen minutes and a couple of hours.

Vernon and I took turns catnapping, because we'd had virtually no sleep at the roadblock south of Maubeuge. We had found out long ago that it was often necessary to go some time without actually getting into your sack in the foxhole and really sleeping. I had learned to sleep sitting in the Jeep, sitting on the ground, and standing up leaning against the wall. I think I could even sleep while walking, as long as I had my hand on somebody's shoulder in front of me.

The firefights were sporadic, with moments of intense firing between our tanks and the German antitank guns. Occasionally, a stray mortar shell or machine-gun fire would impinge in our area, then would let up just as quickly as it started. Flames from burning buildings and knocked-out German vehicles usually shed enough light for me to read my maps.

As the firefights became routine and fairly regular, a strange thing happened. Belgian civilians, particularly the young mademoiselles, would wander out in the streets and give flowers and Cognac to the soldiers. The soldiers would reciprocate with cigarettes and chocolate. Some of the K rations had a small Nestle chocolate bar, and our emergency ration was a large chocolate bar impregnated with some type of bran flake. Needless to say, we soon ran out of K rations and emergency chocolate bars.

It was during one of our particularly long waiting periods that Vernon told me that he would like to get out of the Jeep and talk to one of the soldiers in the truck to the rear. I asked only that he stay within calling distance.

I had to stay awake to be ready when the signal came to start forward again. As I sat in the Jeep glancing at the map, I got extremely drowsy. Occasionally, I would be shocked out of lethargy by the ping of a stray bullet off a wall nearby. It must have been thirty to forty minutes later when I heard the signal coming down from the tank column to wind up. Although the tanks kept their engines running, most of the trucks and other wheeled vehicles had their engines off.

I immediately called for Vernon; there was no response. I got out of the Jeep and walked back to the truck in the rear. There was no driver or assistant driver in the cab. As I passed by the side of the truck, I could hear shuffling and scraping on the steel deck of the truck bed mixed with amorous moans. When I reached the rear of the truck, I saw that the tailgate was up and the curtains were drawn. I called Vernon's name, and the commotion ceased. Vernon emerged with a sheepish look on his face; he was followed by about ten other befuddled GIs.

A young Belgian mademoiselle appeared, straightening out her skirt and blouse, grinning from ear to ear, and chewing gum. As the men opened the tailgate to let her out of the truck, the top of her shoulder-strap purse opened slightly and I could see that it was filled with cigarettes and chocolate bars. She turned and smiled at the young GIs, strolled away, then called back, *"Vive l'Amérique, vive l'Amérique."*

The war seemed to do nothing to reduce the GIs' libido; they certainly took every advantage of getting a little *"couchez avec"* when the opportunity arose. I'm not sure whether Vernon had a turn or not. When he got back in the Jeep, I did not question him; however, I did chew out his butt for getting outside of hearing range. I also told the truck driver behind us that when a combat column stopped, there damn well better be somebody in the cab at all times. I think he understood.

As we approached the center of Charleroi, we came to a bridge blocked by a burning German tank. One of our tank dozers had to push it out of the way so we could continue.

The immediate objective after leaving Charleroi was Namur. One of the main highway systems in Belgium ran through Dinant, on the Meuse River, then northward to Namur. It was felt that the Germans might try to make a stand on the banks of the Meuse, which swung north again east of Liège. For this reason, General Collins ordered the 3d Armored Division to move as rapidly as possible along both sides of the river and to secure whatever bridges they could. With Combat Command A on the north supported by the 1st Infantry Division and Combat Command B south of the river supported by the 9th Infantry Division, the 3d Armored Division advanced at top speed toward Huy, where the Belgian underground had informed us that a bridge was still intact.

With recon elements in front, CCB also advanced at top speed—about thirty-five miles per hour on the road. The M4 Sherman tank, with a 400-horsepower Wright radial engine, was stretching its upper limit even without a governor. Fortunately, by this time, we had replaced a number of tanks with the newer M4A1. It used the Ford V8 in-line engine, which developed 550 horsepower with the governor off. Under ideal conditions, this engine could drive a medium tank at or slightly above thirty-five miles per hour. Some of the GIs in CCA, on the north side of the river, said that the CCB must have been going downhill with a hundred-mile-an-hour tailwind all the way. In any event, they captured the bridge intact.

Liège: The Heaviest Fortified European City

Having secured both sides of the river up to Huy, the division immediately launched an all-out attack toward Liège. The topography of Belgium in this area was different from that of northern France. Instead of broad, rolling plains with wide, straight highways, there were rolling hills and narrow roads. This made it much easier for small German units to set up roadblocks. As we drew closer to Germany, the Germans put up a stiffer resistance.

The division advanced in four columns. Combat Command A, along with CCR and the 1st Infantry Division, made a frontal assault on the city from the west. Combat Command B, along with the 9th Infantry Division, made a long swing to the south, bypassing Liège and curving back to approach the city from the southeast. The assault from the west with the envelopment from the southeast was a classic example of how an armored corps assaults a heavily fortified city. Liège had tremendous Maginot-type underground reinforced concrete fortresses facing Germany. We did not know if the Germans had occupied these forts and turned the guns against us. Fortunately, our rapid advance gave them little time to get ready.

The frontal assault met considerable resistance from a German heavy antiaircraft group. Before this antitank fire could become too severe, Gen. Doyle Hickey ordered an artillery barrage against the gun emplacements. Hickey's command included both the 54th and 67th Armored Field Artillery Battalions, equipped with the M7 105mm self-propelled howitzers. These howitzers could stop in the middle of the highway and start firing immediately, without leaving the road to set the trailer spade into the ground, as with towed artillery pieces. Eighteen guns in each battalion bringing extremely heavy fire onto the German antiaircraft guns soon neutralized them.

Combat Command A and the 1st Infantry moved rapidly into the city amid numerous firefights. Combat Command B and the 9th Infantry came in from the southeast and blocked any German retreat.

On one roadblock, CCB knocked out thirty-five German vehicles and killed a German lieutenant general as he was trying to run the roadblock in his staff car. Another German general was captured about the same time. On another roadblock, CCR knocked out seven German Mark IV tanks as they tried to escape toward Verviers.

On September 9, Joe Collins ordered the 1st and 9th Divisions to take over the 3d Armored Division's positions in Liège and continue the mop-up. The 3d Armored Division was ordered to advance as rapidly as possible toward Verviers.

Verviers to the Siegfried Line

The approach to Verviers was similar to that at Liège. Combat Command A, with two columns, approached and secured the high ground northeast and northwest of Verviers by nightfall. Combat Command B with its twin columns approached the south between Verviers and Theux but met extremely heavy resistance and could not secure its position by nightfall. The men coiled into a defensive position and prepared to attack at dawn the next morning.

At daybreak, CCA continued its advance and entered the city. Combat Command B continued against heavy resistance. At the same time, the forward elements of the 83d Recon bypassed Verviers and headed northeast. Although Verviers was finally subdued after considerable fighting, it was obvious that the resistance was getting much stronger.

The campaign was entering a dramatic new phase. Eastern Belgium, from Verviers to the German border, was taken by Germany in May 1940. This buffer zone, where many German nationals lived, had long been contested. The people spoke both French and German, and many were strongly pro-German. As we raced across Belgium, we would notice Belgian flags hung from the windows of the houses. We now saw a combination of Belgian flags and white flags; the deeper we went toward Germany, the more white flags we saw. The flags were to let us know that the German nationals living in these homes were willing to surrender peacefully; they knew that the Belgians would turn them in to the Americans.

During the initiation of this new phase, Major Arrington called the three liaison officers, Lieutenants Nibbelink and Lincoln and me, into his trailer. Because we would now be moving into enemy territory, we could no longer depend on help from friendly civilians; to the contrary, he said, the Germans would look upon us as invading their homeland and would do everything in their power to stop us.

Arrington warned us that because, as liaison officers, we would travel alone a great deal of the time, especially at night, we were much more exposed than soldiers traveling in a group and that Germans were not above torturing and killing captured liaison officers. This is the reason I had a thermite grenade in my plywood map box, to destroy the box in the event of imminent capture. The major knew that we realized the danger; he just wanted to caution us not to take any unnecessary chances and to perform our job as expeditiously as possible. I appreciated his remarks, because I knew he had our best interests at heart and was doing everything possible to protect us.

We approached the northern reaches of the Ardennes Forest. This area of Germany, known as the Eifel, had narrow roads and heavily wooded hills that extended from the Ardennes up through the Hürtgen Forest.

The next morning, CCB launched an all-out attack against Eupen. Part of Germany prior to World War I but ceded to Belgium by the Treaty of Versailles, Eupen was still really a German town. In May 1940, when the Germans launched their assault through Belgium into France, they took back Eupen. Although the citizens spoke both French and German, the majority of the sentiment was pro-German. Here was where the white flags began to outnumber the Belgian flags.

After overcoming a number of roadblocks and isolated strongpoints, CCB quickly passed through Eupen and headed east. The division was now only a few miles from the German border, and General Rose ordered both CCA and CCB to reconnoiter in force for weak points in the outer defense. Combat Command A reached the outer rows of the dragons' teeth—heavy reinforced-concrete mats, forty to a hundred feet wide and extending three to six feet below the ground—on the German border at a point south of the Aachen–Eynatten Forest and east of Eupen. Lieutenant Colonel Doan's Task Force X probed these outer defenses and reconnoitered through the night preparatory to attacking the next morning.

After overcoming a number of roadblocks and mines, Lieutenant Colonel Lovelady's task force in Combat Command B crossed the German border on the afternoon of September 12 and entered Rötgen. After several firefights, the town fell, and CCB proceeded northward on the road toward Rott and the dragons' teeth. The 83d Recon Battalion sent units to outpost Rötgen, and CCB coiled for the night preparatory to attacking the dragons' teeth at dawn. This was the first time since the Napoleonic wars that a German town had fallen and been held by an enemy. The division drew up before the vaunted Siegfried line, poised to attack. The battle of Belgium was over, and the battle for Germany had begun.

6
Assault on the Siegfried Line

The Siegfried Line

The Siegfried line fortifications, which varied in depth from ten to forty miles and had fairly well dispersed strongpoints, extended from the heavily wooded hills in the Saar region northward along the German border up through Luxembourg. North of there up through the Hürtgen Forest and the beginning of the Rhineland Plain around Stolberg and Aachen, the line narrowed to four to six miles in depth, though the concentration of fortified strongpoints was much greater.

The concept and tactical planning for the Siegfried line were a direct result of the brilliant German general staff and its desire to design a fortified line incorporating all the latest military technology. Unlike the Maginot line in France, which was farther south and limited primarily to the Saar region, the Siegfried line was designed for a new type of highly mobile warfare.

Although fighting a two-front war simultaneously was to be avoided, if possible, German planners recognized that this might be necessary for a short period. Realizing that the French and the British would most likely carry out their commitment to Poland, the Germans decided to build the Siegfried line in the west between Germany and France. It was not only to be the strongest defense line in the world, it was designed to be a launching platform for a major offensive.

The Siegfried line varied in depth depending on terrain and population density. Small villages and towns in close proximity with a concentrated population were incorporated into the defense system.

Many of the small cottages in Hastenrath and Scherpenseel looked like innocent farm dwellings but were actually fortified pillboxes. The basement ceilings were made of twelve- to eighteen-inch-thick reinforced concrete. The basement walls, also reinforced concrete, extended two feet above ground level and had long, narrow gun ports disguised as ventilator slots. The trenches going into the basements zigzagged, so it was difficult to throw in a hand grenade. In effect, these houses were built on top of pillboxes and were so well camouflaged that we had to be right on top of them to detect their true purpose.

The major pillboxes, in the countryside outside the villages, were generally rectangular but were sometimes built in a polygon shape to fit the slope of the land. They varied from thirty to sixty feet across and could accommodate up to fifty men.

The location of these pillboxes at first appeared random, but after close observation we noted that each pillbox took maximum advantage of the terrain. In most instances, the pillbox was located so that a direct assault would bring the attacking force under the fire of two other pillboxes. Therefore, the pillboxes did not necessarily face the direction of the enemy attack but could face any direction that might support another pillbox that was being attacked.

The pillboxes had heavily reinforced concrete walls from three to six feet thick and roofs from three to four feet thick. Their trilock construction consisted of railroad rails placed flange to flange on the bottom layer, with another row at ninety degrees to the first. The rails were approximately six inches apart. Several layers of these were placed in this same pattern one on top of the other. Concrete was poured in between to form an extremely heavy fortress deck that was virtually impenetrable by artillery. A direct hit from a 240mm shell, the largest we had in the field, detonated on top of a pillbox and generated a crater eighteen inches deep and four feet in diameter. An armor-piercing 76mm shell striking the side of the pillbox would generate a hole about ten inches deep and eighteen inches in diameter. If a tank could hit the same spot innumerable times, it might be possible to get a penetration, but in the meantime the tank would be exposed to murderous antitank fire. The best method was to get around to the gun port, where the protection was thinner. Once a pillbox was captured, our engineers would place large explosive charges inside, then they would blow back the roof in one section and neutralize the pillbox.

The aggregate used in the German concrete gave the pillboxes a dull grayish color, which made them blend in perfectly with the surrounding terrain. In front of the pillboxes lay long, continuous lines of dragons' teeth. On top were staggered rows of pyramids, starting about two feet high in front and tapering gradually upward to a height of five to six feet. It was virtually impossible for a tank tread to span them. Thus, the dragons' teeth kept tanks too far away to fire directly at the pillboxes' gun ports but close enough to come under antitank fire from the pillboxes.

The combination of pillboxes and dragons' teeth made an ideal matrix. The Germans dug trenches between the pillboxes, allowing infantry to move freely from one position to another. They used bulldozers to dig large, inverted, tapered wedges, with the dirt pushed into the end facing the enemy. A tank could then enter the pit with its gun barrel barely above ground level. This offered protection for the tank hull and exposed only the gun, the gun mantlet, and the forward part of the turret, with the heaviest armor on the tank facing the enemy fire. It also provided a reasonable degree of camouflage. The tapered pits could be dug quickly, and the tanks could be moved from one position to another. The pits also made ideal positions for 88mm dual-purpose guns.

Farther to the rear were similar positions with artillery and Nebelwerfer multibarreled rocket launchers. Although Nebelwerfers were not as accurate as artillery, their blanketing fire was effective against advancing infantry. Because of the high-pitched noise of these rockets, they were known as "screaming meemies." Interspersed between the pillboxes, communication trenches, and gun pits were a number of slit trenches and foxholes to accommodate machine guns, mortars, and individual riflemen.

Thus, there was no solid line to break through but instead a whole series of positions in tremendous depth. As soon as our troops advanced through one row of defense, they would immediately face second and third rows. Once a penetration was started in a formidable defense such as this, it was absolutely necessary to proceed as rapidly as possible to widen the breach in order to avoid attacks on both flanks of the penetrating unit.

The Siegfried line's intricate series of dragons' teeth, pillboxes, interconnected communication trenches, gun pits, and foxholes supported by an excellent road net provided the Germans with not only an effective defense system but also a base from which to launch a major offensive. We were to learn this during the disastrous German offensive in the Ardennes a few months later.

The First Army pursued the Germans rapidly and tried to intercept them before they could get back into the Siegfried line. Although this was done successfully at Meaux, Soissons, Laon, and Mons, the Germans were still able to extract a number of troops. Our mission was to attack them as quickly as possible, before they could get reinforcements and organize their defense properly.

According to the Armored Force Doctrine, an armored division was not supposed to attack a heavily fortified position but instead wait for a buildup of infantry, artillery, and general headquarters (GHQ) tank battalions, plus airpower, to make the assault. Although General Rose was obviously aware of this, he measured it against the fact that waiting for a buildup would give the Germans more time to reinforce their positions. Knowing that the Germans did not have sufficient troops to man the line in depth, he decided to make an all-out assault as quickly as possible.

Attack Through the Dragons' Teeth

The plan of the attack was simple and direct. Task Force X from CCA was to attack the line at a point east of Eupen and south of the Aachen–Eynatten Forest. Task Forces Lovelady and Kane from CCB were to continue past Rötgen and attempt to attack through that area northward in a flanking movement. On the night of September 12–13, CCA patrols sent out to reconnoiter the dragons' teeth located an area where German farmers had piled up dirt between the "teeth" to make a temporary crossing for farm equipment. The German soldiers had not had time to remove this crossing, but it was assumed that they had mined it heavily.

The assault started at approximately 0800 on September 13. Task Force X sent forward infantry supported by artillery and tank destroyers that fired directly at the gun ports on the closest pillboxes. A flail tank from the 32d Armored Regiment attempted to neutralize any mines buried in the dirt.

The flail tank worked well on level ground, but the underpowered M4 tank did not have sufficient horsepower to operate the flail over rugged ground. As the flail tank got about halfway up the wedge, one of the chains fouled on a dragons' tooth and brought the tank to a halt. The entire crew bailed out and went forward under extremely heavy German fire to disengage the chain. Two other tanks from the 32d Armored Regiment came forward and extracted the flail tank with their towing cables. Combat engineers from the 23d Armored Engineers Battalion, under intense German fire, finally neutralized any mines in the path.

A tank dozer came forward, plowed up a wedge of earth, and filled the space between the dragons' teeth sufficiently to establish another ridge that allowed the tanks to cross. The Germans apparently never anticipated the use of a bulldozer blade hooked onto a tank.

Colonel Doan of Task Force X immediately moved twenty tanks through these paths and approached the pillboxes in support of his infantry. Once the tanks got inside the dragons' teeth, they were extremely effective at firing shots into the pillboxes' gun ports. Elements from the 26th Regimental Combat Team of the 1st Division gave them additional support, and with engineers and artillery they gradually overcame the rows of pillboxes. They not only knocked out pillboxes but also destroyed a number of 88mm antitank guns. That eight of these guns were completely unmanned indicated the German manpower shortage. The shock to the German infantry of being overrun by our tanks contributed largely to the success of this action.

The successful penetration of this first outer layer of the Siegfried line cost CCA dearly. Casualties among the infantry and engineers were extremely high, and ten M4 tanks of the first twenty to cross the dragons' teeth were knocked out by nightfall. Of these ten, eight were set on fire and burned, another example of the relativel weak firepower of the 75mm and 76mm tank guns and the extreme vulnerability of the light armor on the M4 tanks compared to the German armor.

The dug-in German tanks plus the antitank guns and the fire from the pillboxes were awesome. Once again, the Germans continued to fire on a stopped tank until it burned. The flames from two hundred gallons of gasoline plus ammunition and other parts surged into the tank; the turret and the open cupola hatch acted like a chimney. Most of the internal equipment melted and fused together, and the armor was softened by the intense heat. That tank would never be an effective combat vehicle again.

As CCA made its frontal attack across the dragons' teeth just south of Aachen, CCB launched a flanking attack north of Rötgen. The men passed through the northern fringes of the extremely rugged and heavily wooded Hürtgen Forest, which was ideal defensive territory. They finally encountered a roadway through the dragons' teeth that was blocked with cables, mines, and steel reinforcements. Engineers went forward under heavy fire to remove these obstacles so the tanks could pass.

At Schmidthoff, Lieutenant Colonel King's task force made a frontal assault but was repulsed by extremely heavy German fire. A mined roadway, blocked with cables and steel reinforcements, passed through the dragons' teeth at Schmidthoff. After engineers removed the mines and destroyed the reinforcement and cables, the task force attempted to move its tanks through the opening. Just to the left of the roadblock was an innocent-looking farmhouse that was actually a pillbox. The tank column came under severe fire from the rear and the flanks. Only after a heavy firefight was the pillbox knocked out, and the tank column proceeded through the town.

The division was now well into the outer defenses of the Siegfried line. By September 15, CCB had penetrated the second-line defenses as it attacked northeastward. We were headed up the road about a mile south of Kornelimünster, trying to contact Task Force King of CCB. Suddenly, I saw a long white plume of a rocket heading straight up from the woods to the east. At first I thought it was one of our artillery rockets marking the target, but I never recalled seeing such a long white plume. Unlike an artillery rocket, this one kept going straight up and did not arch over. I hollered to Vernon to stop the Jeep, and I got out with my binoculars to inspect the plume more closely.

As it continued its path straight into the heavens, a second rocket slightly to the right of the first started along the same trajectory. Knowing that the German lines were somewhere in the woods to our right, I assumed that these rockets must be theirs and estimated them to be firing from a position approximately three-quarters of a mile to one mile to the east. The rockets continued straight skyward until they disappeared without any evidence of their arching over. It was a relatively clear day, so with my binoculars I could see the entire spectacle extremely well.

Maintenance battalion headquarters was located in Raeren, Belgium, about a mile and a half to the west. When I reported to Major Arrington what I had seen, my buddies made snide remarks that I'd gotten into the German schnapps. But I was vindicated the next day by the G2 report of the Germans having fired the first V2 rockets into Antwerp. We knew about the V2 rockets; the Germans had already fired them at London, the Thames estuary, and other Channel ports. As far as I know, this was the first observation by ordnance personnel of a V2 rocket fired from the ground.

Combat Command A, approaching east, and CCB, approaching northeast, were slowly converging into a relatively narrow front. By September 23, they reached the Stolberg-Aachen area. Stolberg was an industrial city in a deep, narrow valley southeast of Aachen and just north of the Hürtgen Forest.

By this time, the 3d Armored Division and elements of VII Corps had penetrated the last heavy fortifications of the Siegfried line and were in a deep salient in the German lines, in a highly exposed position from both flanks. In barely eighteen days, the First Army, spearheaded by the 3d Armored Division, had dashed from Paris to the Siegfried line and killed or captured many thousands of Germans. In another twenty days, they had fought a desperate battle and penetrated the Siegfried line. The press now called the division the Spearhead Division, a title it had justly earned.

We were completely overextended and had run far beyond the capability of our supply lines. The great majority of our supplies were still coming by truck and pipelines from Omaha Beach. Our supplies of gasoline, ammunition, rations, and vital ordnance supplies were extremely limited. We had even run out of maps. It was necessary for me to mark on my map case with a grease pencil the route we had taken during the day, so I could go back at night with my combat loss report and then return.

The First Army was given the order to halt and set up a defensive position. It was to consolidate it as quickly as possible to allow time for other elements both north and south to straighten out the line and prepare for the next attack. Our division established a line from a point approximately halfway through Stolberg southeast to the high ground on hill 287 and then south to Mausbach.

General Rose moved division headquarters into the Prym House, on the forward slope of a hill on the southern outskirts of Stolberg, well within small-arms and mortar fire range. We weren't sure if the Germans knew that the division headquarters was that far forward. Even though the headquarters received its share of artillery fire, there appeared to be no attempt to destroy the building.

The Division Regroups

The division was exhausted and had been heavily bloodied. Medics from the 45th Armored Medical Battalion did a fantastic job of patching up the wounded, but casualties among tank crews and other combat personnel had been much higher than anticipated. In addition, the loss in tanks and other combat equipment had been staggering. Of the four hundred tanks that had started in Normandy, approximately a hundred were still operational. Although ordnance had replaced most of the losses, the maintenance crews had to make an almost superhuman effort.

The maintenance men together with ordnance men, mechanics, and welders had long since become accustomed to working around the clock in blackout conditions. By using blackout curtains and small Onan portable generators, the crews could do a considerable amount of work at night. We normally didn't like to weld at night, because from the air a flash could be seen in the darkness for several miles. Until the air force introduced the Black Widow night fighters, the only protection we had was from our own antiaircraft guns. Although we tried to do maintenance in areas not exposed to direct small-arms fire, these areas were always exposed to incoming artillery plus an occasional sniper.

The maintenance men quickly adapted to doing field maintenance under all conditions. After a little rain, an open plowed field that had been converted to a VCP became a quagmire once a few tanks and other combat vehicles had run through it. The maintenance men worked in pouring rain and deep mud up to their rear ends. In many small and subtle ways, a strong sense of mutual respect between the combat troops and the maintenance troops developed. Each knew that his survival depended on the other. This helped the division survive under the most horrible conditions.

The Battle of Aachen

The division had now entered a major regrouping. The 1st Infantry Division took over many positions of CCA to the north and shored up our left flank. The 9th Infantry Division shored up the right flank of CCB to the south. The 4th Infantry Division was moving up in the south through the Hürtgen Forest and was experiencing terrible casualties.

Our division had driven a deep salient into the German lines, outflanking Aachen to the southeast. Corps and army medium and heavy artillery was brought forward to join our division artillery supporting the 1st Infantry Division in its assault on Aachen. The XIX Corps of First Army with the 30th Infantry Division and the 2d Armored Division moved in on the northern flank of Aachen. The battle for the city had begun.

The first large city in Germany to come under siege, Aachen was a key strongpoint in the outer edges of the Siegfried line defense system. It was an old and historic city that had been the seat of Charlemagne's government in the ninth century. Charlemagne's body was entombed in the city's historic cathedral. The Allies were determined not to destroy the cathedral if the Germans did not try to make it a strongpoint. Both sides apparently understood this, because the cathedral, although damaged, was left virtually intact. Aachen also contained the famous German Polytechnic Institute, one of the finest engineering schools in Germany.

• • •

The division trains moved forward, closer to the combat units, to perform their functions more rapidly during this buildup period. Maintenance battalion headquarters company moved into an area just north of Raeren. Its billeting officer must have had his head up his rear end because he could not have selected a worse site; it was about two hundred yards wide and situated between two army artillery battalions. To the north was a 155mm howitzer battalion and to the south was an 8-inch howitzer battalion. When I expressed my opinion as to the precariousness of our position, I was told that the move had already been made and we would just have to stay put.

Vernon and I put down our bedrolls beneath Major Arrington's trailer. There were two large armor-plated doors on either side of the trailer that protected the batteries, and we lowered these until they practically touched the ground. We felt that this would make an ideal spot for our bedrolls. We decided that, with all this protection, it wasn't necessary to dig a foxhole. I found out later that this was a big mistake.

The two artillery battalions were laying down intermittent fire in salvos lasting two to three minutes each. First, the 155mm howitzers would let go with a salvo and then stop; next, the 8-inch howitzers would let go with another salvo. This continued throughout the early hours of the evening and until well after dark. The blasts lit up the entire night sky very much like Roman candles.

Suddenly, there was a low whirring and swishing sound followed by a dull thud, then a tremendous crescendo of wracking and crunching. The lack of a high-pitched screaming noise indicated that this was not an 88 or smaller shell but was instead something quite large.

"Damn, Vernon, that's incoming!" I said. "We should have dug that foxhole."

We heard the sound of feet hitting the deck of the trailer above us, and I could hear Major Arrington screaming, "Cooper, what the hell was that?"

"Major, it's incoming and it's big," I hollered. "You better get down here with us."

Arrington came screaming out of the trailer dragging his bedroll and crawled under the trailer to get between the battery box covers with us. As he was straightening out his bedroll, another low, whirring noise started coming in much louder than the first. "Damn," I yelled. "It's right on top of us!"

This time there was no dull thud but instead a horrendous wracking, crunching noise. I felt as though my eardrums were about to burst. Fortunately, my Jeep was parked in front of the trailer and caught most of the blast. The windshield, although it was down and covered, was shattered, and the radiator and tires were destroyed. The entire front of the Jeep looked like a sieve. Part of the major's trailer was also riddled with fragments.

Bitch was snuggled under Vernon's arm, and I thought at first that she had wet the bedroll, but she hadn't. I wasn't sure that I hadn't. There was no question that my Jeep and the armor-plated battery box covers had saved us.

The first round had come in north of headquarters company and just south of the 155mm battalion. The second round had come in on the southern edge of headquarters company, slightly north of the 8-inch howitzer battalion. I thought the next rounds would come right between, in the middle of headquarters company.

Sure enough, the Germans fired three more rounds in quick succession and they landed in the middle of the largest field, where headquarters company was bivouacked. Fortunately, the closest vehicles were about fifty yards away, and the damage was limited primarily to broken windshields and torn tarpaulins.

At daybreak, we could get a better idea of what had happened. The second round had landed across the highway about fifty feet from the major's trailer. There was a railroad track on that side of the road, and the shell landed between the rails. Although this section of track was completely demolished, the combination of the steel rails plus the steel cross ties sometimes used on German rail lines seemed to muffle the effect of the blast. Although I had been correct in my warning about bivouacking between two artillery battalions, it did no good to push the point. I just hoped we all learned from that experience.

With the intermittent firing of the two artillery battalions some five hundred yards apart, the Germans' flash detector was confused. The first round came in to the north of the battalion. The second came in to the south. They split the difference, and the next three rounds zeroed in on the middle, which happened to be right where headquarters company was located.

Examining this area, we found three large craters fifteen to twenty feet deep and forty-five to fifty feet across. The craters actually overlapped one another. We located the base of one of the shells, a 210mm projectile. The largest field artillery we had encountered at that time, the shell had been fired by a 210mm railroad howitzer, located on a track that ran into a tunnel near Eschweiler, eight miles away. The gun was pulled out of the tunnel at night, fired against our positions, then returned to the tunnel at daybreak. This went on for several days before the air force located it, then had P47s dive-bomb and destroy the gun and the tunnel. The ability to fire three large-caliber rounds with overlapping craters from an eight-mile distance was some indication of the extreme accuracy of the German fire control systems.

C Company moved to an area south of Raeren near an ammunition dump. The maintenance company of the 33d Armored Regiment bivouacked a few miles away, just south of Kornelimünster. When I arrived there the next morning to see Maj. Dick Johnson, who commanded the maintenance company and was also CCB's maintenance officer, he was complaining that an 8-inch gun battalion had moved in just north of him.

"Cooper," he said, "I was here first, and those bastards moved in here later and are just going to draw artillery fire on us and make it difficult for us to do maintenance."

"Major, you probably outrank that battery commander captain, so why don't you go over there and tell him to move the guns?" I suggested.

The major grinned and thought about it, although we both knew that the location of the artillery battalions was according to a corps artillery plan and had priority over maintenance. It was obvious, with the buildup taking place, that the areas were going to become even more crowded as artillery, ammunition, and supplies of all types moved as far forward as possible.

As we had predicted, the 8-inch guns fired various missions throughout the day and night. The German sound and flash systems would pick them up and return fire. The Germans had a methodical way of fighting wars, which must have been the result of their discipline. The method must have worked to their advantage many times, but it also worked to their disadvantage, because things tended to become routine. For example, if the Germans fired a mission on a certain target at 1100, they would fire every day at the same time. You could almost set your watch by it. This at least gave us some warning of when incoming artillery was to be expected.

A herd of German cattle occupied a field between the maintenance company and the 8-inch gun battalion, closer to the artillery. Whenever the Germans would start counterbattery fire, some of the rounds would land in the field and kill a cow. As soon as the fire lifted, the artillery troops and maintenance troops who had taken cover in their foxholes would dash into the open field to claim the cow. It was reminiscent of Normandy, when we had smelled the terrible stench of dead livestock in the field. The only solution was to immediately go out and butcher the cow and clean up the remains. This also put fresh beef on the table, which was extremely hard to find at the time.

On this particular day, our maintenance soldiers were determined to avoid the event of the previous day, when the artillery troops had beaten them to a fallen cow. When the counterbattery fire started, one of the maintenance men took his crew and got inside a T2 recovery tank instead of getting into a foxhole. They started up the engine and waited for the counterbattery fire to cease.

Sure enough, right in the midst of the barrage a large cow was fatally wounded. The sergeant immediately moved his T2 across the field while the artillery troops watched helplessly from their covered foxholes. The men opened the trapdoor at the bottom of the tank and one of them sneaked out with a rope sling and attached it to the fallen cow. He attached the other end of the rope to the end of the winch cable, then crawled back inside the hatch as fast as possible. They left the field with the dead cow dragging behind them. The maintenance company had a feast that night with fresh steaks for everyone. To the best of my knowledge, this was the first time in the history of warfare that a battlefield recovery under fire had been made for a dead cow.

• • •

As the buildup continued, Aachen was completely surrounded. An emissary under a flag of truce was sent into the city to demand surrender. The German commander refused, and the battle started in earnest. Task Force Hogan of the 3d Armored Division, attached to the 1st Infantry Division, proceeded to attack from the south and from the encircled east flank. The 30th Division of the XIX Corps, with elements of the 2d Armored Division, attacked from the north and northwest.

There was heavy fighting in some areas, particularly around the hills dominating the main roads in and out of the city. Aachen was pounded with artillery from four divisions plus heavy artillery from both corps and First Army. In addition, the 9th Tactical Air Force made a number of strikes at targets within the city. The German garrison was overpowered, and the commander surrendered after a tough fight.

The G2 received word that the Germans had developed a new secret weapon, a small, remote-controlled robot tank. It was about eighteen inches high, battery powered, and controlled by a wire that played out as the tank moved across open ground. The tank contained a thousand pounds of TNT and could be detonated by the operators, who could be several hundred yards away in a foxhole. A school had been established at Düren to train German soldiers to use this tank.

The G2 sent word to the combat troops to be on the lookout for any prisoners who might have attended this school. He was soon notified that a young captured German soldier appeared to have been a cadet at the robot tank school. He was brought to an abandoned schoolhouse in Mausbach where the G2 was interrogating prisoners. The young cadet, a tall Nordic blond product of the Hitler *Jugend,* turned out to be extremely arrogant and was humiliated that he had been captured alive and not allowed to die for the glory of Germany and his Führer. He refused to answer questions except to give his name, rank, and serial number, as agreed by the Geneva Convention.

Prisoners were sometimes required to do a few calisthenics to keep them in shape and loosen them up a bit. The GIs ran the young German prisoner up the stairway to the second floor of the schoolhouse, then made him jump out the window and slide down the flagpole located next to the window in an attempt to make him talk, but their tactic didn't work. The prisoner continued to express his indignation.

One of the basic tricks when interrogating prisoners of war was to build up the prisoner, then suddenly break him down psychologically. This prisoner was brought down the next morning to where all the prisoners were lined up ready to be loaded onto trucks and taken back to the POW camp.

The young Jewish lieutenant who was in charge of this group had been born in Germany but left the country with his parents in the early 1930s to escape Nazi persecution. He spoke perfect German and understood thoroughly the psychology of the Hitler *Jugend.* When the prisoners were lined up in front of the schoolhouse, the lieutenant was given a list of the prisoners' names. He took a few moments to look over the list, then addressed the prisoners in perfect German. He told them that although they were prisoners of war, the Americans always admired bravery and courage, even among the enemy. He called out the name of the tank school cadet and asked him to step forward. He proceeded to heap additional praise on him in front of his German compatriots. The cadet grinned from ear to ear and constantly swung his eyes to the right and left to make sure that the other German prisoners had understood what the American lieutenant said. The lieutenant then stated that because the Americans were particularly impressed with this type of valor, even from a German prisoner, the decision had been made to accommodate the young lieutenant's wish to fight and die for his Führer. He would therefore be released and returned safely to the German lines.

With that, two MPs, each wearing Red Cross armbands, drove up in a Jeep with a Red Cross flag on it, walked over and grabbed the cadet, one on each arm, and started to escort him to the Jeep. The expression on the young German's face turned from a grin to one of complete and abject terror. He broke down and started crying like a little boy. "*Nein, nein,* I don't want to die for the Führer. *Nein, nein,* I don't want to die, I don't want to die!"

He was escorted back to the schoolhouse, where he told the American lieutenant everything he knew about the robot tank school. In the eyes of the American GIs, he had been completely had. Even his fellow German prisoners laughed at him as he was taken away.

The slow, drizzling rains of the early German autumn continued practically every day. The fields were becoming a quagmire, and it was extremely difficult to do maintenance. A few days after the fall of Aachen, the division trains moved into the city and the maintenance battalion moved into the Engleburt Rubber factory, which had large buildings to be used for shop space and plenty of paved areas. Major Arrington wanted all of the liaison officers to stay in one place so he could find them at a moment's notice. My buddy Ernie Nibbelink found an excellent spot, which turned out to be the factory's telephone exchange. Located on a lower level of the main floor, it had heavy reinforced concrete walls and a concrete roof. We felt reasonably safe here and didn't dig a foxhole. After all this time in the field, we finally moved into a decent building with all the relative comforts of home.

Buildup to the Breakout Through the Siegfried Line

For the first time in four months, the division had a chance to catch its breath. It occupied a narrow front from Stolberg across hill 287 and down through Mausbach. The 9th Division was on our immediate right, and the 4th Infantry Division was south of there in the Hürtgen Forest. The 104th Division had come up on our left flank and relieved the 1st Infantry Division. Although our division occupied a frontline position, it was able to rotate the units periodically and give the combat troops a little chance for rest and recreation.

The buildup was in full swing, and new personnel and equipment replacements arrived daily. Contingents of every artillery and GHQ tank battalion, antiaircraft and tank destroyer units, and all types of supply, maintenance, and ammunition units moved as far forward as possible. The entire area became extremely crowded.

The war in northern Europe, from the landing on the beaches in Normandy to the Siegfried line, had been successful so far. The skilled deployment of infantry, armor, artillery, and airpower made the Saint-Lô breakthrough successful and permitted the armored divisions to exploit the breakthrough in deep, slashing columns across northern France and Belgium and into the Siegfried line defenses in Germany. The assault across northern France became an example of armored warfare exploited to the ultimate state of the art. But as the main weapon of the armored columns, the M4 medium tank resulted in horrendous losses that threw an extra load on the other arms. Only through the combined efforts of our armored infantry, self-propelled artillery, tank destroyer units, and pinpoint bombing by the P47s were our great tank losses partially offset.

The great irony of World War II, as far as the campaign in northern Europe was concerned, was becoming only too apparent. Perhaps the most powerful ground force ever assembled, backed up by powerful strategic and tactical air forces, was being frustrated and taking horrendous losses because its main assault weapon, the M4 medium tank, was vastly inferior to its enemy counterpart. This forced a basic change in the application of our Armored Force Doctrine, which had been so brilliantly conceived a number of years before. Because of our inferior main battle tank we could not utilize this doctrine to its fullest capability.

Armored Force Doctrine was based on two separate and distinct types of armored tactical units. Each unit was organized, equipped, and deployed in the field to accomplish a separate mission.

The GHQ Tank Battalion was normally attached to an infantry division and supported it in assaults on fortified postions. The original thinking was to have the GHQ Tank Battalions equipped with a heavy assault tank with sufficient frontal armor to enable it to resist enemy antitank fire. The Germans had long since recognized this need and had developed turretless versions of their Mark IV, Mark V, and Mark VI tanks. Without the extra weight of the turret mechanism, heavier armor could be provided. The assault version of the PzKw VI, known as the *Jagdtiger* (Hunting Tiger) had a 128mm high-velocity antitank gun and 13 inches of frontal armor and weighed approximately 64 tons. This was twice the weight of our M4 and it was obvious to us that the M4 was not even remotely in the same ballpark as this awesome monster.

An American heavy tank had been developed in the early years of the war, but it was soon abandoned and all efforts were concentrated on the M26 Pershing. Patton's recommendation to concentrate instead on the M4, because we needed a fast medium tank and because tanks were not supposed to fight tanks anyway, was a disastrous decision based on inflexible military thinking. Patton was the ranking Armored Force commander and had an extreme flair for getting his way.

Patton's view was opposed by the combat commanders who had served under him in North Africa, and to even the most inexperienced second lieutenant tank platoon leader it was obvious that if our Armored Force Doctrine said that tanks were not supposed to fight tanks, the Germans would do just the opposite and oppose our tanks with their heavier tanks whenever possible. Even though this policy had been reversed by General Eisenhower when he saw our terrible losses in Normandy, it was too little too late, and we still had not received any M26 heavy tanks by early November 1944, though they were desperately needed.

The armored division was a highly mobile, self-contained arms unit capable of ranging deeply behind enemy lines for at least three days without additional supplies. Once a breakthrough had been made by the infantry and GHQ tank battalions, the armored division could penetrate deeply behind enemy lines. Even though the Armored Force Doctrine said that the armored division should avoid enemy tanks where possible, the original planner certainly would have insisted that the divison be equipped with tanks equal to or superior to the enemy tanks, should the occasion arise for them to engage each other. The idea that the M4 should be given preference over the M26 because of its superior speed was a great fallacy. Although the M26 Pershing outweighed the M4 Sherman by some 15 tons, its 550-horsepower motor compared to the 400-horsepower motor of the Sherman gave it a higher horsepower per ton ratio and thus an equal or greater speed on the highway. In addition, its longer wheelbase and wider track gave it a ground bearing pressure approximately half that of the M4. This bearing pressure was similar to that of the German tanks and made it much more maneuverable in open country.

Though lacking an adequate main battle tank, the armored division was often called on to perform the missions that would normally have been assigned to a GHQ tank battalion. Besides lacking an adequate assault tank, the GHQ tank battalions apparently had insufficient training in combined operations with infantry. The armored division had its own armored infantry and was accustomed to working with it in a symbiotic relationship where each depended on the other. This made for an excellent working relationship, when a combat command was attached to an infantry division or a regimental combat team from an infantry division was attached to an armored division.

As the buildup neared completion in early November 1944, it was obvious that another massive breakthrough was being planned. General Eisenhower had observed that if the Germans attempted to take a defensive stand with the narrow Rhineland and the Rhine River to their rear, they were taking a serious risk. With our great air superiority, the Rhine crossings could be neutralized and the Germans trapped on the west bank of the river.

There were, however, several reasons for the Germans to take this position. The Siegfried line was still virtually intact and had been penetrated deeply by the First Army only in the Aachen-Stolberg area. A large percentage of German electric power came from the steam-driven, brown coal–fired electric utility plants on the Rhine Plain between Bonn, Cologne, and Düsseldorf. The loss of these plants would be a major disaster to the German war effort. Unknown to us, the Germans needed the Rhineland to launch their planned Ardennes campaign. In addition, the Germans, particularly Hitler, saw the invasion and occupation of German soil as anathema.

It had rained practically every day and the ground was saturated, making movement by tanks and other armored vehicles extremely difficult. The inability of our medium tanks to negotiate soft ground had been recognized some time before, and field service modification kits had been sent forward to be installed on the tanks.

The kits consisted of three-inch-wide steel grousers, which were attached to the track connectors on each track block on both sides. This gave an overall width of twenty inches compared to thirty to thirty-six inches on German tank tracks. I contacted Dick Johnson with the 33d Maintenance and arranged to have their supply truck pick up the boxes of grousers at the ordnance battalion headquarters company. The grousers finally got down to the tank crews, who installed them on their own tanks.

The tank crews were enthusiastic about the grousers, which did help somewhat, but the ground was so completely saturated that the grousers only partially solved the problem. Our tanks still got stuck easily. The problem was that the grousers were designed so they did not come in full contact with the ground until the tank had already penetrated the outer crust. Thus, the breakthrough of the crust had already occurred and the tank could still sink down further due to the shearing action. I'd venture to say that the fields around Kornelimünster, Mausbach, and Breinig are still filled with leftover grousers and spare locknuts.

Our front line between Stolberg and Mausbach extended across the top of hill 287. On top of the hill was a German pillbox we had captured and used as an observation post. From an open-top concrete bunker adjacent to the pillbox, we could observe the back slope of the hill. The German frontline positions were seventy-five yards down the slope and east of the pillbox.

During this two-month lull, the buildup continued on both sides, although the view from this frontline position gave little evidence of it. There were often exchanges of small-arms and mortar fire. In the intervening times between these firefights, the whole area was relatively calm.

Looking down the hill from the bunker, we could see a roadway running roughly parallel to our front line and connecting the small villages in the valley below. They had obviously been evacuated of all German civilians, although we occasionally saw cattle grazing in the valley. This pastoral scene would be rudely interrupted when one of the cows would suddenly explode. There were mines all over the area, and whenever a cow blew up the forward observers would try to pinpoint it on the map. From the frequency and randomness of the explosions, it was apparent that numerous minefields were scattered throughout this entire area.

Between our lines and the German lines and about a hundred yards north of the pillbox was a large slag dump. A small clump of trees stood at the bottom of the forward slope and the dump. A German infantry company had taken cover in these trees and come under heavy artillery fire. The point detonating fuses on the 105mm howitzer shells were set off when they struck the tree branches, and the midair explosion caused the troops on the ground to get the full effect of the blast. About 150 bodies were piled up under the trees, and numerous bodies were scattered across the crest of the hill and down the slope behind the German lines. Some of the bodies had been there for two months, and the stench from them was terrible.

I received a new Jeep to replace the one that had been damaged by shell fire at Raeren. I also got a new driver. Vernon received a well-deserved rest, then was transferred back to C Company.

My new driver, a young soldier named White, was vigorous and enthusiastic about his job. He could hardly wait to get to the front line and see all the excitement. I explained that his job was to take care of the Jeep and keep it ready to move on a moment's notice twenty-four hours a day. Combat was not glamorous; our job was to keep a low profile. There would be plenty of excitement to go around.

When Vernon transferred back to C Company, he took our little dog Bitch with him, because they were attached to each other by now. In the four months we'd had her, she had matured rapidly. She soon met many German boy dogs, became pregnant, and had a large litter. Vernon gave the puppies to many of his buddies in C Company. I'm sure that her progeny are scattered throughout western Germany and did their share in cementing long-term German-French relations.

The first time I took White forward, we went to the pillbox on hill 287. I wanted to talk to the forward observer and get some idea where the mines were located, because I knew that when the attack started, our tanks would eventually have to go through this area. We left the Jeep about a hundred yards west of the crest of the hill and proceeded on foot. I told White to stay inside the pillbox to avoid the occasional random shells that fell near there. He could look through the vision slots on the back side of the pillbox to see what was going on and keep an eye on the Jeep.

The artillery observer was out on the open parapet with his battery commander's (BC) scope looking down the valley toward the German positions. He had his maps out and was marking targets as I approached him.

We saw some movement about a quarter mile down the forward slope of the hill. Three white objects were moving among the German positions; upon close examination through his scope, we saw that they were German medics. They wore large, stolelike white vestments that covered their chests and backs completely and were stuffed into their belts. Red crosses approximately eighteen inches high were on both the front and back of the vestments, and their helmets were solid white with red crosses front and back. This garb gave them much greater visibility than our medics had; they wore only armbands with small red crosses and helmets with red crosses painted in white circles on both sides.

The German medics moved freely from one foxhole to the next tending to the wounded. Our artillery observer made no attempt to fire on them as long as they were exposed. I'm not sure the Germans had the same respect for our Red Cross. I remember too well when the Germans fired on the clearly marked half-track ambulance back in Villers-Cotterêts, killing all aboard.

Suddenly, there was a tremendous explosion on the earth mound right behind us. We both hit the deck immediately. I remember feeling a tug at the back of my combat jacket as I fell down. An incoming 81mm mortar shell had struck the parapet behind us. I reached over my shoulder to see if I'd been hit and discovered that my right shoulder epaulet on my combat jacket had been severed by one of the flying mortar fragments. With the exception of being dazed for a few minutes, I was unharmed. Although I could not hear what the artillery observer was saying, I could tell by the expression on his face that he was also okay.

I returned to the bunker and stuck my head inside to tell White we were getting ready to leave, but he was not there. One of the men inside said he had left a few minutes ago and thought he'd gone back down the hill to the Jeep. I looked around but didn't see him anywhere. I continued to call his name, without any response. After several minutes I saw a lone figure emerge around the south side of the pillbox. It was White all right, and he was carrying a rusty M1 rifle covered with mud. I explained that he had not only exposed himself unnecessarily but had jeopardized the lives of our infantrymen dug in around the pillbox. Because he was only seventy-five yards from the German front lines, he could have easily been killed and drawn fire on our other positions in the vicinity.

The chewing out I gave him shook him up; he had no idea of the seriousness of what he had done.

"Look, Lieutenant," he said, "I found an American rifle on the field and brought it back."

I knew then that White was an extremely naive young soldier. I explained to him that there was no shortage of M1 rifles and that risking a life was not worth his find. I continued to press hard on this point to make sure it didn't happen again.

After examining the rusty, mud-covered rifle, I figured it had probably been on the ground for at least two months. There was a live round in the chamber, and both the bolt and the safety were rusted tight in the firing position. I knew it wouldn't be safe to bring it back to the maintenance company in this condition. I held the rifle at arms' length, pointed it over the hill toward the enemy line, and pulled the trigger. It fired perfectly, and the reaction sheared loose the rust on the bolt and inserted a new round in the chamber. I then unloaded the rifle, gave it to White, and told him to take it back to the small-arms section. They could clean it up and reissue it. I had always felt that the Garand rifle was an excellent gun, and this certainly confirmed it. General Patton reportedly called it "the ultimate weapon of World War II."

The battle plan called for another major combined-arms operation, similar to the Saint-Lô breakthrough. With the massive use of airpower, artillery, armor, and infantry, we were to shatter the German frontline positions and break out onto the Rhineland Plain.

To accomplish this mission, VII Corps was assigned five infantry divisions (1st, 4th, 9th, 83d, and 104th) and two armored divisions (3d and 5th), more than half of First Army's strength. The VII Corps front line extended from the middle of Stolberg, southeast across the back slope of hill 287, down to Mausbach, and into the northern part of the Hürtgen Forest. The initial objective was to break out of this line, capture Eschweiler and Düren, and secure a bridgehead across the Roer River, which was the last barrier before the flat portion of the Cologne Plain.

Just prior to the initial attack, all the division's tanks were incorporated in the division artillery fire plan. Each tank platoon was given an aiming point and the proper elevation and deflection of its guns to strike specific target areas. Excess ammunition was stored alongside the tanks for use during the initial barrage. After the barrage, the tanks could move into their attack positions with a full load of combat ammunition. The tanks firing as artillery gave the division a total firepower of thirty-six artillery battalions. Combined with the artillery of the other divisions plus attached corps and army artillery, the VII Corps had a total firepower of ninety artillery battalions.

The tanks and other armored vehicles were in reasonably good shape from a maintenance point of view. Any tanks that had survived since Normandy had had a hundred-hour check, and all badly worn tracks had been replaced. In Stolberg some of the tankers had gotten sacks of cement from an abandoned cement factory and made up a crude mixture of concrete for patches to reinforce the front glacis plate. The patches, which the men reinforced with chicken wire and angle iron, were three to four inches thick. Other tankers used sandbags, logs, or anything else that might offer added protection.

The Assault to the Roer River

The buildup was now complete, and the infantry and armor were in position and ready for the attack. During September and October, the infantry assaults through the Hürtgen Forest had been extremely costly. It had been estimated that a major assault through the forest would cost an additional ten thousand infantry lives. This apparently contributed to the decision to use the 3d Armored Division for a direct frontal assault. Although this was completely contrary to Armored Force Doctrine, it was felt that an armored division must be used as the initial assault force due to the inadequacy of the GHQ tank battalion and infantry division combination.

The Germans had taken advantage of this interim to reinforce their side of the line. They had pretty well evaluated our M4 battle tank and realized that the gun and the armor were vastly inferior to those of their Panther and Tiger tanks. They also knew that our tanks would get stuck more easily in soggy terrain, and persistent rains had kept the ground completely saturated. With this knowledge, they developed an extremely effective defense plan. They heavily mined all of the open terrain on the back side of hill 287 and the fields surrounding the villages below.

The German line on top of hill 287 was barely seventy-five yards from our positions in the pillbox and extended down the hill southeast toward Mausbach. When placing their first row of mines, the Germans did something that we had never encountered. Instead of placing the mines in front of the outer infantry line, as was normally done, they placed them slightly behind their forward infantry outposts. Thus, our combat engineers would have to infiltrate these outposts at night to locate and remove the mines. This was extremely difficult if not virtually impossible. The Germans planned to hold these outposts as long as they could; only when the pressure became too great would they withdraw. This would leave our troops exposed to completely intact minefields.

The first objective was to break out of this area and secure the bridgehead across the Roer River at Düren. To accomplish this, the 3d Armored Division was to penetrate the minefield on the back side of hill 287 and seize three villages in the valley below, about a mile away. These villages—Werth, Hastenrath, and Scherpenseel—were heavily fortified and lay in a triangular fashion across the main north-south communication lines for the German troops in this area. Combat Command B of the 3d Armored Division was selected to make the initial penetration.

The morning of November 16 was overcast with patchy ground cover. The initial attack started at 1115 with the assault of thirteen hundred heavy bombers and six hundred fighters against Eschweiler and Langerwehe. This was followed by seven hundred medium bombers and a thousand heavy bombers attacking targets farther to the east.

From the revetment at the pillbox on hill 287, I could see a group of P47 dive-bombers attacking German fortifications at the base of a concrete observation tower approximately a mile and a half across the valley. The German antiaircraft fire was extremely intense, and I could see the tracers weaving like giant luminescent snakes. When a dive-bomber makes its pass, it must fly in a straight line before releasing its bombs. The planes are extremely vulnerable at this point, and one of the planes was struck just as it turned down into a dive. Although it was on fire, the pilot continued on his dive path until he had released his bombs and fired his machine guns. He pulled out of the dive at the last minute and headed back westward streaming smoke and flames. I never saw a parachute and was not sure whether he made it back or not. Everyone who witnessed the incident realized that it took a lot of guts to fly into a solid wall of flak the way that young pilot did.

Simultaneously with the heavy air strike, the ninety battalions of field artillery opened up, concentrating particularly on the villages. Combat Command B assembled just south and west of hill 287. As the task forces proceeded over the crest of the hill and passed through our infantry lines, they were exposed to the full effect of the German minefields.

Each task force had one flail tank. As the flail tanks crested the hill, they passed through our infantry line directly into the minefields. Although the tanks had to contend not only with mines but with an extremely soggy field, they made an initial good showing. The flying chains detonated several mines, and the explosions created additional craters. But finally, due to the combination of the muddy fields and the fact that the horsepower needed to turn the flail took too much power away from the tracks, both flail tanks became mired in the mud. They made excellent targets and were soon knocked out.

The second tank in each column had no choice but to go around the flail tanks and continue the attack. A tragic domino effect followed. The first tank proceeded around the flail tank and made its own way for several yards before striking a mine and becoming disabled. The next tank bypassed the first tank and tried to go its own way for several yards, then it struck a mine and became disabled.

This process continued until eventually one tank got through the minefield and proceeded with the attack. The next tank behind it tried to follow the same path, and sometimes it would get through the minefield successfully. However, by the time the third tank tried to come through in the same tracks, the soft ground would mire the tank so deeply that it would stick, in spite of the "duck feet" we had bolted on the track connectors. All the stuck tanks became sitting ducks for the murderous German antitank fire. The Germans continued to fire at the tanks until they set them on fire. When the crew tried to bail out, they immediately came under concentrated automatic weapons fire.

These brave tankers knew that the tanks would be at an extreme disadvantage in the muddy minefields, but they pressed on with the attack. This was one of the most courageous tank attacks of the entire war. It started with sixty-four medium tanks, and we lost forty-eight of them in twenty-six minutes. A proportional number of soldiers died in this terrible fight.

By nightfall, Task Force 1 had reached the vicinity of Hastenrath after taking tremendous losses. One column started out with nineteen tanks, including a flail, and ended up with four by the end of the day. The other fifteen were lost in the minefield. The surviving tanks were further exposed because the infantry had a difficult time coming forward to support them. The minefields were also heavily infested with antipersonnel mines. These were deadly to the infantry, who were under extremely heavy small-arms, mortar, and artillery fire.

In the fighting around Hastenrath and Scherpenseel, the tankers, without adequate infantry support, performed almost superhuman acts of heroism to hold on throughout the night. It was reported that one of the tankers, in his tank on a road junction, was the only surviving member of his crew but was determined to hold his position at all costs. A German infantry unit approached, apparently not spotting the tank in the darkness. The lone tanker had previously sighted his 76mm tank gun down the middle of the road. He depressed the mechanism slightly and loaded a 76mm HE. As the Germans advanced in parallel columns along each side of the road, he fired. The HE shell hit the ground about 150 feet in front of the tank and ricocheted to a height of about 3 feet before it exploded.

The shock took the Germans completely by surprise. The American tanker continued to fire all the HE he had as rapidly as possible, swinging the turret around to spray the German infantry, who were trying to escape into the fields on both sides of the highway. Loading and firing the gun by himself was extremely difficult, because he had to cross to the other side of the gun to load and then come back to the gunner's position to fire.

After exhausting his HE and .30-caliber ammunition, he opened the turret and swung the .50 caliber around on the ring mount and opened fire again. He continued firing until all of his .50-caliber ammunition was exhausted, then he grabbed a .45 submachine gun from the fighting compartment and opened fire with this. After using all the ammunition from his Thompson and his pistol, he dropped back in the turret and closed the hatch.

He opened his box of hand grenades and grabbed one. When he heard German infantry climb onto the back of the tank, he pulled the pin, cracked the turret hatch slightly, and threw the grenade. It killed all the Germans on the back of the tank and those around it on the ground. He continued to do this until all of his hand grenades were gone; then he closed the hatch and secured it.

By this time, the German infantry unit apparently decided to bypass the tank. From the vicious rate of firing, they must have assumed that they had run up on an entire reinforced roadblock. When our infantry arrived the next day, they found the brave young tanker still alive in his tank. The entire surrounding area was littered with German dead and wounded. This, to me, was one of the most courageous acts of individual heroism in World War II.

By the next morning, the engineers had cleared some of the mines on the forward slopes of hill 287. They put up taped markers so the T2 recovery crews could come forward. As we went through the path to examine each tank, we had to be extremely careful. Although the major fighting had ceased in this area, we were still subjected to periodic small-arms and mortar fire. The recovery crews would take cover behind the tanks when the firing started; as soon as it lifted, they would resume trying to hook up the tanks and get them out.

In addition to the sporadic fire, there was still the danger of mines. In some cases there were unexploded Teller mines under some of the knocked-out tanks. Assuming that there might be mines under all the tanks, the recovery crews hooked a long cable from the T2, which was parked about a hundred feet away, then slowly pulled the tank by its winch. If a mine under a tank exploded, the tank would be further damaged but the maintenance crews would be relatively safe inside their T2 vehicle.

The maintenance crews, who had to expose themselves many times in situations such as this, took every reasonable precaution. They first went for the tanks that were merely stuck in the mud, because they had their tracks intact and were easier to pull out. If a tank struck a mine and broke a track, generally one or more bogey wheels were damaged and temporary repairs were made.

While we worked on the tanks, a line of infantry crested hill 287 and headed down through the minefield. Their rifles were fixed with bayonets and they were ready for action. This turned out to be the second mop-up wave of the 104th Infantry Division. The first wave had gone through earlier and was engaged in bitter fighting in the Hastenrath area working with our Task Force 1. Lieutenant Colonel Mills, the Task Force 1 commander, had been killed on November 18 in this action and was replaced by Colonel Welborn. We were delighted to see soldiers from the 104th Division, because we knew that it was a crack division commanded by Gen. Terry Allen. He had previously commanded the 1st Infantry Division, which was also in this operation and had a reputation as one of the best divisions in the army.

As the infantrymen passed through us, they executed considerable skill in fanning out on the flanks of the slag pile and the woods on our left. As soon as they entered this area, they had to dislodge the Germans with a lot of bitter hand-to-hand fighting. They cleaned up the area with dispatch and took out a number of prisoners. Firing into our area immediately tapered off, and we were considerably relieved.

Sooner or later you develop an almost super sixth sense. You know that an artillery or mortar shell is coming toward you before you hear the whining and before the *wrack wrack* sound when the shell strikes the ground in an exploding crescendo. I have often tried to analyze this sixth sense. I believe it has something to do with the high-angle trajectories of the mortars and howitzers. The sound from the gun barrel travels in a straight line faster than the projectile, which reaches you an instant later. I believe that one intuitively learns to recognize the difference between the sound of the muzzle blast when the projectile is aimed directly toward you and when it is aimed at an angle away from you. I'm not sure if this is correct, but I know that understanding this enormously increases one's chances of becoming a survivor.

Captain Bew White, motor officer of the 391st Field Artillery Battalion and second-ranking maintenance officer in CCB below Maj. Dick Johnson, came down with his recovery vehicle headed toward the Hastenrath area. He told me they had lost one of their forward observer tanks and he was going down to see about it. I told him that the VCP was being set up at Mausbach on the highway. Lieutenant Colonel Garton, commanding officer of the 391st Armored Field Artillery Battalion, was also in command of the artillery group supporting CCB in this operation. As White's commanding officer, Garton would raise hell until he got back his forward observer tank. In an operation of this type, the artillery has its own forward observer tanks that go with the task force to pinpoint the artillery fire.

The loss of a forward observer tank meant that we also lost a tremendous amount of concentrated artillery fire; thus, replacement was vital. German tankers, even buttoned up in their Panther and Tiger tanks, were extremely leery of the 105mm howitzer. A direct hit on the frontal or side armor by a 105mm would have little effect on a German tank, but a plunging hit on the top of the tank, where in some cases the armor was only a quarter of an inch thick, would be disastrous. In a situation like that at Hastenrath, with the tanks beyond the infantry support, the forward observer could call for overhead airbursts directly on their position. The tankers buttoned up inside would be relatively safe, but the fire would be devastating to any German infantry trying to close in on the tanks with bazookas.

By the middle of the day, the Mausbach VCP was rapidly filling with shot-up tanks. The T2 recovery crews did a superhuman job extracting these broken and battered tanks from the minefield. In some cases, the tanks were so completely mired, up to the middle and tops of the bogey wheels, that the tanks acted like huge suction cups. It was necessary to dig small slit trenches under the back and sides of the tanks to let air underneath and break the vacuum. Although each T2 recovery vehicle had a powerful fifty-ton winch on the back, and using a single pulley made it possible to get a hundred-ton drawbar pull, sometimes it took two T2s hooked together to get a tank unstuck.

When I went back to maintenance battalion headquarters, I reported to Major Arrington that we had lost forty-eight tanks in twenty-six minutes in the minefield. We had recovered all but eight, which were badly burned and still in the minefield. He asked me how many I thought we could repair, and I told him I didn't know but we had a lot of work to do. He said he was going to dispatch a detachment from B Company to assist Captain Grindatti from C Company with this extra work. Arrington immediately called Captain Sembera and instructed him to get more tanks on the way, because he did not know how many we would need.

Captain Tommy Sembera went back to army ordnance with the "W" numbers of all the tanks burned in the minefield, plus the numbers of others that had already been cannibalized. This should have been enough to get replacements started. Tommy, however, had one major disadvantage in dealing with the people in army ordnance. He was the only armored division ordnance property officer who was a captain. The table of organization for an armored division called for the ordnance property officer to be a lieutenant colonel. In another one of his screw-ups, Colonel Cowhey had deviously given this position to one of his personal friends and had Tommy actually perform the duties. Although Tommy had been the ordnance property officer for at least two years back in the States and in England and had done an excellent job, he had remained a captain because no other vacancy was available. Because the 3d Armored Division had sustained the highest tank losses of any other armored division to date, he was forced to compete with other officers of higher rank for new tanks. It was only due to the fact that Tommy had an excellent record and had done a superior job of liaison with army ordnance that he was able to perform his duties effectively. He apparently had established a high degree of credibility with the First Army ordnance people, because he was usually able to get us the tanks we required.

Once all the damaged vehicles were brought to the VCP, the maintenance people worked around the clock. Of the forty-eight tanks initially knocked out, we were able to repair all but thirteen. This was done in three days, faster than the G1 could bring up the necessary replacement personnel. This was a perfect example of the tremendous effect that a well-coordinated maintenance operation could have on an armored division's combat effectiveness.

As the infantry came up and consolidated positions around Werth, Hastenrath, and Scherpenseel, CCA was committed with elements of the 1st Infantry Division toward Langerwehe, a heavily fortified objective north and east of Eschweiler. Here again the tanks were unable to negotiate the extremely muddy fields. In one task force, twelve out of thirteen tanks became stuck in the mud. Had it not been for the support of the infantry, the task force would have suffered many more losses. The infantry pushed on through the stalled tanks and advanced forward without the direct fire support of the tank guns. Although the infantry had excellent artillery support, they undoubtedly suffered much higher casualties without the tanks. After heavy fighting, Langerwehe fell and CCA returned to division control.

Next, CCR was committed with elements of the 9th Infantry Division. The objective was to straighten out the line and bring it up to Düren on the Roer River. The line of advance was from Langerwehe through Obergeich and Geich to Echtz.

The tanks again encountered the terrible combination of mud and minefields. This slowed them considerably, and they were unable to give the infantry adequate support. At one point, one of the task forces encountered six antitank guns dug in on one flank supported by three mobile German tanks. Although CCR theoretically had many more tank guns available, the higher velocity of the German antitank guns plus the superior guns, armor, and maneuverability of the German tanks put them at a decided disadvantage.

The capture of Hoven allowed VII Corps to complete this particular phase of the operation and bring the line up to the west bank of the Roer River. By December 15, the entire 3d Armored Division had been pulled out of the line and put back in a rear area for a well-deserved rest and maintenance period.

The Failure of the November Offensive

Although the American First and Ninth Armies had penetrated the Siegfried line, the assault that began on November 16 had been a grave failure. The Ninth Army to the north had the mission of making the main effort in an attempt to break through the last vestiges of the Siegfried line, cross the Roer River, and fan out onto the Cologne Plain. VII Corps was to protect the Ninth Army's right flank and capture Cologne, the largest industrial city in the Rhineland and an important rail and road communication center. The final objective was to secure bridgeheads on the Rhine River and attempt to trap the main elements of the German army on the west bank.

The operation failed for a number of reasons. The American armies had advanced extremely rapidly after the Saint-Lô breakthrough. The Germans had done an excellent job of demolishing the docks and harbors along the English Channel. The only usable port at that time was Cherbourg, and the distance by truck was almost six hundred miles through France and Belgium and into Germany. To make things worse, the chalklike ground of western and northwestern France became saturated after two months of almost continuous rain. This was particularly true around Reims, one of the main central supply hubs of the entire western front. The ground and roadbeds would no longer support heavy traffic, and under the constant pounding of tanks, trucks, and other vehicles the roadbed in many areas completely collapsed.

To offset these problems, the army organized what later became known as the Red Ball Express. The communication zone (COMZ) troops had thousands of two-and-a-half-ton GMC trucks running bumper to bumper twenty-four hours a day. Because the air force completely dominated the skies with the new Black Widow night fighter, contrary to all training the trucks ran with their headlights on as fast as they could go.

The army had long since lost confidence in the use of GHQ tank battalions working with infantry to achieve a major breakthrough, so they had used the armored divisions to perform this function. This was completely contrary to Armored Force Doctrine, and it dissipated the armored divisions' strength.

With no heavy assault tank with wide tracks to negotiate the muddy fields, the attack on November 16 resulted in disastrous losses. In addition to CCB's loss of forty-eight out of sixty-four tanks in twenty-six minutes, two combat commands from the 2d Armored Division lost approximately a hundred tanks under the same conditions in the Jülich area as they approached the Roer River. These losses were unacceptable, and the two divisions could not maintain their combat effectiveness under such conditions.

Few, if any, military historians have ever understood the importance of our not having the M26 heavy tank in time for the November offensive. Many combat soldiers felt that the initial assault on November 16 would have succeeded if we had had the Pershing, with its better protection and better mobility in muddy terrain. It would have been possible to break through the Cologne Plain and capture the bridgeheads on the Rhine River. Major elements of the German army would have been annihilated on the west bank of the Rhine, and the Ardennes attack might have been preempted. By that time, we would have been behind the German panzer units building up for the offensive. The Battle of the Bulge may have never taken place, some 182,000 German and American casualties might have been averted, and the war could have ended five months earlier.

This of course is pure speculation; however, it is based on the tragic experience of many armored and infantry troops. After the tankers saw their buddies slaughtered in our M4 tanks when they tried to engage the heavier German tanks, they could not help but agree.

7
The Battle of the Bulge: Phase I, the German Attack

Status of the Division Prior to the German Attack

For the wheeled vehicles of the 3d Armored Division, the rest and maintenance period meant replacing tires and changing engines, particularly in many of the GMC trucks. Although the heavy-tread tires did not wear out, they had to be replaced primarily because they were either shot up or severely damaged by the mortar shell fragments on the roadways. When an HE shell explodes on a roadway, it generally breaks up into many small slivers with sharp points on both ends. Unlike a nail, which lies flat on the road, a sliver often has one point facing upward. The rolling action of a heavy-tread tire forces one of the points through the wall of the tire. Instead of causing a simple puncture, a fragment usually tears a large gap in the casing, so the tire has to be replaced.

In the 3d Armored Division, with all of its attached units, there were approximately 1,800 combat vehicles and 2,300 wheeled vehicles. To perform maintenance on all the diverse types of vehicles required a major commitment of personnel. In addition to the maintenance battalion, which had more than 1,000 men, there were another 1,000 men in the maintenance companies of the armored regiments plus the platoons and maintenance sections of other units, giving us a total of 2,000 men directly involved in maintenance. Add to this another 8,200 drivers and assistant drivers, who performed first echelon maintenance on their own vehicles, including tire changes, track changes, and minor repairs, and you can get some idea of the tremendous number of people required to keep a reinforced heavy armored division rolling.

Although this may appear to be an unusually large commitment, the combat maintenance problems of an armored division in the field were staggering. There is no comparable commercial enterprise. For the wheeled vehicles, the maintenance problems were exacerbated by their being driven many miles in muddy and rough fields in four-wheel drive. When they came up on the highway for a short period, their drivers would often fail to disconnect the four-wheel drive. Because there was no slip mechanism in the final drive to accommodate the difference in front- and rear-tire wear, this put a severe overload on the entire engine and power train.

All the wheeled vehicles were heavily overloaded, particularly the GMC truck. Although it was rated at two and a half tons, it normally carried from four to ten tons, even in off-road conditions. Under these loads, truck engines had to be replaced every ten thousand miles, and it didn't take long to put on that many miles. With 850 two-and-a-half-ton GMC trucks in the division, this in itself was a major maintenance problem.

For the combat vehicles, the overwhelming maintenance problem was by far the repair and replacement of battle-damaged vehicles. On the M4 tanks, with the Wright R975 radial engine, we had the persistent problem of spark-plug fouling, when the tanks idle their engines while standing still. Many of the older tanks had been knocked out by this time and had been replaced with the newer M4A1 tank with a Ford V8 water-cooled engine.

One problem we had thought might be major never materialized, the replacement of the tank tracks. One of the best features about our tank design was the track system. Back in the States, during garrison training and maneuvers, we were able to get approximately twenty-five hundred miles on a set of M4 tracks. The tracks were reversible and could be run on one side, then reversed and run on the other side. The tanks that we received in England, before going into Normandy, had heavy rubber grousers imbedded on one side of the track and they could no longer be reversed; however, the extra rubber still gave us good mileage. This was an excellent track design and far superior to anything that the Germans had. Their tracks used hardened steel blocks and hardened pins, which resulted in greater friction and wear. However, few of our tanks lasted in combat long enough to use up a set of tracks.

Each tank had a set of steel grousers that could be put on the track blocks over the holes in the track pins, which were spaced about every five or six blocks. These grousers did help somewhat in mud however, on snow and ice, they would break through to the road and cause a large reverse bump between the track blocks. This would strain the rubber doughnuts in the opposite direction and tend to cause the track to wear out prematurely at these bumps. It also created an extremely rough ride and was hard on the bogie wheels and suspension system. The tank crews had been instructed to use these grousers only in off-road conditions, but this was obviosly impractical because tanks constantly went on and off the road. An alternate solution used one-half-inch square steel blocks, about two inches long, welded to the bottom of the wedge screw on the track connector. This welded pin extended down about one-quarter inch to three-eights inch below the bottom of the track surface. It did appear to penetrate ice and hard-packed snow to a certain degree and seemed to help quite a bit as the snow and ice on the roads began to build up. It was not completely effective, but it was the best we had to offer at the time.

The 3d Armored Division's unusually large maintenance organization had other, unanticipated benefits. When the combat commands went forward to exploit a breakthrough, each had its own ordnance maintenance company, in addition to the maintenance company of the armored regiment and the maintenance sections of each separate battalion and company. A large percentage of the officers and men in this maintenance group knew one another and had worked together as a team in maneuvers and training for three years back in the States and in England.

Major Dick Johnson, commanding officer of the maintenance company in the 33d Armored Regiment, was the ranking maintenance officer in Combat Command B. It was my responsibility to coordinate the maintenance effort between Major Johnson's group, the ordnance maintenance company attached to the combat command, and the ordnance battalion in the division trains to the rear.

As the combat command moved forward, it often had motorized infantry battalions from the infantry divisions and separate artillery battalions and other corps-level combat units attached to it. The combat command often moved thirty to forty miles a day, and it might take the main elements of the infantry divisions several days to come forward. The infantry division's maintenance sections followed behind the main body, which left the elements attached to the combat command without adequate heavy maintenance support. We soon learned from experience that it was necessary for the combat command maintenance group to assist the attached units in addition to doing the work for the combat command's organic units.

During the campaign from Paris to the Siegfried line, the 3d Armored Division's maintenance group supplied the major maintenance for the entire forward elements of the corps. This commitment was a major contributing factor in the continued success of the corps during such extended operations. Without this, the corps' progress would have soon ground to a halt.

The German Attack

On the morning of December 16, I walked from the maintenance battalion headquarters, located in the main office building of the Engleburt Rubber factory in Aachen, to our shop area across the street. I was careful to give a wide berth to two 500-pound American unexploded bombs (UXBs) lying about a hundred feet apart in the parking lot. These bombs were considered extremely dangerous and were avoided until the ordnance bomb disposal crews could get rid of them.

As I approached the shop building, I saw my buddy Lt. Ernie Nibbelink, liaison officer for CCA, coming toward me. He appeared excited about something.

"Cooper, have you heard the news? The Krauts have broken through south of us near Malmédy and are going like hell. Arrington just got word; it came down from division."

My initial reaction was that this couldn't be more than a local operation. We had the Germans pinned down on the Roer River and had been beating their butts off. But I was soon proven wrong. In a short time, the rumors were going like wildfire. The Germans had dropped paratroopers in isolated groups behind our lines. Groups of German SS troops, wearing American uniforms and riding in American Jeeps, had infiltrated our lines.

The reaction at CCB headquarters was confused, and the situation map was sketchy. Apparently, the Germans had launched a massive assault along a broad front ranging from the Losheim gap in the north, near Malmédy, as far south as Luxembourg, just north of Echternach. This distance of some sixty miles was covered by only three divisions. An average of twenty miles of front per division was far too much to be covered. Because this sector had been considered relatively quiet, it had been used to give new troops combat experience before they were exposed to heavy fighting.

The 106th Division, which had just been committed to combat for the first time, entered the line on December 14, the day before, to replace the 2d Infantry Division. The battle-hardened 2d Infantry Division had pulled out of the line to move north to attack the dams on the Roer River at Schmidt, long been considered a prime target. The 106th Division moved into the positions previously occupied by the 2d Division on the Schnee Eifel, a series of heavily wooded hills just inside the German border. The 2d Division had prepared elaborate bunkers, foxholes, and trenches, and the 106th Division occupied these same positions.

The 14th Cavalry Squadron screened the area just north of the Schnee Eifel. This was a relatively wide area, and in some cases the outposts were as much as a mile apart. SHAEF had sixty-four divisions covering six hundred miles from the English Channel to the Swiss border. With some divisions in reserve, the average division had ten miles or more of front to cover. When forces concentrated for an offensive, certain areas would be even more lightly protected.

The German Ardennes offensive had brilliant planning and extremely tight security. On the morning of December 16, the Germans launched a massive assault with three armies abreast. Although the weather was extremely overcast and bad for flying, the Germans committed a thousand Luftwaffe planes, the largest force we had seen since the early days of Normandy. They used this air force for reconnaissance, for dropping groups of paratroopers, and, as the weather cleared, for attacking the highways, particularly at night. They also committed fighters to oppose high-level American bombing.

The initial assault against our frontline troops was overwhelming. With widely dispersed units, the Germans infiltrated, cut off, and surrounded many of our forward elements. In spite of this, many units formed small groups that put up a courageous rear guard. Stubborn resistance by these American units disrupted the tight German timetable during the critical phases of the attack and enabled SHAEF to bring reserves into play.

Back at maintenance battalion headquarters in Aachen, everything was in a mad scramble. All available men made an all-out effort to get every tank, half-track, and armored vehicle back on the line. The division was put on full alert and prepared to move immediately. We were told that the 7th Armored Division, our sister division at Camp Polk, from XIX Corps had already moved toward Saint-Vith. We had many buddies in the 7th Armored Division and were shocked the next day to hear that the first combat command to arrive in Saint-Vith to team up with remnants of the 106th Division had been completely overrun and shattered by superior German armor.

Although the Germans had been delayed, it was soon obvious that they had made a broad and deep breakthrough. Combat veterans in American armored divisions had long known that it was futile to try to stand directly in front of a major German panzer attack; this understanding had finally seeped up the chain of command.

Because of this German armor superiority, our task forces had to develop special tactics. As a combat command moved forward, the task forces would contact the German column and attempt to set up a roadblock reinforced with tanks, infantry, and self-propelled artillery. At the roadblock, the tanks could sometimes take a defiladed position for added protection against German firepower. Other tanks and infantry from the task force would attempt to move out on the flanks and, once the German column was stopped, subject it to heavy flanking fire, where our tank guns were most effective against the lighter German side armor.

Our task forces also used the M36 tank destroyer, when it was available. It had a 90mm gun with a muzzle velocity of 2,850 feet per second. This was still less powerful than the German PzKw VIb King Tiger's 88mm gun and was not effective against the Tiger's six-inch glacis faceplate. Sometimes, it would ricochet off the faceplate of a Panther. The M36 had only an inch and a half of armor on its front glacis plate and one inch on its sides. It also had an open-topped turret, which made it vulnerable to overhead airbursts from artillery.

The large gasoline dump at Stavelot was a prime objective of the German 6th SS Panzer Army. From there, they and the 5th SS Panzer Army would proceed northward past Liège, secure bridges across the Meuse River, and drive northward to Antwerp, cutting off the American First and Ninth Armies and the entire British 21st Army Group. Had this been successful, it would have been a military disaster for the Allies. The Germans were so short of gas at the beginning of this attack that the first parachute landing had to be delayed twenty-four hours because the paratroopers' trucks ran out of gas trying to get to the airfield on time. The capture of the gasoline dump at Stavelot was absolutely essential to the Germans.

The Germans had trained a special brigade of English-speaking soldiers, scrounged from the entire German army on both fronts. They were equipped with American Jeeps and American uniforms and weapons even down to dog tags and GI long underwear. They also carried identification taken from dead American soldiers and prisoners. Their mission was to infiltrate rapidly through the American lines and, in conjunction with paratroopers, attempt to secure bridges across the Meuse River.

We used an identification method known as "password and parole." When our sentries challenged an individual, they asked for the password. If he knew this, he was challenged a second time to give the parole. If he knew this, he would be allowed to pass. A new password and parole was issued every twenty-four hours.

Somehow these infiltrated Germans secured the correct password and parole, many of which began with the letter *W*. Because most Germans had difficulty pronouncing *W*, pronouncing *V* instead, we thought this might give them away. The Germans had apparently been cautioned about this and had overcome the problem. So we also asked simple questions that only an average American would know, such as who is L'il Abner? name five American candy bars, and who is Babe Ruth? Any German soldier who could name these was pretty sharp.

In an incident near Spa, a sentry in an ordnance heavy maintenance company stopped an American 99th Division Jeep carrying four well-dressed GIs. They knew the password and parole and seemed to pass all the other preliminary tests, so the sentry was getting ready to let them pass. About this time, a lieutenant came out and saw the four men in the Jeep. He asked where they were going. They said they had just come out of the line and were going for rest and recreation in Liège. The lieutenant figured that no GI came out of the line with clean clothes and a clean-shaven face. He also knew that all leaves had been canceled and that the 99th Division was fighting for its life.

He called the corporal of the guard, and the men were taken in, questioned, and strip-searched down to their bare skin. One of the young Germans apparently was an officer and had kept his German identification with him to get back inside the German lines. The unit commander immediately convened a general court-martial, and the German soldiers were tried in accordance with the Geneva Convention, which stated that any soldier caught behind enemy lines in enemy uniforms could be shot as a spy. The men were all convicted and, with First Army notification, were taken out and shot that night. Justice was swift and final in wartime.

At least these Germans had been given a fair trial, which was more than our soldiers received just east of Malmédy. A number of American soldiers were captured by a German SS armored column, marched out in a field, and shot in cold blood with machine guns. This became known as the Malmédy Massacre. After the word got out, American GIs had little sympathy for German POWs.

The American Defense

Back at SHAEF, it was obvious that the Germans had driven a wedge between the First and Third Armies. General Bradley's 12th Army Group headquarters down south in Luxembourg could no longer maintain contact with First Army in the north. General Eisenhower reluctantly decided that Bradley would hold on to Third Army and get what assistance he could from General Devers's 6th Army Group while the First and Ninth Armies would come under the control of General Montgomery's 21st Army Group.

From the 7th Armored Division's decimation at Saint-Vith, it was obvious that any attempt to directly block German armor was futile.

SHAEF developed a simple and direct battle plan to counter the German offensive. First, the hinges on the flanks must be held at all costs. The 99th and 2d Divisions on the Elsenborn Ridge on the north would be reinforced as quickly as possible. At the same time the southern hinge and the 4th Infantry Division near Echternach were also reinforced. The First and Ninth Armies on the north would pull out all available divisions and swing them south into the line, one at a time, to seal off the northern flank of the German penetration. At the same time, the Third Army on the south would send all available divisions to seal off the southern flank. No major defense positions would be established directly in front of the westward movement of the main German elements.

Montgomery was ordered to bring British troops to the west side of the Meuse near Dinant and prepare to make a stand. The Germans would have to commit troops to protect their flanks as they penetrated, and the deeper they penetrated the weaker the main forces would become. As soon as the northern and southern flanks were stabilized and the Germans had overextended themselves sufficiently, the American counterattack would attempt to cut off the base of the German salient and surround and destroy the German remnants.

On December 18, the 3d Armored Division was ordered to move south to Eupen. A German paratrooper unit had dropped into some woods south of the town on the road extending toward Malmédy and the Elsenborn Ridge. The paratroopers threatened the 1st Infantry Division and the other units on the hinge, so CCA sent down a task force to engage them. The paratroopers were soon eliminated, and CCA dug further into its positions.

The 30th Infantry Division had previously been ordered to secure Stavelot, which lay directly on the main line of advance of the 6th SS Panzer Army. In the wooded area just north of Stavelot was a large First Army gasoline dump containing 3 million gallons of gasoline. This would have given the 6th SS Panzer Army sufficient gasoline to go into Antwerp. On the night of December 19, CCB was ordered southward to the Spa and Stavelot area to back up the 30th Infantry Division.

Combat Command B left the Mausbach area late in the afternoon of December 19 and headed sixty miles south to Verviers, Spa, and Stavelot. They moved all night. The scattered snow soon turned to freezing rain, making the roads sheets of ice. All the vehicles had small blackout lights both front and rear. These consisted of a small housing with a slot about an inch long and about an eighth of an inch wide. In the dark, the lights were supposed to be visible at a distance of sixty yards. With the fog, mist, and sleet, the lights were barely visible more than a few feet away. It was impossible to maintain a normal sixty-yard march order. To get twelve hundred vehicles on the road and moving, it was necessary to jam them bumper to bumper and move as rapidly as possible.

The movement was a pure nightmare. Despite the system of guides and sentries that the MPs had worked out on short notice, there was still lots of confusion and a constant stop-and-start situation all night long. The intervals were extremely erratic, and often after prolonged stops the vehicles would get stretched out. When this happened, the vehicle in the rear would drive rapidly to catch up, but in the mist and darkness it often came upon another stopped vehicle and banged into the rear of it. If a two-and-a-half-ton GMC truck happened to hit a three-quarter-ton weapons carrier, it would simply knock it off the road. If a tank skidded into a Jeep, it would have squashed it flatter than a pancake. I made sure I didn't get in front of a tank that night.

The problem of unsnarling the wrecks, taking care of broken-down vehicles, and keeping everything moving in an orderly manner was the responsibility of the maintenance groups. The last vehicle in each section of each column was a maintenance vehicle. Following each column were ordnance wreckers and crews to take care of anything that the unit maintenance crews could not handle themselves. By dividing the maintenance into various levels and echelons, a particular problem could be taken care of at the lowest level as expeditiously as the facilities available would allow. This way the heavy ordnance maintenance crews and wreckers were required to take care of only the major problems.

In addition to this, we had our regular routine breakdown maintenance. A column of twelve hundred vehicles, approximately half of them tanks, half-tracks, and other combat vehicles, would normally experience 150 to 200 breakdowns during a night march of fifty to sixty miles. When this happened, the vehicles would be repaired on the shoulder of the road. If this could not be done quickly, crews were told to stay with the vehicles, and the ordnance maintenance heavy units from the rear of the column would get to them in due time.

Sixty percent of the combat command had arrived in the assembly area by daybreak on December 20. The remaining vehicles were scattered along the highway, and it was late in the afternoon before the majority of them arrived. It took an entire day before the worst wrecks were cleared up. In a few isolated instances, drivers got lost, and the entire crews used this as an excuse to shack up in some remote Belgian farmhouse. One oddball GI from the maintenance battalion got lost and wound up at Liège. When the MPs apprehended him six weeks later, he was wearing an Eisenhower jacket with captain's bars and both air force and ordnance lapel insignias. The MPs became suspicious because he was obviously out of uniform. He was returned to maintenance battalion custody and could have been charged with desertion in the face of the enemy, which was a capital offense. The charges were later reduced to extended AWOL and impersonating an officer. He was given a section 8 (incompetent for military service) and a dishonorable discharge.

The army, like any other cross section of the American population, had its share of misfits. Almost all soldiers, even lieutenants (if you can believe it), were prone to goof off from time to time. This acted as a stress relief valve to offset some of the fear and terror that gnawed at the guts of the soldier in combat. All the average American soldier wanted was for the war to end so he could go home. In spite of this, the great majority of American soldiers did their duty with great courage and valor, as proven by the terrible sacrifices they made.

In spite of all the planning, the night of December 19 was one of violent contrasts for the maintenance people. There were long periods when the crews, working under blackout conditions, would have to crawl under a tank or other wrecked vehicle to hook up a towing cable. In some instances a tank or truck would be on its side, and the men would have to crawl in rain-soaked ditches to hook up the cables. The first priority was to get the combat vehicles on the road, then the wheeled vehicles still able to run, and finally those that had to be repaired in place or towed to the next VCP. My job was to stay behind the tank column, find out where it was going, and offer ordnance contact as soon as the firefight began. In spite of all the breakdowns and wrecks, the road march soon settled down into a typical start-and-stop situation.

During one of the long waiting periods on the road, I reflected on the situation. This was the first time we had actually seen the enemy achieve a major breakthrough in our lines. Rumors were flying. The Germans had broken through on a broad front with twenty to thirty divisions and were still going strong. They were killing prisoners. German paratroopers had dropped behind our lines and German soldiers in American Jeeps and uniforms were infiltrating our lines.

The situation was highly fluid, and we never knew exactly where the enemy was. A definite change in the mood of the men was evident. Although morale was still good, there was a great deal of anxiety because this was our first experience in a major retreat. I began to understand how the German soldier must have felt during the greater part of the fighting from Normandy up to the Siegfried line. Although a retreat is difficult for everyone, it must have been much harder on the infantry than on the armored troops. After all, we spent most of our time behind enemy lines when we were advancing. The main difference here was that instead of advancing most of the time, we were going backward. That's one hell of a difference.

Stavelot–Trois Ponts–Stoumont–La Gleize

After arriving in Spa on December 20, CCB immediately went into action. It was attached to the XVIII Airborne Corps, and Maj. Gen. James Gavin ordered us to support the 30th Infantry Division in its attack to retake Stavelot and prevent the Germans from getting to the gasoline dump. At the same time, CCB was to attempt to establish a line south of Stavelot to further extend our northern flank.

Combat Command B advanced southward in three columns. Task Force Lovelady, the eastern column, advanced from Spa down the middle of the gasoline dump to the intersection of the road be-

tween La Gleize and Stavelot and from there to the western side of
Stavelot to support the 30th Division's attack. Part of the column
went southward to extend the defense line. Task Force McGeorge
in the middle secured La Gleize. Task Force Jordan on the west advanced through the rugged woods to secure Stoumont and extend
the line farther.

When I arrived in Spa, I immediately drove through the main part
of town to the top of the hill, where CCB had turned off to head
down through the gas dump to Stavelot. The dump, which spread
over several square miles and was well camouflaged from the air, consisted of five-gallon cans in thousand-can stacks about fifty yards apart
along both sides of small firebreak roads that spread in a geometric
pattern throughout the forest. A reinforced quartermaster truck
group had been ordered forward to move the gas out of there as
quickly as possible and take it to another dump across the Meuse
River in France, where it would be safe from the German advance.

A GMC truck could handle only two hundred five-gallon cans, so
this would have taken three thousand truckloads. The quartermaster group had brought up a number of ten-ton tractor-trailer trucks
and parked them along both sides of the main road in Spa. The plan
called for the GMC trucks to load the gas in the dump, unload it onto
the ten-ton trucks, then return for another load. As soon as the tractor-trailer was filled up, it was supposed to take off as rapidly as possible, unload the gas, and make a return trip.

The quartermaster troops had worked out a system for loading
the GMC trucks. They worked in four-man teams. Each truck had a
small portable manual roller conveyor about twenty feet long. The
truck was backed up as close as possible to the gasoline stack. Two
men got on top of the stack and two men were in the truck with the
conveyor stretched between them. The men on the stack would load
the cans onto the conveyor, which angled slightly downward, and the
other two men would pick the cans off the rolling conveyor and stack
them in the truck.

When left to their own devices, the American GI could always
come up with an innovative solution. Pretty soon, the GIs started
loading the trucks to a boogie cadence. They were spurred on not
only by competition among the various trucks but also because the

991st Field Artillery had started firing 155mm shells over their heads onto a road junction south of the dump.

I had gone about a hundred yards down the road into the dump when one of these GMC trucks loaded with gas came screaming around the curve heading straight toward me. My driver, White, pulled onto the shoulder of the road; the truck missed us by inches. The expression on the truckdriver's face was frozen as he came wheeling by, and I knew he wasn't going to stop for any Jeep. We pulled back on the road and drove another fifty yards or so when another truck came screaming out of the dump.

After repeating this five or six times, I finally contacted the quartermaster lieutenant in charge of the group. I told him I was the 3d Armored Division maintenance liaison officer and was trying to contact some elements of CCB near Stavelot. I asked him if he could hold a couple of these trucks for a few seconds until I could get by them.

He looked at me with a sheepish grin. "Lieutenant, I had to sweat my damn guts out to get these guys to come in here in the first place and unload this gas, and I sure as hell can't stop them now. If I can just keep these guys coming fast enough and unloading this gas to keep it away from the Krauts, I'll have done the best I can."

I surmised by his bearing that he was a brand-new second lieutenant right out of officer candidate school and was probably greener than I was. I could have pulled rank on him and chewed his butt a little bit, but I knew that it probably wouldn't do much good. And I couldn't blame the quartermaster troops for being nervous about those 155s being lobbed over their heads. After all, if one of them fell short in the dump, it could have been a disaster. I realized that any further attempt to get through the dump by that route was futile. I turned around, went back to Spa, and found another route.

One of the startling things about the Battle of the Bulge was how rapidly the rear-echelon service troops responded to the situation. By December 20, four days after the initial assault, the German breakthrough was fifty miles wide and thirty to thirty-five miles deep. SHAEF's defensive tactic of sealing off the flanks was forcing the Germans to penetrate deeper and in turn commit their own troops on the flanks, while at the same time seeking out a weak point where they could swing north and cross the Meuse River. Thus, when Kampfgruppe Peiper of the 6th SS Panzer Army took Stavelot, elements of the 30th Division came to retake Stavelot, seal off the gas dump, and establish a line on the northern flank. Because this flank was still highly fluid, the 30th Division was able to block off only the main road from the north through Stavelot. It was not possible for the 30th Division to block off all the firebreaks. As a result, the 6th SS Panzer Army constantly sent patrols to try to get through one of these lanes and bypass the 30th Division's positions. Until the 30th Division arrived north of Stavelot, the only thing standing between the Germans and the road to the gas dump were several small detachments of COMZ troops.

These consisted of engineers, signal, ordnance, quartermaster, and antiaircraft troops ranging in size from five to twenty-five men. The men carried .30-caliber M1 carbines, which had about half the range of the Garand but were still good weapons at close range. Every available man, including cooks, bakers, clerks, runners, mechanics, and drivers, was pressed into service.

One such group on the road from Spa to Stavelot consisted of a young engineer construction lieutenant with some engineer and antiaircraft troops together with a 90mm antiaircraft gun and one machine gun. They were the only roadblock north of Stavelot on this particular highway to the gas dump. They put the 90mm antiaircraft gun in a defiladed position off the left shoulder of the road and depressed the gun barrel to where it was just barely above the pavement. They placed the machine gun on the other side of the road, then set up small groups of riflemen in foxholes on both sides of the road. The total group consisted of no more than ten to twelve men, but they had a well dug in fortified position.

The 90mm, like the German 88, could be operated as an antitank as well as an antiaircraft weapon. The group had both armor-piercing and HE ammunition. There were numerous roadblocks of this type around the area, so whenever the advance guard of one of the German task groups approached they would immediately draw fire. Not realizing the size or nature of the roadblock, the German units would try to bypass and infiltrate around the roadblock. In so doing, they would encounter another roadblock from another small group of Americans dug in along one of the small fire lanes or by-pass roads. Because the Germans had no way of knowing whether these were outposts of a major defensive position or just merely in-dividual roadblocks, they were slowed considerably—enough to al-low the 30th Infantry Division and CCB of the 3d Armored Division to secure the gas dump and establish a strong position along the northern flank.

The hauling of the gas continued at a feverish pace, spurred on by accelerated artillery fire. As Task Force Lovelady approached the junction on the road between La Gleize and Stavelot, it ran into in-creasing German opposition. A firefight in this area destroyed a small German convoy of three ammunition trucks and three antitank guns. The American column split into two groups, one heading eastward toward Stavelot and the other southward toward Trois Ponts. Just north of Trois Ponts, the group ran into a heavy armored column consisting of Panther and King Tiger tanks from the 1st SS Leib-standarte Adolf Hitler Panzer Division, considered the toughest panzer unit in the entire German army. Our lightly armored M4 Shermans didn't stand a chance against these German behemoths, and we immediately lost our four lead Sherman tanks. Task Force Lovelady withdrew slightly, established roadblocks, and called for heavy artillery fire.

In one incident, an M12 gun carriage with its 155mm GPF rifle loaded came around a bend in the road and suddenly found itself face to face with a King Tiger. Fortunately, the 155 was pointed di-rectly at the base of the King Tiger's turret. The gun commander gave the order to fire. The 155 struck the King Tiger at the base of the gun mantlet where the turret joins the deck. The explosion rup-tured the thin top deck armor and blew the turret off the tank, in-stantly killing the entire crew. Had the shell struck a few inches lower on the front glacis plate, it would have exploded harmlessly, and the King Tiger would have been able to drill the M12 from end to end with its high-velocity 88. Such were the fortunes of war.

Back north in the gasoline dump, the boogie cadence picked up a terrific rate of speed and the quartermaster crews started loading those damn trucks like crazy. No sooner was a truck loaded than off it went. I found out later that as the artillery fire increased some of the drivers panicked and kept going when they got to Spa, not stopping to load the gasoline in the large 10-ton semi-trailers. Like a race horse grabbing the bit in his mouth, they went off in every direction except toward the Germans. Some of these gas trucks wound up at Liège, Antwerp, Brussels, and various points in northern Paris.* At least the damn Germans didn't get it. This was still a remarkable undertaking, when one considers that it took First Army over two months to accumulate this much gas and it took the quartermanster troops some 24 hours to get it safely away from the Germans.

In the meantime, the other two task forces of CCB proceeded southward in two columns. Task Force Lovelady withdrew north from Trois Ponts and Petit-Coo and proceeded down a secondary road to Parfondroy preparatory to a joint attack on Stavelot with the 30th Infantry Division. It was here that they discovered the massacre of innocent civilians by the brutal SS troops of Kampfgruppe Peiper. Numerous bodies of old men, women, and children were scattered around the village; they had been shot by the SS. The 30th Division troops in Stavelot told us that they had encountered similar massacres there. Word of these massacres undoubtedly contributed to the shortage of live SS prisoners taken by American GIs.

The battle of Stavelot raged back and forth for several days. Before CCB got there on December 20, the 117th Regimental Combat Team of the 30th Infantry Division engaged German *panzergrenadiers* with heavy King Tiger tanks, without any forward support of their own. Because the 117th Regiment was spread over a large area, their flanks were constantly threatened.

Company A of the 117th Infantry, commanded by Capt. John Kent, found a number of fifty-five-gallon drums loaded with gasoline. Kent told me later that his men removed incendiary rounds from .30-caliber machine-gun ammunition and loaded them in their Garand rifles. When a German tank column emerged from the narrow streets of Stavelot and started up the hill, the GIs rolled several drums of gasoline down the hill, then fired incendiary bullets into

*A lot of the gas wound up on the French black market in Paris.

the gas drums, which immediately erupted into a blazing explosion. As the crew attempted to bail out of the lead tank, they were met by a fusillade of small-arms fire.

When the GIs found the roads frozen too hard to plant mines, they would take a mine and tie a light rope to the cage. They would place the mine in a ditch on one side of the road with a GI on the other side holding the rope. When a tank approached, they would pull the mine across the road in front of the tracks. The tank would strike the mine, breaking the tracks. When the crews bailed out, the GIs would cut loose with small-arms fire and kill the crew members before they could get off the tank.

In the meantime, a major battle had developed on the northern flank, and CCB and the 30th Division were joined by the 82d Airborne. The entire force came under the XVIII Airborne Corps, which brought up additional artillery and other supporting troops.

Both Task Force Jordan and Task Force McGregor were stopped by heavy German tank and antitank fire. Task Force Jordan withdrew slightly, regrouped, and overcame resistance in Stoumont. Jordan then proceeded toward La Gleize to join up with Task Force Mc-Gregor coming down from the north. After an extremely heavy firefight, the German resistance was overcome and the entire German column was put out of action.

This operation along the Stavelot–La Gleize–Stoumont line appears to be the first time that the main armored thrust of the 6th SS Panzer Army was engaged head-on by a major combination of American armor and infantry. They were stopped dead. They not only failed to capture the gasoline dump, which could have been the most valuable prize of the entire campaign, they were forced to extend their efforts farther westward and expose their ever-lengthening flanks on the north. This, in turn, weakened their forward thrust as they constantly committed troops to hold this flank against American pressure.

8

The Battle of the Bulge: Phase II, the Counterattack

The Germans Regroup

By December 24, the situation in the Stavelot–La Gleize–Stoumont area had stabilized, and CCB was relieved and reverted back to 3d Armored Division control. In the meantime, 3d Armored Division headquarters with elements of CCR had moved on the night of December 19 from Stolberg to the vicinity of Hotton.

They had to contend with the same horrible driving conditions of ice, sleet, and freezing rain, and when they arrived at Hotton the next morning they had numerous vehicles scattered up and down the seventy-mile route of march. It was an enormous effort for the maintenance people to unsnarl this mess and get the damaged vehicles repaired and back on the road. With CCB at Stavelot and CCA still committed south of Eupen, the division was vastly understrength. The division's mission was to establish contact with the 82d Airborne to the east along the Grandménil-Manhay-Hotton highway and at the same time try to contain the flow of German armor north until more reinforcements arrived.

The Battle of the Bulge now entered the critical second phase. The plan to hold the hinges north and south of the bulge appeared to be gaining success. Kampfgruppe Peiper, leading the 1st SS Leibstandarte Adolf Hitler Panzer Division, had failed to capture the gasoline dump and had suffered a crushing defeat. To the south, the 101st Airborne Division and elements of the 10th Armored Division doggedly defended Bastogne. Even though they were completely surrounded, they refused to surrender. General Patton's Third Army had launched an all-out assault to relieve Bastogne. Both the northern and southern flanks appeared to be stabilizing somewhat, but the area between Bastogne and Saint-Vith was wide open, and German armor and *panzergrenadier* units were still going strong.

The virtual decimation of Kampfgruppe Peiper and 1st SS Panzer Division cost the Germans their most powerful attacking force. It appeared that the emphasis was now being shifted to the 5th Panzer Army, and the 116th Panzer Division had the mission to head north and seize the bridgehead across the Meuse River on the way to Antwerp.

On the morning of December 20, the 3d Armored Division rushed into the gap between Hotton and Manhay to confront this advance. With less than a third of its strength—both of its major combat commands were committed elsewhere—the division was thrown into the maw. General Rose faced some critical decisions.

Generally speaking, our intelligence about German movements was good. Rose knew that the Germans probably had less of an idea of American dispositions. For the 3d Armored Division to be in the Aachen-Stolberg area on December 19 and suddenly appear seventy miles away the next morning took the Germans completely by surprise; they didn't realize that this was less than a third of the division. With our well-organized motor transport and maintenance system, American armor had a vast maneuver and logistic superiority over comparable German units. The Germans never quite comprehended this.

Here again we see the advantages of the heavier American armored division. The 3d Armored Division had a total strength of 390 tanks, 232 of them M4 Shermans. Although vastly inferior in armor and firepower, the heavy armored division had as many tanks as two and a half German panzer divisions. Rose's 60 medium and 30 light tanks, together with accompanying units and artillery, gave him a lean and mean Combat Command R.

3d Armored Division at Hotton-Manhay

General Rose already had a reputation as an extremely aggressive division commander who had great confidence in his troops. He had his staff come up with a fast-moving, innovative plan.

At noon on December 20, the 3d Armored Division attacked southward against elements of one panzer and two *volksgrenadier* divisions. The attack called for an advance along the broad front from

Hotton to Grandménil. The three American task forces moving southward and the Germans moving northward had a series of meeting engagements.

The terrain in this area of the Ardennes was extremely rugged. The ability to advance was limited, and sometimes columns would come around a bend facing each other less than a hundred yards apart. It was as if two blindfolded prizefighters suddenly found themselves in the middle of the ring and their blindfolds were removed. The guy who threw the first punch had the advantage.

If the lead German tank was a Mark IV, the American M4A1 with its 76mm gun and power traverse turret had a good chance. The German turrets were manually operated, and we could generally swing faster and get off the first shot quicker. If the lead German tank was a Tiger or a Panther, we had to back up, get out of there, and set up a roadblock.

A tank commander reported that he had come face-to-face with a Panther that had its gun turret turned ninety degrees from the forward position. He fired the first round from the 76mm gun and struck the Panther square in the middle of its forward glacis plate. There was a tremendous flash of sparks, like a grinding wheel hitting a piece of steel. When it was over, the tank commander realized that the round had ricocheted and not penetrated the tank. He quickly reloaded, fired the second round, and struck the glacis plate again as the German slowly turned its turret in his direction. Before the Panther could get its gun zeroed in on the M4, the tank commander got off a third round, with equal results. The Panther was finally able to fire its high-velocity 75mm, which penetrated the M4 tank like a sieve. Fortunately, the tank commander survived to tell this story.

Although the heavier Panther and King Tiger tanks were far superior in firepower and armor, our small task forces had additional capabilities, which tended to offset this. Our infantry rode in M3 half-tracks with one-half-inch and one-quarter-inch armor on the front and the sides. With three machine guns on each half-track plus their semi-automatic Garand rifles, our infantrymen had considerably greater firepower than comparable German units. The M2 half-track had a door in the back and mounted an 81mm mortar that could be fired directly from the half-track. It could also be removed and fired from the ground. Each task force also included several M16 half-tracks with quad .50-caliber machine guns and M15 half-tracks with a single 37mm automatic gun and two .50-caliber machine guns. This gave the task force a tremendous amount of automatic fire-power. Armored and infantry firepower was supplemented by M7 105mm self-propelled howitzers, which generally rode on the tail of the column. Even though these task forces were small, they were highly mobile and could pack a hell of a punch if they got into a fire-fight. The task force commanders realized they were light on armor and they could not stand much of a chance when engaged by major panzer units.

For the next few days, the situation was highly fluid. With the exception of certain isolated supply units, such as the 7th Armored Division trains at La Roche, there were no major American combat forces in this area other than the 3d Armored Division. Its three columns advanced south as rapidly as possible. Once they contacted the enemy, they tried to slow down the enemy's advance. As the overwhelming enemy strength built up, they withdrew.

General Rose's mission was to establish a screen between the 82d Airborne on the east and Hotton on the west, where the 84th Infantry was due to arrive soon. All three task forces began to encounter heavy German resistance and started to withdraw slowly. The Germans brought in the 2d SS Panzer Division with the mission of driving up highway N15 toward Manhay and screening the flank of the 5th Panzer Army to the south. The 2d SS Panzer Division had become notorious for the cruel massacre of more than six hundred innocent French civilians including women and children during the earlier days of the invasion.

Task Force Hogan had proceeded southward from Soy to a point three miles south of Samrée. As the German pressure began to build, the task force slowly withdrew to higher ground at Berisménil, where they were completely cut off and surrounded by German panzer units. They set up a strong perimeter defense, and from this high ground could observe the movement of the German troops down below and fire on them while directing other division artillery into this area.

This was a constant thorn in the Germans' side. A young German officer under a truce flag approached the outer perimeter defenses. He was met, blindfolded, and escorted to Colonel Hogan's command post. His message said they were surrounded by three divisions and would be totally destroyed if they did not surrender. Hogan told him in his polite Texas drawl to go to hell, and the German returned with his mission unfulfilled.

The weather was beginning to abate somewhat, and there were patches of clear sky mixed with the clouds. An attempt to resupply Hogan's unit with an airdrop missed the target completely. Another attempt was made to fire medical supplies in empty smoke shells. When this too failed, the situation became more critical. After four desperate days, General Rose ordered Hogan to destroy his equipment and evacuate as many of his men as possible.

To destroy his equipment without giving away his plans to the Germans, Hogan could not burn it or use demolitions. To the well-trained maintenance crews and gunners, the solution became obvious. All American teenagers know that when you get angry at your buddy and want to get back at him, you put sugar in his gas tank to destroy it. This is exactly what they did to all the engines. At the same time, they destroyed the firing pins of the tanks and the artillery pieces and buried the breechblocks in the dirt. They also dismantled many machine guns and heavy weapons and scattered their parts.

Finally, the men blackened their faces and under the cover of darkness began to slip out in groups of ten to twenty. Colonel Hogan had a difficult time walking in his air force boots, but he finally got back safely to our lines. When questioned by General Rose as to why he was the last man out, Hogan could have given him some heroic textbook answer. Instead, in his typical Texas drawl he said, "General, my damn feet hurt."

Task Force Hogan kept the 116th Panzer Division from exploiting its quick advantage in obtaining bridgeheads across the Ourthe River. All three task forces slowed the Germans considerably and disrupted them until American reinforcements began to arrive.

On the morning of December 21, Combat Command A reverted back to division control followed by CCB on December 24. They were joined by two regimental combat teams from the 75th Infantry Division and some other units. The 3d Armored Division was practically up to the strength of a full armored corps.

The 2d SS Panzer Division, joined by elements of the 12th SS Panzer Division, had driven up through Manhay and occupied Grandménil. When they attempted to turn west and tried to outflank the 3d Armored Division, they were stopped cold and driven back. After major assaults and much back-and-forth fighting with small task groups, the line began to stabilize. The time had come to regroup and build up for the counterattack.

German Air Attack

When CCB reverted back to the division on Christmas Eve, I decided to return to the maintenance battalion headquarters company and deliver my combat loss report. I had heard that orders were issued to deliver at least one hot dinner on Christmas Eve or Christmas Day to all troops if possible. I was tired of eating cold K rations and 10-N-1s by this time.

Headquarters company maintenance battalion had moved into a large rock quarry in Aywaille. The quarry, big enough to hold the entire company and all its vehicles, was approximately half a mile square and had walls extending fifty to sixty feet above the quarry floor, which was relatively even and made an ideal working area. The entrance was down a gradual slope of crushed stone. A number of buildings provided cover for work areas.

By a rare coincidence, we arrived at headquarters company shortly before chow. I told my driver, White, to get the vehicle gassed up and checked out, get himself some chow, and be prepared to leave on a moment's notice.

The officers' mess was set up in a lean-to next to one of the buildings. I sat down at the table looking forward to a good meal. I couldn't remember when I'd last had a real hot meal served in a chow line.

Suddenly, a low, rumbling noise erupted out of nowhere and exploded into an awesome crescendo as a low-flying plane came screaming over the quarry. A sentry rushed in and told Colonel Mc-

Carthy that it was a German fighter plane but it was flying so low and so fast that our antiaircraft gunners didn't get in a shot.

There were disadvantages to being in a defiladed position such as this. The antiaircraft gunners had no visibility over the edge of the quarry, so they couldn't see an approaching plane until it was right on top of us. Everybody ran out of the quarry shed and immediately took cover. We expected the plane to make a wide turn and come in on a strafing run. I found a perfect foxhole, about three feet wide by four feet deep by ten feet long, where a large block had been removed. There were similar holes all around the quarry, and they were soon filled with men.

After what seemed to be eons of time waiting for the German fighter plane to return, although it was actually less than a minute, we heard a low, rumbling noise. It was music to our ears. Directly overhead was a large group of B17 heavy bombers flying at about twenty thousand feet. We could see them clearly because the clouds had disappeared the night before and the sky was crystal clear for the first time in weeks. There were three squadrons staggered in a V formation. To the rear we could see other groups following. This was the first day since the German offensive began that large masses of American bombers were out to attack.

In my fascination at looking at these beautiful planes, I forgot momentarily about the German fighter plane. My binoculars were in the Jeep, so I strained my eyes to look up at this magnificent sight. The lead squadron, some twelve Flying Fortresses, was directly above the quarry and was leaving long contrails like a series of diamond necklaces in the sky. The column extended as far as the eye could see over the horizon. The sight was further enhanced by the eruption of dozens of small, flashing lights, like snowflakes rotating in the sun, around the planes in the lead squadron.

My fascination turned to horror as suddenly the lead plane in the squadron exploded in midair. Another explosion cut the tail off one of the Flying Fortresses; the main body of the plane tumbled toward the earth as the tail section slowly fluttered back and forth like a maple leaf descending in the breeze. Another explosion sheared off the entire wing of one of the Fortresses, and it spiraled toward the quarry. Two other B17s with their engines on fire broke out of the column and started spiraling like wounded birds struck with flaming arrows. The spirals became tighter and tighter as the planes plunged headlong to earth.

I was so engrossed by this sight that it was some time before I could discern nine German fighter planes lined up perpendicular to the direction of flight to the first squadron. They were flying several thousand feet to the rear of the lead squadron, just far enough to be out of range of the .50-caliber machine guns of the tail gunners. The rocket-firing German fighters were accurate. Out of twelve planes in the lead squadron, they shot down five.

The skies filled with parachutes. I counted twenty-five in the air and figured that approximately half the crews had escaped. The sky was also filled with the debris of broken, twisted airplanes as they plummeted downward. There were landing gears, engines, pieces of wing, parts of fuselages, and even bombs falling. Some of the bombs, even though they were unarmed, exploded on impact with the ground. Fortunately, none of them landed directly in the quarry. As if in some giant apocalypse, the heavens literally exploded, raining a deluge of fire upon the earth below.

The Flying Fortress with its right wing sheared off struck the ground about fifty yards beyond the edge of the quarry. The explosion rocked the ground as the gasoline and the bomb load went off. A column of flame and debris erupted some thousand feet into the air, scattering parts in all directions. Had the bomber crashed into the hard stone floor of the quarry, the blast might have annihilated our entire company.

Anytime an airman parachuted down in our area, we sent out patrols with medics to pick him up. When the patrol reached the fallen tail section of the Flying Fortress, they noticed a body in the tail gunner's seat. The medics had to forcibly break the hatch to remove the body. Apparently, the tail gunner had not been able to escape because the crawl zone between his position and the rest of the plane was crushed flat.

As the medics removed the tail gunner from beneath the canopy, they discovered that he was still alive. They put him on a stretcher and after a quick examination determined that he had no wounds. When he regained consciousness, he told the medics that he thought he'd fainted.

Another parachute was about five hundred feet in the air and descending earthward when we noticed what appeared to be a section of wing falling directly on top of him. We screamed and waved frantically to get him to slip his chute to one side. He obviously did not hear us. The wing continued downward, shearing the parachute in half; the young airman fell to his death. It was terrible to think that he had parachuted safely from twenty thousand feet, then was killed by this falling piece of debris.

Yet another parachute was heading directly into the middle of the quarry. And this brought on something I did not believe could happen. I had heard of instances like this but did not think that they actually occured. When it was about a thousand feet above the quarry, a lone German ME109 fighter dove down and headed straight toward the parachute with all of its machine guns wide open. We screamed and hollered and waved our arms to try to warn him, but we couldn't fire any antiaircraft guns because we were afraid of hitting him. He saw us, and kicking violently he slipped his chute to one side. The German plane missed him on the first pass.

The German pilot was apparently obsessed with killing this helpless young airman, because he made a second wide turn and came back for another pass, firing the machine guns again. By this time the parachute was much lower, and the German pilot was so intent on cold-blooded murder that he crashed into the side of the quarry in a terrible explosion. If there was ever a case of retribution in war, this was it.

The medics brought in the airman, who turned out to be a bombardier. He had not been hit. His worst injury was a frozen foot as a result of having kicked off his flying boot when he was trying to slip his chute. All these airman were taken to the aid station and evacuated back to the army hospital.

In spite of the falling debris and exploding bombs and aircraft, our company in the rock quarry received no major injuries or damage. I finally figured out what the German plane that had buzzed the quarry a few minutes before the air battle started was doing. It was a low-flying reconnaissance plane radioing back the position of the lead bomber squadron. Because our bombers were still over friendly territory, they had not picked up any fighter escort.

If I'd had a color movie camera and could have laid on my back in my stone foxhole, I could probably have gotten the most spectacular aerial battle of the war on film. I realized the terrible risk the young bomber crews took. Air battles are sudden and last only a few seconds or minutes. Like all combat, you are killed outright or wounded or you survive to fight another day.

My Driver, White, Is Wounded

As CCB moved into the Hotton-Soy area, it relieved some of the pressure on CCR, which had been severely battered. Company C of the maintenance battalion moved into Werbomont to give CCB closer support. Werbomont was south on highway N15 between Harz and Grandménil.

I decided to spend the night at headquarters company and join C Company the next morning. My driver, White, wanted to visit some of his buddies, and I told him it was okay, so long as he was ready to move out at a moment's notice. I returned to the section of the building next to Major Arrington's trailer and put down my sack there.

That night, lying in my sack, I reflected on Christmas Eves past. I didn't think about where I would be next Christmas, or if I would be. I don't suppose anyone ever understands what goes on in a soldier's mind in combat. We conjure pleasant memories of the past, think about the present in a fleeting moment, skip over the immediate future, and dwell on long-range possibilities. In this way, we can do what is necessary yet at the same time maintain a low anxiety level about the immediate future. This is how the soldier survives physically and emotionally. This process must be magnified many times for the combat infantryman or tanker who is constantly exposed to enemy fire. It mounts up, in various levels, for those of us in maintenance who are exposed to direct fire only periodically.

Before I went overseas, my mother sent me a small book entitled *Prayers for the Day*. It was divided into 365 days, each dated with a separate section of scripture and a prayer for each day. My mother could open her copy to a given date and read the same prayer I was reading. That night, I was comforted by reading the Christmas story about the birth of Christ, and I thought what a beautiful idea it was for my mother to give me the book with excerpts for us to share. I was thankful to almighty God that my parents had taught me Christian values. The faith based on these values was essential to my survival both physically and emotionally.

After chow the next morning, I went to find White. The Jeep was gone and White was nowhere around. Some of the men who had been with him said that Warrant Officer Macklin had come over around midnight and asked White to drive him to division headquarters rear to deliver a report. Neither White nor Macklin had returned, and no one knew where they were.

I was angry that Macklin had taken my Jeep without asking. He knew that liaison officers had to be prepared to move out at any time. Checking with headquarters company, I found out that White had been seriously wounded and had been evacuated to the army hospital. My first thoughts were that White had died. Because it was extremely difficult to get information about wounded evacuated to an army hospital during combat, it was several years after the war before I heard that White had survived. Here is what happened.

The Luftwaffe had committed well over a thousand planes to the Ardennes offensive. As in Normandy, it concentrated its attacks at night. This was the first night with clear weather, and the planes attacked every target site, as our planes had done during the daytime.

Because the roads were covered with ice and there were no leaves on the trees, my Jeep must have looked like a dark object moving across a mirror. As it approached a crossroad on its way to division headquarters, a rocket-firing ME109 came screaming down in a strafing run. A rocket exploded alongside the Jeep on the driver's side. The blast blew the Jeep off the road into the ditch, and some of the fragments struck White behind his left ear at the base of the skull. Fortunately, there was a Red Cross ambulance at the crossroads, and Macklin and some of the aidemen loaded White into it. Macklin was apparently uninjured, but the Jeep was damaged. I felt terrible about White being wounded, particularly not knowing at the time whether or not he had survived. We had developed a bond that is understood only by soldiers in combat who live together on a daily basis and depend on each other for survival. I would miss him.

A Problem with Frostbite

For the next few days, the division consolidated its position. The 2d Armored Division to our west was mopping up the 2d SS Panzer Division, which it had caught on the road at Celles and virtually annihilated. Our maintenance people worked feverishly to get everything ready for a new offensive. The maintenance effort was complicated because we had no buildings or hard ground to work from. Company C, located in Werbomont, was scattered in this small village and set up shop in the rolling fields between the farmhouses. It was bitterly cold; if a mechanic tried to grab a hand tool without his gloves, his skin would stick to it. Yet wearing heavy gloves while working with hand tools makes it hard to get down in the small recesses on a tank engine.

Even under these conditions, the maintenance people were lucky compared to the combat infantrymen and tankers trying to hold the line. The continuous cold weather had frozen the ground, and it was difficult to dig a foxhole. In some cases the infantrymen and combat engineers used grenades to penetrate the ground.

By this time, the driving was becoming hazardous. The constant packing of the snow by the tanks and other vehicles had created sheets of solid ice. Even with the metal grousers, some tanks would slide like a sled if they attempted to stop on a slope. We constantly used our wreckers to get tanks out of the ditches and back onto the roads. For several days, it snowed almost constantly, and the buildup on some of the little-used side roads would reach two to three feet.

Major Arrington issued me a new Jeep to replace the damaged one, and I was assigned a new driver. Private First Class Wrayford, a tall country boy from Louisiana, was a good driver and mechanic and took a great deal of pride in keeping the Jeep in first-class condition. He transferred the contents of the damaged Jeep to the new one. From the looks of the driver's side on the old Jeep, White had apparently lost a great deal of blood and it was a miracle that he had survived.

In transferring to the new Jeep, I was surprised to find how much equipment and other articles I had accumulated. We had two bedrolls, two backpacks, a wooden map box with a thermite grenade inside, two ponchos, my binoculars, a case of 10-N-1 rations, and a case of K rations. I was issued a .45-caliber 1911 automatic pistol and shoulder holster. Wrayford had a .30-caliber carbine mounted in a bracket on the windshield. In addition we had one 1903 Springfield bolt-action sharpshooter's rifle, two .30-caliber M1 Garand rifles, a box of hand grenades, and two German 100-meter *panzerfausts*. Whenever we overran a German column, we would find some *panzerfausts* lying around. An excellent weapon for an individual, it could be fired one time and then discarded. It did not have the range of our bazooka, but it had much greater penetrating power. I explained to Wrayford that in the event of imminent capture, we definitely wanted to get rid of the *panzerfausts*, because the Germans had been known to kill American soldiers if they found German weapons on them.

I had also accumulated various other loot, such as German cameras, pistols, binoculars, and many miscellaneous items picked up along the way. (Technically, all of these items came under the classification of military contraband and thus were legal.) We traded these items constantly with other soldiers to upgrade our stock.

The snow continued to fall as we drove. We came to a snowdrift about three feet deep on a small side road and thought we could get through it. Wrayford put the Jeep in low-low gear and we started out, but the buildup of snow in front of the Jeep formed a wedge and eventually lifted the wheels right off the ground. The Jeep wouldn't budge in either direction. We got out and started digging until a command and reconnaissance car with a winch on the front came down the main road near us and we flagged it down. One pull of the winch and we were free. I told Wrayford that I hoped we'd learned a lesson; if this had happened when we were following the combat units, we would have been in deep trouble.

The Belgian château at Pair that the headquarters maintenance battalion had moved into was the most luxurious quarters we'd had to date. During this part of the Ardennes offensive, when the situation was somewhat static, we would put the Belgian family in one part of the house and take over the rest. In this way we could get our men inside and at the same time take care of the civilians.

The Belgians were usually cooperative and welcomed us. They realized that we were fighting for them, and if the Germans had been occupying the area they would have probably been thrown out in the cold. Even the combat elements in forward areas tended to concentrate around the small villages, in order to keep as many men inside as possible. The men living in foxholes on the line and in the outposts suffered terribly in this cold weather.

During the early part of the Ardennes campaign, the soldiers were equipped with combat boots with a heavy composition sole, an unfinished heavy leather upper, and a smooth leather extension on the top that buckled about halfway up the calf. With one or more pairs of heavy GI cotton socks, the boots were adequate for normal conditions. They were, however, completely inadequate for the frontline soldier standing in a foxhole. In the constantly alternating sleet, rain, and snow, the foxholes often filled with water. Standing in the water for many hours at a time, without being able to walk around, caused serious circulation problems in the feet and lower legs. Wet feet would begin to swell, and severe pain would incapacitate the soldier. This was known as trench foot, which caused many casualties. In some cases the swelling became so severe that gangrene set in, and some men lost parts of or, in extreme cases, both their feet.

At first, the army was completely unprepared to cope with this. It wasn't until almost the end of the Ardennes campaign that we received shoepacs, which were much better. They had a heavy rubber bottom and sides, similar to an overshoe, a one-inch heavy felt innersole, and high leather tops that extended halfway up the calf. They were completely waterproof at the bottom. Worn with extra socks and sized to provide plenty of room for our feet to move around, they worked well. The Germans wore a similar boot that had been developed after their experience on the Russian front.

One night at Pair, I was getting ready to get in the sack and had removed my combat jacket, shirt, trousers, and boots. All that was left was my long underwear and socks. I never took off my socks unless I could change into a new pair. New socks were rare, so this wasn't too often.

My feet were usually numb during the day when I was outside in the cold, but they would warm up and the feeling would return once I got inside. I would rub my feet with the socks on before getting into the sack. This night I noticed that my feet were unusually sore, particularly on the bottom. On removing my socks, I noticed large black splotches on the ball and heel of both feet.

The next day, Captain Myzak, our battalion surgeon, examined my feet and told me I had bad frostbite spots and should go to an army base hospital for treatment. Apparently, the constant exposure of my thin-soled boots on the steel floor of the Jeep had caused the frostbite. I pleaded with the captain not to send me to an army hospital, because I was afraid I would be temporarily transferred out of the division and might never get back. I felt just the opposite of Brer Rabbit in the briar patch.

He offered to treat me at the combat aid station. With a scalpel he gently peeled the outer callus layer of skin from the spots on both feet. The spots consisted of dried blood from ruptured capillaries; it had come to the surface and frozen. I supposed this was nature's way of protecting my feet from further freezing. Then he swabbed my feet and bandaged them with gauze soaked in antiseptic. I was cured after lying flat on my back for the next couple of days, and I went back to duty wearing the new shoepacs.

The (VT) Proximity Fuse

All of our plans were proceeding for a major counterattack. VII Corps of First Army was to attack southward along highway N15 from Grandménil toward Houffalize while Third Army attacked northward from Bastogne to Houffalize. The meeting at Houffalize should cut off any remaining German troops west of there.

VII Corps consisted of the 75th, 83d, and 84th Infantry Divisions and the 2d and 3d Armored Divisions. The 3d Armored Division on the east and the 2d Armored Division on the west were to pass through the 75th Infantry Division and, supported by the 83d and 84th Divisions, make the major attack southward toward Houffalize. With the U.S. Army's only two heavy armored divisions supported by three first-class infantry divisions, VII Corps had the maximum available capability.

One of the best-kept secrets of World War II, next to the atomic bomb, was the proximity fuse, or VT fuse—or pozit fuse, as it was commonly known. It was an improvement on the traditional overhead time-fire fuse, which until then had been considered one of the deadliest fuses.

The traditional time-fire fuse contained a series of annular powder rings that could be adjusted in length to provide a fairly exact time when a shell was supposed to explode. This adjustment was made by inserting the head of the fuse into a fuse cutter, which changed the length of the powder train so that the fuse would explode at the proper time. By knowing the range and the velocity of the shell, according to the number of charges used, the gunner could look at a chart and tell the exact setting to get the shell to explode at a prescribed number of feet in the air.

When a shell exploded in the air, a cone of fragments struck the ground with a devastating effect on the soldiers in the exposed area. Even soldiers in foxholes were vulnerable to this type of fire. To get the shells to explode at the optimum height overhead, an observer had to see the shell exploding and adjust the time fire accordingly by radio. This meant that the attacking group must have the enemy under observation.

The proximity fuse contained a small battery-powered radar system that was armed when the projectile fired from the tube. As the projectile approached the ground, the radar bounced the signal back and caused the fuse to detonate at the desired height. This was much more reliable than the traditional time-fire fuse. It also did not require an observer to actually see the explosion. This fire could be directed deep into the enemy's rear against artillery and other targets that were not under observation.

The proximity fuse had been developed and used two years earlier by the navy in the Pacific. It had been effective against Japanese aircraft. Any rounds that failed to fire fell harmlessly into the ocean. To the best of our knowledge, neither the Japanese nor the Germans knew about this fuse.

The decision had been made to use the proximity fuse in the opening assault of this counterattack. It would be the first time it had been used in massive artillery barrages.

On New Year's Day, Major Arrington called in the liaison officers and briefed us on the new fuse. We were to contact the artillery units in our combat commands and brief them. I contacted the 391st Field Artillery in CCB and told them about the new fuses, which were to be drawn at the ammunition point that day. I passed along all the technical data I had, which was relatively simple. The fuse was to be used in place of the time-fire fuse and required no further adjustments. Upon firing, the impact of the propellent charge armed the fuse. When the round reached a certain height above the target, it would automatically detonate. If the projectile was fired into a wooded area, tree branches might set off the fuse. I didn't tell them anything about the radar system; the less they knew, the better, in case they were captured.

The next morning, the day before the counterattack was due to start, people from the division G2 section brought a civilian down to the forward line. He was dressed as a typical Belgian farmer with heavy boots and a greatcoat that hung almost to his ankles. He wore heavy wool mittens and a wool cap with flaps that pulled down over his ears. He had a small, thin radio mounted on his belt but also supported by shoulder straps. The straps had slip-type loops, so if he raised his arms as if to surrender, the loops would disengage the belt and the straps, and the radio would fall, hopefully undetected. He also carried several large envelopes filled with some type of chemical powder. He said he could rub this powder on his coat along with dry snow and the reaction would change the coat's color. He had the password and parole for the next several days. After being briefed by the commander of the forward infantry company, he passed through our lines and wandered off into the woods between the German outposts.

His mission was to infiltrate German lines and radio information back to us about their positions. This was courageous, because the Germans would summarily execute him if he was caught. This is just one example of the many instances in which the Belgian underground assisted the U.S. Army.

The proximity fuse had been issued to all the artillery in both the First and Third Armies. The attack on the morning of January 3 was preceded by a horrendous artillery barrage. Using the proximity fuse, we got airbursts with 155mm and 8-inch shells directly over Houffalize. Although our forward elements were still five to eight miles from Houffalize, the Germans thought we had already broken through and were less than a mile from the city. We would have to have been that close to get direct observation from the surrounding hills. This created a panic among the retreating German troops and further added to the terrible congestion trying to jam through the narrow streets of Houffalize. This panic fed upon itself, and the traffic jams created further targets for the devastating airbursts.

The American Counterattack

By this time, the U.S. Army had gained a great deal of experience in planning a frontal assault. General Collins realized that the GHQ tank battalions and infantry did not have sufficient armored power to make a major assault in open country, where the enemy could bring large concentrations of fire against them.

From December 30 through January 3, the enemy, realizing our next possible move, had prepared a series of strongpoints in depth over the rolling open country immediately in front of us. The main line of advance went through this area for about three miles. The next couple of miles consisted of heavy woods, then open country again.

The planned tactics for this operation used the armored division with additional infantry to make the initial assault across the open country. When they reached the woods, with its narrow roads and logging trails, the infantry passed through the armored division. Once clear of the woods, the armored division again moved ahead of the infantry. This tactic seemed to take advantage of the best capabilities of both the infantry division and the armored division.

Accompanied by the extremely heavy barrage using the proximity fuses, the attack started on the morning of January 3. The 3d Armored Division and 83d Infantry Division were to the east of highway N15, and the 2d Armored Division and 84th Infantry Division were to the west. Because the German main effort had been to the north in this area, when we started our counterattack southward we were still opposed by scattered remnants of three German panzer divisions and two *volksgrenadier* divisions. They put up a terrific fight.

The Germans were past masters at defense against armor by using their own armor skillfully. They took every advantage of their su-

perior armor and used the buildings and rubble of the small fortified villages to conceal their tanks and self-propelled guns. Even
when attacking one of these strongpoints with a combination of infantry supported by armor and preceded by a quick, heavy artillery
barrage, we still sustained heavy losses in our tanks.

The losses probably would have been much greater had it not
been for the M7 self-propelled 105mm howitzer. Able to fire for effect immediately from almost any position, the M7 could put down
a deadly fire of proximity fuse overhead airbursts. It could also fire
white phosphorus shells, which put out a lot of smoke and inhibited
the German observation. I have always felt that the M7 gun carriage
was one of the most effective weapons we had.

With the weather beginning to clear up, we got more and more
support from the Ninth Air Force P47 dive-bombers. We had to be
extremely careful in calling for air strikes because of the close proximity of our troops to the Germans. In a fluid situation such as this,
it was easy for the air force to be confused and bomb the wrong targets. We were always excited to see the air force come in because we
knew that the Germans would really catch hell.

The heavy armor losses we had sustained so far in the Battle of
the Bulge resulted in a critical shortage of tank crews. The M4 Sherman normally had a five-man crew: the driver; the assistant driver,
who rode next to him and manned the ball-mount .30-caliber machine gun; the assistant gunner, who sat on the left side of the turret and loaded the main gun; the gunner, who sat on the right side
of the turret and fired the gun; and the tank commander, who sat
at the rear of the turret and operated the radio.

There was a small cupola with a periscopic sight in the hatch
cover directly over the tank commander. When the tank was under
artillery fire, the tank commander kept the hatch closed and buttoned up; however, the tank often rode with the hatch open for better visibility.

As casualties became more acute, we first had to eliminate the assistant driver. This denied the tank the use of the ball-mount machine gun, which was particularly effective against infantry. Later on,
we had to eliminate the assistant gunner, and the tank commander

had to double as the loader. This gave us a three-man crew, a bare minimum to operate a tank.

On the afternoon of January 8 at Werbomont, C Company was getting seventeen tanks ready to issue to the troops. Some had been knocked out previously and been repaired; some were brand-new tanks sent from army ordnance as replacements. It was our job to get the tanks ready and find crews to man them.

The 33d Armored Regiment had sent us seventeen tank crewmen who had limited experience with tanks in combat. These men had come in as replacements themselves only a few days before. The G1 had sent thirty-five men who had just gotten off the boat in Antwerp a few hours earlier and didn't seem to have received previous indoctrination. We asked how many had previous experience with tanks, and they all replied negative. Most had never been in a tank or even close to one.

We selected thirty-four men and split them into two-man crews. These men, along with the drivers, made up seventeen three-man crews for the tanks. They were all given a brief orientation of what a tank was all about and shown various items of equipment, the machine guns, and the ammunition boxes. The tanks had already been filled with gasoline and were lubricated and ready to go.

Several artillery mechanics took the tanks to the edge of the field. They swung the turret to one side and loaded the guns with armor-piercing ammunition to prevent any explosion. Each crew member got to fire three rounds with the main gun. (The men had already had basic training, so they were familiar with machine guns.) This was all the training that time permitted before they were taken to their units by guides from the 33d Armored Regiment. It was about 1500.

Going down to the 33d Armored Regiment at about 1900 it was discovered that of the seventeen tanks issued, fifteen had been knocked out and destroyed along the side of the road. I was unable to find out how many, if any, of these young crew members had survived. This tragedy was destined to be repeated many times.

By January 9, the 3d Armored Division had completed the first phase of the operation and reached the edge of the heavily wooded area. The 83d Infantry Division passed through and cleared the woods for the next two to three miles. By January 13, the woods had been pretty well cleared of *panzerfaust* crews and mines along the small logging trails.

The division passed through the woods and through the infantry again, then started on its last and final push across the open rolling terrain, which was heavily fortified. For the last ten days, the Germans had fought a bitter rear-guard action, and we had advanced ten miles to the southern edge of the woods. On the thirteenth, the division passed through the 83d Infantry Division again, then proceeded toward its final objective: to cut the main highway east from Houffalize, then occupy the high ground in the vicinity of Brisy.

The Germans fought bitterly to keep us from cutting off their final escape route. German tanks and armored infantry jammed the highway and set up heavy fortified positions around Stommeln. On January 15, Combat Command B set up a roadblock just east of Stommeln, cutting the German escape route. They then proceeded southward to Brisy and occupied the high ground north of the river.

Having achieved our final objective, we held this ground, and the 84th Infantry and 2d Armored Divisions bypassed us to the west and proceeded toward Houffalize. On January 16, in the vicinity of Houffalize, elements of the 84th Infantry Division made contact with the 11th Armored Division proceeding northward from the Third Army, completing this phase of the Ardennes campaign. On January 20, our division moved into the Barvaux-Durbuy area for rest and rehabilitation.

The maintenance and supply units worked feverishly to get the division back up to strength. There were no trained tank crew replacements; all came from the infantry recruit pool. These men were integrated with the survivors of existing tank crews and given intensive training for the next few days. At least they had a much better chance for survival than the young crews brought down to us at Werbomont on January 8. Captain Tom Sembera secured our proper share of replacement tanks and other vehicles. We were now beginning to get a number of the new M4A1 medium tanks with a 76mm gun and a 550-horsepower V8 Ford engine.

Casualties

The Battle of the Bulge drew to a rapid and final conclusion. By January 28, the Germans had been driven back to their original line of departure. The fighting had been savage, and both sides were heavily bloodied. The approximate casualties were 81,000 Americans and 100,000 Germans. The 3d Armored Division alone, from December 16 through January 20, lost 125 M4 medium tanks, 38 M5 light tanks, 6 M7 self-propelled guns, and 158 half-tracks, armored cars, and other vehicles.

On Leave to Reims

After a few days in our new rest area, the division commander directed that as many officers and men as possible be given time off for rest and relaxation. During a visit to one of the ordnance depots at Reims, Captain Sembera was approached in the joint officers' mess one evening by a young captain who had noticed the captain's 3d Armored Division Spearhead shoulder patch. He also noticed the ordnance bomb insignia on his lapel. The captain identified himself as my brother George, and asked Sembera if he might know me.

Sembera broke out in a broad grin. "Hell, yes, I know him. He's one of my old buddies. He's always bitching to get him more damned tanks. He's liaison with CCB and loses more tanks and fouls up more than anybody else. He really gives me a hard time. He's one of the reasons I'm back here."

George told him that he was an executive officer in one of the quartermaster truck groups stationed in Reims and gave him his address. The next time I saw Tommy, he told me about meeting George and gave me the address. Until then, I knew that George was somewhere in France but had no idea where. All I'd had was his APO number.

After a few days in the rest area, things seemed to be going a lot better, and I asked Major Arrington if I could take a couple of days to go back to Reims to visit my brother. The major told Captain Ellis to cut an order sending me to Reims for three days on official ordnance business, so it wouldn't count against my leave. When I told Wrayford we were going to Reims, his face lit up. "Lieutenant, I'm going to have to shave extra good this time."

Wrayford got water from one of the decontamination trucks and even managed to wash the Jeep. We straightened all our gear as best we could, then took off like a couple of foxes going to a chicken reunion.

We left maintenance battalion headquarters at Pair and headed toward Werbomont. The weather had warmed up considerably, and most of the ice and snow had melted. On the route through Marche and Sedan to Reims, the roads were littered with both American and German vehicles but mostly tanks and half-tracks from the German 2d SS Panzer Division.

The main highways in this part of France were straight and broad and lined with poplar trees. They were paved with blacktop in the country and with Belgian block near villages and small cities. I first thought that this would be an ideal area for a road net for the COMZ communication. To my surprise, however, the roads were in terrible condition. There were stretches along the main highway varying from a hundred yards to a quarter mile long where the road had completely collapsed due to heavy military traffic. We passed numerous engineering construction battalions rebuilding the roads, using both German prisoners and French civilians to help them.

After arriving in Reims, we located the headquarters of George's quartermaster truck group. Although I had written down the address that Tommy gave me, I had committed it to memory many times. It was 32 Rue de Moisson and was located in an elegant neighborhood. The street contained a number of beautiful eighteenth-century French town houses with walled formal gardens in the backyard, similar to many English homes.

Number 32 was a three-story house, the highest on the street. It had an impressive gray granite facade with carved lintels over the door and windows. The upper windows had small balconies with wrought-iron grillwork. I knew that if George had anything to do with selecting these billets, he had chosen this one, because he always liked to go first class. We parked the Jeep in front and went inside.

The hallway had a black and white Italian marble floor and walls paneled and festooned with bronze sconces and French paintings. I was impressed, especially after having lived in barns and the cold stone basements of Belgian farmhouses. Even the château at Pair, where headquarters company was located, paled in comparison to this beautiful home.

A corporal sat at a desk in the main hallway, and I asked him if Captain Cooper was in. He said his office was upstairs just to the right of the stairway. I told him I was his brother but to be sure not to tell him.

He kind of grinned and picked up the phone. "Captain, some beat-up-looking lieutenant down here wants to see you."

As the corporal escorted me upstairs, he told me that the house used to be a French bawdy house accommodating German officers. The walls were covered with erotic paintings of nude women in nefarious poses.

As I walked into the room, George was busy reading. When he raised his head, he looked shocked; he hadn't known whether or not I was alive. It had been back in November when Sembera told him I was okay. We embraced warmly and both started talking at once. I told him that Sembera had given me his address and I'd just decided to come see him. In the meantime, Wrayford and the corporal had struck up an acquaintance. George told the corporal to get Wrayford some quarters, clean clothes, and a shower, then to take him over to the NCO club and show him around.

We went over to George's quarters, around the corner and several doors down the street. It was a three-story French house facing the street with an entrance hall that went straight through to a garden in the rear. There was a spiral stairway, a large potbellied stove located on the ground floor, and a stovepipe that extended all the way up three floors through the roof. This apparently was the main source of heat for the entire house.

George said that Madame Fochée, the matriarch of the family, lived downstairs with her husband and three young children. The army had taken over the two upper floors. His room was on the third floor and looked out on the rear garden. After about two hours of intense conversation, we had exhausted all of our news and brought each other up-to-date on our respective lives for the last two years. He showed me pictures of my niece, Dotsie, who was now a year old. I remembered her birthday, October 3, because it was the day we had arrived in England in 1943 and was also the day before my birthday.

That evening we went to the joint officers' mess club. The next three days I had plenty of good food, Cognac, and fine wine. Wrayford and the corporal apparently got along well and spent time seeing many of the charms of Reims. We were both sorry to see our visit end. It had been like a breath of fresh air injected into the devastation of war.

A Mark V German Panther that was knocked out of action at Normandy. An American M36 tank destroyer with a 90mm cannon penetrated the face plate from 100 yards.

A Mark V German Panther destroyed in Normandy by an M4 Sherman's 76mm gun (hit on the left flank side), near Le Dézert, France (St. Lo sector), July 1944.

An American tank knocked out near Fromentel, France, 18 August 1944.

A Mark V Panther destroyed by overhead artillery fire at Le Dézert in Normandy, July 1944.

An M4 Sherman that was struck in its turret ring, near Ranes, France, 1944. Both turret and hull are damaged, thus making the tank unrepairable.

A closeup of shell marks in frontal armor of a Panther Mark V, which was struck twice by a 76mm shot at close range, at Le Dézert, France, July 1944.

A T2 armored recovery vehicle towing a disabled M4 Sherman.

One of only two Super Pershing M26A1E2 tanks built, being test fired in Niederaussen, Germany. Weighing 53 tons, its 90mm-70 caliber gun fired at 3850 feet per second. It was the most powerful tank in World War II.

An M26 Pershing G7-32AK approaches the bombed Cathedral Plaza in Cologne. A German Panther Mark V had just knocked out an M4 Sherman.

An M26 Pershing comes around a corner and faces a Panther tank, (not in photo). The Panther expects the M26 to stop before firing but gunner Clarence Smoyer's tank had a gyro-stabilizer which let him fire when moving.

The first shot struck the base of the gun mantelet and deflected down through the deck armor killing the German gunner and setting the tank on fire. Smoyer fired two other shots to the flank. Three Germans burned in the tank, while two (seen running) escaped death.

This Mark V Panther burned for two days.

Infantryman of the 3d armored division advance toward Cologne Cathedral.

Assistant driver of M26 sitting on Panther turret. Assistant Gunner loader John Dereggi, standing to the right, holding rifle.

General Maurice Rose was killed in action on 30 March 1944 by a young German tank commander when the 3d Armor division enveloped the Ruhr Pocket. There were 380,000 German prisoners of war taken in this battle.

A Mark VI King Tiger shot in its rear engine back plate by an M4A1 Sherman. This tank was part of the group that emasculated our entire task force south of Paderborn on 30 March 1944. We believed that this was the tank that killed General Rose.

American 8th Infantry division infantryman examining the German Panther tank. Three tankers of the German crew's burned bodies were still in the tank.

This Mark VI Tiger tank ran out of gas and was captured in Central Germany.

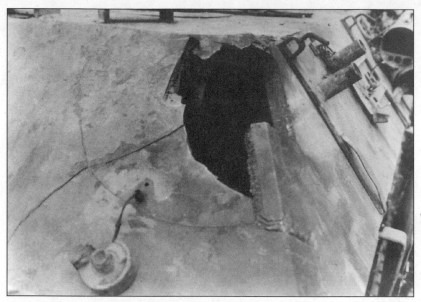

A closeup of a shell that penetrated the back side of the face plate of a German Mark V Panther.

Three M4 Sherman tanks that were destroyed in street fighting in Paderborn, Germany.

9
Back to Germany

Return to Aachen

On February 7, the division moved back to occupy Aachen, Stolberg, Mausbach, Werth, and Hastenrath, areas we had so bitterly fought over back in November. In the meantime, the 104th Infantry Division had consolidated this area and driven up to the west bank of the Roer River at Düren.

The maintenance battalion moved back to the Engleburt Rubber factory in Aachen, where we had buildings and plenty of paved areas to do maintenance. When we got there, the liaison group made a mad dash for the telephone exchange. With its heavy concrete walls and roof, it was obviously the safest place in the factory.

The weather had cleared up considerably. Even though the rains made the fields muddy, it was still better than the snow and slush of Belgium. Many of the tanks were bivouacked in the muddy fields surrounding the small villages, but the maintenance company of the 33d Armored Regiment had moved back into Mausbach, where there were many paved areas in the middle of the village. Although the division was still within enemy artillery range, the Germans were apparently trying to conserve their ammunition in preparation for our upcoming offensive.

The headquarters building of the Engleburt Rubber factory was posh even by German standards. The largest tire manufacturing company in Germany, it had been working around the clock making tires for German combat vehicles and trucks. Because of this continuous operation, the company provided elaborate living quarters for its top executives. It had a beautiful paneled dining room complete with linen napkins and tablecloths, crystal, and sterling silver flatware. There were adjoining bedroom-and-bath facilities.

The liaison group arrived back at Engleburt before the rest of the headquarters company, so my buddies Lincoln and Lucas made a quick emergency requisition for tablecloths, crystal, and silver flatware. Having lived there before the Ardennes campaign, we knew about these elaborate facilities and wanted to make sure that they were shared with the liaison group before Colonel McCarthy and Major Lawrence could claim the entire layout.

By this time, we had obtained one of the giant blowtorches that came with each German tank. Apparently, the low-octane fuel made the big V8 Maybach engines extremely difficult to start in cold weather. The Germans used these torches to preheat the manifold prior to starting up. They had to be careful doing this; they could set the tank on fire if there was the slightest fuel leak.

The blowtorches, which we took from any shot-up German tank we found, made good trading material; they were in much demand as a source of heat.We could fire one up and shoot a flame about three inches in diameter and ten feet long. The flame would heat a room in a matter of seconds, especially if the flame was oscillated back and forth. Living fairly high on the hog, the liaison group felt well fixed for the time being.

Trading with the Enemy

The factory also held a cache of German schnapps and good French wines. The liaison group made sure they got their share. One evening after an elaborate meal, we decided to explore the building further. It was a split-level in the area near the telephone exchange. Our quarters were partly above- and partly belowground. Below us were at least two levels of subbasement with heavy reinforced concrete floors and walls. The building itself was a natural fortress. In one of the lower-level basement rooms, we discovered many German file cases. Some of them were marked with what we thought was the German equivalent of "confidential." This naturally tweaked our curiosity and we immediately opened them and started examining the contents. As ordnance officers, we had been instructed to be on the lookout for intelligence on enemy industrial technology.

I was stunned by the contents. Correspondence and documents between English firms and Engleburt, dated from 1940 through 1943, indicated that business went on as usual. All correspondence was in both English and German, attached together in the same file. It was obvious that the Germans and English were placing orders and transferring checks and money, apparently through Swiss banks. I was shocked to find out there were English businessmen dealing as merchants of blood when their own soldiers plus their American allies were engaged in a desperate fight for their lives. We reported these findings to Colonel McCarthy. After checking them out, he notified G5 (military government), which in turn instructed us to impound the documents until further notice.

A few days later, a lone German civilian came to headquarters and asked to see the commanding officer. Although he was shabbily dressed, as most civilians were at that time, his bearing and manner suggested that he was well educated. He told Colonel McCarthy that he had orders from G5 to get the records in the basement.

Colonel McCarthy smelled a rat and immediately detained the man. He called G5, which sent a couple of MPs to take the man away. We speculated that he might have been one of the ex-Engelburt executives trying to get hold of the records and destroy them before they could be turned over to a war-crimes commission. I never knew the final outcome of this matter, as we turned over all records to G5 when we left Engelburt.

The Western Front: February 1, 1945

The Allied armies occupied virtually the same positions we had on December 16, prior to the Battle of the Bulge. The dams on the upper reaches of the Roer River had finally been captured, and the flooding caused by the damaged control valves on the dams had now subsided. We were preparing for the final assault on Germany.

Rumors about strategy flew, particularly among the junior-grade officers. The general plan called for an advance along the entire front. The main effort was to be made by the 21st Army Group across the Rhine River, north of the Ruhr Valley. The First Army was to cover the southern flank of the 21st Army Group's Ninth Army, and the Third Army would in turn cover our southern flank. The

6th Army Group would consolidate the Saar area and the upper Rhine.

We all knew that the Germans had suffered a terrible defeat in the Battle of the Bulge, although not without horrendous losses to our side. We also knew that the Russians on the eastern front had taken the major brunt of the war so far, although there had been little activity there for some time. It appeared now that the Russians finally were beginning to get things going.

Much of what went on during this time didn't make much sense to the junior officers. The real esprit de corps of a good outfit is based largely on the faith that the younger soldiers have in commanders. In the 3d Armored Division, that faith was well placed. We had, with a few exceptions, an excellent officer corps.

Although we did not know it at the time, considerable friction existed between General Eisenhower and Field Marshal Montgomery. The Combined Chiefs had already decided that Montgomery and his 21st Army Group would make the major effort in the north. Somewhat reluctantly, Eisenhower went along with these plans. General Bradley and his officers resented Montgomery's arrogance and felt they had made the main effort since Normandy.

The senior Allied commanders ranged from one extreme to the other. Montgomery was conservative and would hesitate to attack until he had overwhelming superiority. He was also arrogant and was constantly trying to build up the importance of his 21st Army Group. On the other end of the spectrum was the extremely aggressive Patton, who believed in attacking at the first opportunity. He was really in his element when his armored columns could range far and wide in exploiting a major breakthrough. However, he had little patience with infantry assault operations, and when he was not immediately successful he became frustrated.

General Bradley had actually served as Patton's subordinate in Sicily; however, Bradley's tactical brilliance and steady judgment had caused Eisenhower to select him to command the 12th Army Group. Under Bradley, Gen. Courtney Hodges of First Army had served as an enlisted infantryman in World War I and had later gone to West Point. Through his hard-bitten determination, he advanced through the ranks to become an army commander. Although he had none of Patton's flamboyance, his steady judgment earned him the un-yielding loyalty and respect of his subordinates. Hodges, more than any other army commander, understood the use of armored divisions and infantry divisions reinforced with GHQ tank battalions and how each could be used to maximum advantage. Always unassuming and never pushing for undue publicity, Hodges had a combat record that was unequalled or little understood by the general public.

One of the cardinal principles in warfare is that the units that are opposed by the most powerful enemy units suffer the greatest casu-alties. At the same time, if they are successful, they can also inflict the maximum casualties on the enemy. The First Army suffered more casualties than any other American army and inflicted the greatest casualties on the Germans. It was also responsible for the capture of the greatest number of German prisoners.

General Simpson's Ninth Army was activated in September 1944 from a cadre of battle-hardened divisions from First Army. It was part of the 12th Army Group until the Battle of the Bulge, then was as-signed to Field Marshal Montgomery's 21st Army Group. General Devers's 6th Army Group, with the American Seventh Army and the French First Army, had landed on the southern coast of France and driven northward to the Saar region and the Vosges Mountains. The French First Army did a good job when actually concentrating on fighting the Germans. Its commanders were so concerned about the French place in history that they were often involved in political dis-putes with both Devers and Eisenhower.

Ordnance Problems

The buildup for the final assault was now proceeding rapidly. I spent a great deal of time going back and forth between the Engleburt fac-tory in Aachen and the maintenance company of the 33d Armored Regiment at Mausbach. One day in Mausbach, Maj. Dick Johnson told me that a tank from the 2d Battalion was having difficulty in keeping 75mm rounds in the main ammunition storage box un-derneath the turret. He said this condition had appeared in other tanks before, and no one knew what was causing it.

The ammunition was stored in the racks with the projectile to the rear and the cartridge case sticking out the front for easy removal.

Small, spring-loaded metal clips engaged the rim of the cartridge and kept the round in place. For some reason the rounds were dislodging when the tank stopped. If the primer happened to strike a sharp object, the rounds could explode prematurely.

The main ammunition rack was a fabricated aluminum box approximately three feet wide, two feet high, and three feet deep. It had a series of three-inch longitudinal tubes nested together in several rows to accommodate thirty-four rounds of 75mm tank ammunition. Although the ammunition box was enclosed in quarter-inch armor plate with split-type doors down the front, the rim clips were supposed to hold the ammunition in the rack with the doors open.

The maintenance crew hadn't checked this out very well, because the trouble was obvious once I got inside the tank and examined the front of the rack. This particular tank had thirty rounds of 75mm tank ammunition and four bottles of Cognac. The tank crew had decided that this was a good place to store their extra Cognac. The diameter of the bottle of Cognac was slightly larger than that of the ammunition. There was enough clearance in the tube to allow the bottle of Cognac to go in, but not without stretching the clips beyond their yield point. The weakened clips would no longer hold a round of ammunition. The crew had apparently removed the Cognac and replaced the 75mm ammunition in time for another inspection, but the day I came they were not expecting an ordnance inspection. We replaced the clips and corrected the condition.

When confronted, the crew defended their actions. "This ammunition is no damn good anyway against a German tank. If the going got too rough, we could hide behind a building and break out the Cognac and at least ease some of the pain."

I couldn't help but realize the tragic irony of what they said. The crew was reprimanded by their company officers, and Major Johnson put out notification that the practice must cease immediately. Although it could seriously threaten the crew members' lives, I don't believe it ever stopped completely.

Captain Bew White, maintenance officer of the 391st Field Artillery, which was normally attached to CCB, told me they were having difficulty with 105mm howitzer shells firing erratically. Although the division was out of the line, the artillery fired support from time to time for the 104th Infantry Division, which was holding the line on the Roer River at Düren.

The firing chamber in the breech end of a 105mm howitzer is bored in several diameters. The initial part is bored to a specific diameter and tapered to allow the cartridge to be easily inserted. This diameter must be large enough to allow the free passage of the cartridge case and yet small enough to allow the cartridge case to expand against it when the round is fired, and to allow obturation (a sealing action that traps combustion gases).

Just forward of the cartridge chamber is the head space, with a smaller diameter than the cartridge chamber and of sufficient bore and length to accommodate the rotating band. Just forward of the head space is the forcing cone, the area where the tapered lands start from the diameter of the rotating band and decrease slightly along a tapered length of approximately two inches until the lands reach a diameter to accommodate the projectile's bourrelet (the main diameter of the projectile itself). The lands are in effect longitudinal ridges approximately a quarter inch wide, separated by grooves of equal dimension and of sufficient number to cover the entire circumference of the barrel. The groove between the lands is approximately an eighth inch deep, and the diameter from the top of the lands back into the head space is gradually tapered for a length of approximately one and a half inches. These lands and grooves are formed with a spiral broach that is pulled through the barrel.

When the propelling charge fires, the pressure forces the shell forward and the soft top of the rotating band is cut by the tapered forcing cone. This imparts obturation to the front of the shell and at the same time causes the shell to rotate, giving it stability as it leaves the end of the barrel. This forcing cone, the most critical part of the gun barrel, receives the greatest wear.

In addition to the shearing action of cutting the rotating band, the forcing cone is subjected to corrosion from the fulminate of mercury used in the primers, and from the high temperature and pressure inside the barrel. This corrosion causes pitting, which further weakens the lands in the forcing cone to the extent that they shear off for several inches inside the tube itself. When this happens, the grooving in the rotating band becomes erratic. This in turn causes the projectile to lose obturation and wobble when it emerges from the end of the barrel. In some cases, the rotating band is so severely damaged that it comes off in flight and the projectile starts tumbling, which throws it off its trajectory. A tumbling projectile could drop short and kill our own troops.

Upon examination, it was revealed that all the gun barrels in the 391st Field Artillery were in bad shape. In some cases, the lands were sheared off for twelve to eighteen inches. I reported this immediately to Major Arrington. Lieutenants Nibbelink and Lincoln reported similar conditions in the 67th and 54th Armored Field Artillery Battalions. A detailed ordnance inspection revealed that all of these gun tubes were badly worn and should be replaced. Major Arrington called Captain Sembera and requested that he immediately requisition fifty-four 105mm tubes.

Army ordnance couldn't believe that the gun barrels were worn as badly as we reported. They told Captain Sembera that they were sending forward a first lieutenant who was an ordnance "expert" on gun barrels from Rock Island Arsenal. When Sembera introduced him to us in the liaison group, I recognized him immediately, although I'm not sure he recognized me at the time. After a short while, we developed a good rapport. The lieutenant was Joe Dortman; we had been classmates in 1939 during ROTC summer camp training at Aberdeen Proving Ground. He was an academic type, kind of flaky, extremely naive, and the butt of several practical jokes. By today's standards, he would be considered a nerd. I told Nibbelink and Lincoln about my experience with Dortman back at Aberdeen; I wanted to make sure they didn't let the cat out of the bag, because we wanted to make sure we got those replacement gun tubes.

At Aberdeen Proving Ground that summer, we had 150 ordnance cadets from nine different ROTC units. We were split up so we would get to know the men from other schools. My three tent mates were from the University of California at Berkeley, Cornell, and the University of Cincinnati; the tent next to us had my buddy Barnett from Georgia Tech. Dortman, an MIT man, lived several tents down. He always sounded off the right answer before anybody else when the instructor asked questions during lectures. He was also somewhat arrogant, and the rest of us began to resent him.

We were given seating assignments at the eight-man tables in the mess hall, and Dortman was assigned to the same table with Barnett and me. During the day, we were on a tight schedule. In the mornings we would attend lectures together and after lunch we would be assigned to small groups and visit various weapons sections. The day's activities were good grist for the table conversations that evening.

One evening Barnett asked what I'd done that day.

"Oh," I answered with a slight grin, "we visited the white rat section down at the south end of the proving ground."

Barnett winked back. "Oh, what do they do down there?"

"They've developed a highly intelligent breed of gopher rats," I replied, "and they put them through a rigorous training program."

"What kind of a training program are you talking about?" Dortman demanded.

I notched up the ante. "They use the rats to assist in cleaning out the antitank guns before they fire them."

"What do you mean they assist in cleaning out the guns?" replied Dortman.

He was beginning to swallow the bait, so I quickly replied. "They take these white rats and breed them specially for size and weight and color, also for the quality of their fur. When the rats are fully developed, they train them in different mazes to see if they'll follow commands and directions. After they're thoroughly indoctrinated, they're dipped in a cleaning solution and put into the chamber of a 37mm gun. A soldier holds up a piece of cheese at the other end of the gun tube. As the rat scrambles after the cheese, he thoroughly swabs the inside of the barrel, cleaning out the dirt and Cosmoline.

"Just before he reaches the end of the barrel, the soldier pulls the cheese away and the rat drops into another cleaning bath, then he's routed back through the chamber again. Sometimes it takes two or three passes before the gun barrel is clean, provided he doesn't get the cheese in the meantime. If he grabs the cheese before the soldier can pull it away from the end of the muzzle, he'll stop and eat the cheese and won't be interested in cleaning the gun. If he completes his mission properly, he gets the cheese as a reward."

Dortman looked stunned as he took this in. I was sort of stunned myself to think he actually believed the story. I had never told such a lie in my life.

The other fellows sitting around the table looked about to explode. I figured we'd better do something in a hurry, so I started out again.

"You remember last week when we went down to see them fire the big fourteen-inch gun? Well, Dortman, do you know how they cleaned it out? They used a rare breed of Texas jackrabbit, and instead of cheese they dangled carrots at the other end of the barrel. I understand it took six jackrabbits and about three bushels of carrots before they got that gun clean."

This last comment was too much. I think Dortman realized he'd been had. For the next few days, he was kind of cold and aloof, and I realized he must have thought I was some kind of nut. Before we left camp, however, things had settled down and we parted as good buddies. This was the last I had seen of Dortman until he showed up for the artillery inspection in Germany.

When we got down to the 391st Field Artillery, I took Dortman to see Bew White, and we went over to one of the batteries and started inspecting the guns. Dortman had brought with him a special inspection mirror, consisting of a telescopic stainless steel tube with an angular adjustable mirror on the end; it looked like an enlarged version of a dentist's inspection mirror. By stretching the stainless steel handle to its full length, Dortman could inspect the bore of the gun barrel.

The first gun we inspected was heavily pitted around the forcing cone, and the lands were ripped out eighteen inches forward of this area in a jagged fashion. It was obvious that the gun should be replaced.

Dortman couldn't believe this and asked to see the gun book. Each artillery piece had a gun book that was kept with it at all times; the crew entered the number of rounds and the size of the charge fired each day. After an extremely heavy barrage, the crew could look at the number of rounds left and tell how many had been fired. A good gun crew chief kept these books up-to-date, so he could have a relative comparison of the condition of his gun tube at any time.

The 105mm ammunition was designed as a separate loading round. This meant that the brass cartridge case and the projectile would come apart. Each new round contained seven individual charges. Each charge consisted of a small bag of smokeless powder. By removing the bags, the crew had the option of firing from one to seven charges, depending on the range of the target. By entering this information into the gun book on a daily basis, one could quickly calculate the comparable number of service charges (the equivalent of firing the full seven) that had been fired.

After looking at the gun book, Dortman said, "These guns are supposed to fire seventy-five hundred service rounds, and they haven't fired nearly that many. What the hell have you been doing with these guns?"

The crew chief spoke up. "Lieutenant, as you know, the seventy-five-hundred- service-round charge rating is based on firing at four rounds per minute. When we're firing a red-hot mission, we fire at least ten rounds per minute."

Dortman was incredulous that a gun could be fired this fast, but after witnessing several rapid-fire missions called by the 104th Infantry Division, he became a believer. All of the other gun barrels were in similar or worse condition. Dortman told Captain Sembera that he would recommend that First Army replace all the gun barrels immediately.

As Dortman was leaving, he relaxed and smiled. "Cooper, I never have forgotten how you and Barnett pulled my leg about those white rats."

I relaxed myself and told him that I'd been uptight during his whole visit, hoping he hadn't held it against me. As he left in his Jeep on his way back to First Army, I couldn't help but get in a last-minute remark. "You know, if we ran some of those white rats through these gun tubes, they'd probably come out looking like striped-butt tigers."

As I was leaving VII Corps headquarters at Eupen, I saw two young boys standing near my Jeep. One of the great tragedies of war is the profound effect it has on children. Because Eupen was a border town and had been transferred back and forth four times in the last thirty years, the children were bound to be confused as to whose side they were on. The two boys looked to be about four and eight years of age, and I figured they were brothers. Many of these children spoke French and German and also understood a little English.

I figured I'd been targeted for a handout. The older one blurted, *"Avez vous du chocolat?"* (Do you have some chocolate?) The younger one blurted something about *schokolade* (the German word for chocolate). The older boy understood that the Americans and the Belgians were on the same side, whereas the younger boy, having been born during the German occupation, had no idea about sides; he was German and proud of it.

"You Belgian or Deutsch?" I asked.

The older one quickly replied, *"Me Belgique."*

The younger one steadily persisted, *"Me Deutsch, me Deutsch."*

"Non, non, he mon frère, he Belgique, just like me," the older one replied quickly. The younger one shook his head and stubbornly insisted that he was German.

I was about to explode with laughter and could carry on the charade no longer. In the meantime, Wrayford had already broken out several chocolate bars and we divided them evenly between the boys. As we got in the Jeep to drive away, I noticed the older boy nudge the young one. They both waved and called out, *"Vive l'Amerique."* War makes children grow up fast.

The constantly diminishing tank crews became increasingly aware of the M4's weaknesses. They took every means available to reinforce the front glacis plate. They stored spare track blocks and bogey wheels there, but this was not sufficient. Some crews put sandbags on the glacis plate; others used a combination of logs and sandbags laced together with chicken wire.

At Stolberg, the crews continued their efforts at the abandoned cement factory, making concrete armor. Although these measures may not have been effective, I'm sure they had a great psychological effect on the crews. The concrete may have done some good, but this was probably offset by the added weight, which crunched the forward bogey wheels and slowed the tank considerably. The crews felt this was worth it if they could get more protection. Like drowning men, they would grab at any straw that might save them. They were desperate to survive.

The First New M26 Tanks Arrive

During the first week of February, Major Arrington called in the three liaison officers to brief us on a pleasant surprise. Within the next few days, we would receive our first shipments of the M26 Pershing heavy tank, films of which had been shown at Tidworth Downs in 1944. Although information on the new tank was limited, Major Arrington gave us everything he had and told us to brief the tank units.

We did not want to make the same mistake we had made on the M4 Sherman tank. Prior to the invasion, we had innocently informed the tank units that the M4 Sherman was a much better tank than it actually proved to be in combat. This was due to false information and to pure ignorance on our part.

The Pershing was the first completely new American main battle tank of World War II. Both the M3 medium with the 75mm gun in the hull and the M4 Sherman with the same short barrel 75mm in a rotating turret were built on the basic tank chassis of the old M2 medium tank, which had been developed back in the late 1920s and early 1930s at Aberdeen Proving Ground.

The M26 was a radically new design with an entirely new chassis. It was longer, wider, and lower than the M4 Sherman and had a gross weight of some forty-seven and one half tons compared to 34 tons for the M4 Sherman. Although it was heavier than the Sherman, its longer and wider track gave it a ground bearing pressure of three to four pounds per square inch compared to seven pounds per square inch for the Sherman. This meant that the M26 would go over rough, muddy ground in which the Sherman would get stuck. The track was supported by large, overlapping bogey wheels suspended on torsion bar spring systems. This was the old Christy system, which had been developed by the Americans some twenty years previously and had been adopted by the Germans and the Russians. The Christy system allowed a much wider track, and also the torsion bar suspension had a greater amplitude than the old coil spring system on the M4 Sherman. This system permitted a much easier ride over rough terrain at higher speeds, and the increased amplitude gave the tank better traction going over rough ground or ascending rugged slopes. All American tanks that came after the M26 Pershing used the Christy system.

The M26 was the closest thing we had to the German Panther. It had four inches of cast steel armor on the glacis plate at forty-five degrees, whereas the Panther had three and a half inches of plate armor at somewhat less than thirty-eight degrees, the nominal angle below which armor-piercing shot would ricochet.

During our ordnance ROTC training, there was considerable debate among the experts as to the value of cast armor versus plate armor. American metallurgists who advocated cast armor claimed that it could be made more homogeneous; therefore, once the projectile started to penetrate, it had a work hardening effect that could limit the depth of the penetration.

The plate armor advocates claimed that it was roll forged, which produced an elongated, high-tensile-strength grain in the direction of rolling. The surface of the plate could then be case hardened; this, backed up with the high-strength elongated grain boundaries underneath, produced a superior grade of armor.

Having no expert knowledge, I based my conclusions only on actual observations of tanks knocked out in combat. From more than a thousand tanks, both American and German, that had been knocked out in combat, I do not recall ever seeing one where a 75mm or larger projectile started to enter the armor and failed to penetrate. The American cast armor on the tanks resisted penetration of armor-piercing shot from .30-caliber small-arms projectiles up through 37mm armor-piercing projectiles; however, once the 75mm or larger projectile started to penetrate, it would normally go through.

In fact, the first tank that was brought back to our VCP at Airel in Normandy was struck by a German 75mm PAK41 on the top radius of the turret just forward of the tank commander's periscope. The angle at the point of impact could not have been more than fifteen to twenty degrees; however, the projectile penetrated two and a half inches of armor and ripped an eighteen-inch gap at the top of the turret, which tapered down to an inch and a half further back. The fragments from this impact showered down on the tank commander and killed him. When I saw this, I was shocked by the power of the German antitank guns. Although all of the turrets for the M4 Sherman tank were cast armor and some of the earlier hulls were cast armor, most of the hulls were plate armor.

Other than the fact that the M26 tank armor was cast and the Panther's was plate armor, the armor was comparable in thickness on the sides and the rear. However, the armor on the top deck of the Pershing varied from one inch down to half an inch, whereas the armor on the top deck of the Panther was only about a quarter of an inch thick.

The M26 turret was equipped with power traverse, far superior to the manual traverse of the Panther. It also had a gyrostabilized gun control, which enabled a tank to fire while moving and have the gun remain fairly level. The M4 Shermans had this gyrostabilizer, as did the M5 light tanks, but our tank crews appeared hesitant about using this system and preferred to fire from a stationary position. In some instances, our Sherman crews could get off two or more shots against a Panther before the Panther could get its gun around to fire on the Sherman. Unless the shots fired by the Sherman hit the Panther on the side or the rear, the Sherman would usually be knocked out by a single shot from the Panther.

The 90mm M1 gun in the Pershing fired a heavy projectile at a relatively low muzzle velocity of about 2,750 feet per second. The Panther's 75mm, whose muzzle velocity was 350 to 400 feet per second higher than this, probably had a slight edge in penetrating capability. In one incident, the projectile from a 90mm M1 gun struck a Panther directly on its glacis plate at a range of less than 300 yards, and the projectile ricocheted.

The Pershing had a 550-horsepower Ford in-line engine. This gave the tank a higher horsepower-per-ton ratio than the heavier Panther, which had a Maybach engine with approximately the same horsepower. The Maybach was a good engine; however, the Germans had to use such low-octane fuel that it was difficult to start the engine in cold weather. This was why the German tanks carried blowtorches. The Pershing's higher ratio made it more mobile and faster than the Panther. Overall, the two tanks were evenly matched, but the Pershing's mobility was somewhat neutralized because the Panther often fired from stationary and sometimes dug in positions whereas the Pershing was usually moving on the offensive.

Of the first twenty Pershing tanks to arrive in the European theater of operations, ten went to the 2d Armored Division and ten went to the 3d Armored Division. We issued five to each of our armored regiments.

After a thorough checkout, we took one of the new Pershings up a hill in the vicinity of Mausbach and set up some preliminary firing tests. The forward observers set up their BC scopes and picked out some German targets about a mile away in a section of Düren, across the Roer River. As a safety precaution, we set up tapes at about a forty-five-degree angle from the front of the tank and extending back about a hundred feet on either side.

The 90mm gun had a muzzle brake similar to the one on the Sherman's 76mm gun. The brake was a heavy steel casting on the front end of the gun barrel with a clearance hole through the center to allow the projectile to pass. On either side were dual blast deflectors, which deflected the blast to the rear and sides. This reversal of the gun blast offset the recoiling forces to the rear. Because the space inside the tank turret is limited, the recoil distance from the rear on the gun must be confined to nine to twelve inches. The muzzle brake makes this possible.

Anyone standing inside the tapes could not only have his eardrums ruptured, he might be killed by the shock of the blast. This same situation occurred with the Sherman's 76mm gun, but the effect was magnified considerably by the power of the 90mm gun. Although our armored infantry soldiers knew about this, we had to make sure that anyone attached from other divisions was also warned.

The Roer River Line

Across the Roer at Düren lay level farmland. At first it appeared to be ideal tank country, but these flat, open spaces also provided excellent fields of fire for the dug in and camouflaged German tanks and antitank guns. The Germans had had two months to prepare these positions, and they did it in a superb manner. A series of zigzagged trenches ranging from seventy-five to two hundred feet long overlapped one another. Interspersed among the trenches were a series of two- and three-man foxholes used for machine-gun nests and mortar pits.

There were also numerous dug in positions for dual-purpose 88mm guns, self-propelled guns, and tanks. The tanks and guns were located so that anyone assaulting one of them frontally would come under the fire of two others, to the left and right. There were numerous pits farther to the rear that could be occupied by self-propelled guns and tanks that were driven out of their forward positions.

Among the trenches and antitank positions were numerous minefields. Realizing by now that American armored divisions tended to go cross-country to try to flank strongpoints, the Germans made sure that all avenues of approach were covered with minefields. In some cases, the Germans put mines behind the forward trench line so the engineers would have to face the German infantry before they could get to the mines. This was similar to the positions on hill 287 near Stolberg during the November offensive. The flood waters of the Roer were now beginning to subside, although the flatlands across the river were still saturated.

American and German forces used widely different methods when holding a dug in position. The Americans tried to maintain extreme flexibility and move about constantly, putting out patrols to capture prisoners and at the same time confuse the enemy about our intentions. The Germans tended to fall into routines and seemed to perform certain operations every day at the same time. Their predictable actions undoubtedly saved us many casualties.

A rifleman with the 104th Division was stationed at an outpost on top of a two-story building about forty yards from the west bank of the Roer River at Düren. These outposts were manned by two men who were relieved periodically on staggered shifts. This meant that a soldier would spend half his time with a soldier who had been on the outpost previously and the second half with a new soldier who had just come on.

Late one afternoon, a new soldier arrived at the outpost. The soldier already present asked the new soldier if this was his first time in combat. The new soldier replied that he had just been transferred from the communications zone and was excited and anxious to see some action. The older soldier told him he'd see plenty, and soon. He pointed out the various German positions and explained that although there would be random mortar and artillery fire from time to time, there would be several mortar rounds fired on their position at 1830.

The young soldier was confused. "How do you know it's going to be at eighteen-thirty?"

"They always fire at eighteen-thirty. You can damn near set your watch by it."

The older soldier then showed the new man where to take cover and told him if things got too hot to just follow him. He said he'd learned from experience that the German 81mm mortar was a high-angled weapon with a low muzzle velocity. The sound of a muzzle blast travels in a straight line faster than the flight of the projectile. A soldier could hear the mortar blast before the projectile reached him. Within the receiving arc, the sound of the mortar blast was much like a cork popped from a champagne bottle. At no other point around the periphery of the border did it sound like this. When a soldier hears that particular sound, he is in the middle of the target area and may have just two to three seconds to take cover. A good infantryman can cover a lot of ground in that time.

Sure enough, at 1830 the mortar fire started coming in. The first rounds landed on a roadblock to the right of them down in the street. When the older soldier heard the cork pop out of the bottle, he yelled, "Let's go." He took off down the steps to the basement, and the younger soldier followed close behind.

The incoming round struck the high parapet over the edge of the roof, and the blast went over their heads. As the older soldier reached the bottom step, he was struck a violent, wrenching blow by a large object. Knocked to the floor, he lost his helmet and gun. He soon realized that the blow was the young soldier behind him, following close on his heels. As he tried to collect his senses, he yelled, "Are you all right?"

A belated but firm reply came back. "You beat me this time, but now I know the way."

Sleeping on a UXB

On the night of February 22, the day before the attack was to start, the RAF launched a massive air raid on Berdorf, Elsdorf, and Nieder-aussen, the major fortified towns on the way to Cologne. British night air raids normally began with Mosquito bombers at low level dropping flares to mark the target, followed by the bombers dropping incendiary bombs.

Because the target area was only fifteen to twenty miles from Aachen, we went up on the roof to watch. The bombers flew in single file to unload their bombs. Although there were many lines of planes for the different targets, it still took well over an hour for some thousand planes to drop their bombs. The planes at the head of the columns would unload incendiary bombs and start large fires, and the planes after that would drop high-explosive bombs.

The Germans had reinforced their antiaircraft defenses considerably. In addition to the dual-purpose 88mm guns surrounding the area, they had numerous batteries of 40mm Bofors and 20mm Oerlikon antiaircraft guns. Searchlights pierced the misty skies with their incandescent beams. The raging firestorms, the thousands of red incendiaries leaping up from the ground and merging in an apex, the crisscrossing of the shafts of lights, and the crescendo of exploding 88mm shells was an awesome sight. It was as if some giant diabolical Christmas tree was raining death and destruction from its boughs.

After the raid was over, we started back across the roof near the elevator house to the stairs leading below. Suddenly, my buddy Lieutenant Lincoln grabbed my arm and pulled me aside. "Look out, Cooper, you're about to step in that hole!"

Glancing down, I saw a hole in the roof approximately fifteen inches in diameter. We went downstairs to see what it was. As we approached the area on the third floor, we saw the same size hole, which was repeated on both the second and first floors. Finally, in the basement, we saw the same neat, round hole and could tell by the clear, sharp cut at its edge that the object had been traveling at a high speed when it struck the basement floor.

Trying to recall everything I had learned at bomb disposal school, I surmised that this was a 500 pound unexploded American bomb (UXB), which was probably buried twenty to thirty feet below. It had obviously been in the building since the American air raid in October. There were several other American UXBs lying around in the yard. This type of bomb was extremely dangerous; the men were told to avoid them, if possible, and leave them for bomb disposal crews.

Working around unburied UXBs on the ground was one thing, but having them in the building where you and two hundred other

men were living was a different matter. As the only officer in the
maintenance battalion who had attended bomb disposal school, I felt
I should tell Colonel McCarthy immediately. When I informed him,
he told me to keep my mouth shut, that we were moving out in the
morning and he didn't want to create a panic.

Lincoln and I both agreed that he was right. After all, that bomb
had been in the building for five months and was there during our
first bivouac in Aachen before the Battle of the Bulge. Of the several thousand American bombs dropped on Aachen during the September and October assaults, there were probably well over a hundred American UXBs in the city. Had we tried to move the battalion
in the dark to another area, it would have created confusion, and
we might have moved to an area even more heavily infested with
UXBs.

We left the next morning without further event. Sometime after
the war, German prisoners removed the bombs under the supervi-
sion of American bomb disposal officers. At least they did not have
to concern themselves with booby traps buried underneath the
fuses, as the Germans had done with the bombs they dropped in
London.

New Maps of Germany

When we first entered Germany back in September, we had been
moving so rapidly that we had run out of maps. Many a time I would
take a grease pencil and mark the route on my plastic map case as I
followed a tank column. I would try carefully not to smudge the
markings, because they were the only thing I had to go on when I
returned at night some thirty miles to our division rear.

When we captured Liège, we discovered a German map factory in
full production. We moved a signal corps cartography group into the
factory, and they started making maps for the American army. From
then on, we were issued maps before each new major operation.

We had just been issued maps covering the entire Rhine Plain to
Cologne and also through central Germany to Berlin. We all figured
that this was the big one, the final assault to destroy the German army
in the west and meet up with the Russians somewhere in central Germany.

The signal corps map group in Liège did such as excellent job of supplying us with new maps that they soon ran out of map paper. Military maps require high-quality, heavy paper. With tens of thousands of brand-new German maps available, the signal corps began to print our maps on the back side. This seemed to solve the shortage. Each liaison officer received a complete set of maps tied together in one big roll.

I unrolled my maps, spread them out on the hood of my Jeep, and started separating them according to type: 1:125,000 scale, 1:62,500 scale, and 1:10,000 scale. Then I started folding them and classifying them in numerical order. The 1:125,000 maps, in color, were to be used as large situation maps. The 1:62,500 maps, also in color, were used by the tactical commanders to plot advances. The 1:10,000 maps, in black and white, showed details of individual houses in the villages and were used as close-in tactical maps.

As I folded some of the 1:125,000 color maps, I noticed a lot of blue on the back of two of them. Upon closer examination, I was surprised to see that these were maps of southern England prepared by the Germans for the invasion of England in June 1940. They covered the area from the Thames estuary down through Weymouth and Bournemouth, the ports from which we had embarked. The maps continued farther west and covered all the major potential invasion sites on the English Channel.

When I saw these maps, I remembered when we had first arrived in Codford in September 1943. We had been assigned quarters formerly occupied by the area's British Defense Command. The liaison officers had been assigned individual desks, and as I cleaned out my desk I noticed that the main drawer was jammed. I got it unjammed and saw a folded map caught between the top of the drawer and the bottom of the desktop. When I finally got the map out safely, I damn near collapsed when I saw stamped in large red letters the word "Bigot-Amgot," the British code word for "top secret."

This map should have been kept under double lock and key. I knew that a lowly first lieutenant had no business with it. Although I was excited and I am sure my hands were shaking, I was not too excited to take a careful look at it. Fortunately, I was by myself. The map covered an area south of Codford, which was in Wiltshire, extending along the coast for about fifty to sixty miles. The British camp to which we had been assigned was apparently some type of command headquarters for the defense of this area. The map showed the location of every unit from battalion down through company, platoon, squad, and outpost.

From my limited knowledge of defensive tactics, I could see immediately that this entire area was grossly undermanned; it was covered by only about a thousand soldiers instead of the usual five infantry divisions plus at least one motorized or armored division in reserve. The map showed a battalion area where a division would have been expected, and a company where a full regiment should have been. The defenses gradually diminished to the point where they had to actually cover the beaches. There were not enough outposts to cover all the exits from the beach. It appeared that there were outposts manned by at least an automatic weapon with a couple of men spaced at intervals of a mile or more along the cliffs above the beaches. They apparently used some type of messenger on a bicycle to communicate among these outposts. This British map was dated June 1940 and covered a small portion of the same area of the German map that I had just been issued.

I have often wondered if the German decision to invade England would have been affected if they'd had a copy of this map when they made their German maps in Liège. A single German division could have completely overwhelmed the pitiful British defenses shown on this map. Later, I couldn't help but realize the great irony of being issued a map to invade Germany that had been printed on the back of a German map that would have been used to invade England.

When my mind finally returned to the real world in Codford, I wondered what to do with this map. How could I explain how it came into my possession? If I turned in the map to Major Arrington, he would have to pass it along to a higher authority, and eventually it would wind up in British hands. Probably some young British lieutenant who was as green and inexperienced as I and about my age would wind up in a general court-martial. I would be called as a key witness, which might require my transfer out of the division.

I was even afraid to show it to my buddies Lincoln and Nibbelink for fear they might advise me to turn it in. I finally chickened out. I wrapped the map in some other papers, sneaked it down to my cubbyhole in the Quonset hut in the bachelor officers' quarters, stuffed it in my little potbellied stove, and burned it. This is probably one of the dumbest things I ever did. It would have been a rare memento.

10
Battle of the Rhineland

Attack Across the Rhineland

Military historians have often agreed that until you've fought the German army, you have never fought a real battle. We had fought the German army, we had fought a real battle, and we had defeated the Germans. We had been heavily bloodied and suffered severe casualties. The Germans had suffered even heavier casualties than we had; however, we had a healthy respect for the German soldier and we realized now that Germany would not surrender until we had defeated all their armies and occupied all of their territory. We expected a bitter struggle right down to the end.

The final major assault across the Roer River and into the Rhineland was designed to destroy as much of the German army as possible and forge a bridgehead across the Rhine to make a major assault on the Ruhr Valley. It was felt that capturing the Ruhr would destroy German industrial potential and help bring the war to a speedy conclusion.

The plan called for VII Corps to attack on a relativly narrow front in the Düren area. After the 104th Infantry Division established the initial bridgehead across the Roer River, the 3d Armored Division was to pass through the infantry and advance to the Erft Canal, about twelve miles away, and establish a bridgehead there. The waters of the Roer River had subsided, but the fields were still soft due to the constant rain over the past few weeks. The armored columns tried to stay on the roads as much as possible. Although the British gave us night bombing support, the low-hanging clouds did not permit the massive high-level daylight bombing that we had had at Saint-

Lô. We did, however, have excellent support from 9th Tactical Air Force's P47 dive-bombers. They were constantly overhead during daylight.

Before the attack started, the entire tank force of the 3d Armored Division was deployed as artillery. The nearly four hundred tanks together with the artillery units was the equivalent of forty-five to fifty artillery battalions. With the L5 Piper Cubs skirting the overhanging clouds, the artillery delivered extremely heavy fire. We had learned our lessons well. For a narrow front of less than two miles, this was an awesome amount of artillery fire. The effect on the enemy was catastrophic.

The day before the Roer River offensive started, we received new 1:10,000 scale black-and-white maps showing the details of the villages, roads, and surrounding fields. At least twenty-four hours before these maps were issued, low-flying recon fighters had passed over and photographed the entire area. These photographs were rushed back to the signal corps map section, which made red overlays of the enemy fortifications. The maps were marked on the bottom, "Enemy installations as of February 21, 0900 hours."

I didn't see how they got the maps to us so quickly. The maps showed the most minute details, with the zigzagged German slit trenches marked in red. They also showed antitank guns, artillery emplacements, dug in tank emplacements, and even individual foxholes and machine-gun emplacements.

I later asked a signal corps mapmaker how he could tell whether a foxhole held a machine gun or a rifleman. He said that the rapid fire blast of an automatic weapon left a trace in the ground several feet long. This pattern was distinctly different from that made by a rifleman firing one shot at a time. In addition, he could sometimes see the pockmarks of freshly turned earth where mines had obviously been planted.

After a heavy artillery barrage, the infantry made the initial assault at 0300 on February 23. The first crossing was made using small assault boats. The infantry soon established a bridgehead in Düren against heavy resistance. An infantry assault on a heavily bombed-out city is extremely risky, because the rubble makes ideal fortifications. The Germans fought tenaciously, and our infantry suffered considerable casualties before they dislodged the Germans from the main part of the city. The engineers followed immediately and started putting up pontoon bridges. After the light personnel bridges were established, they started putting in heavy-duty pontoon bridges to accommodate tanks and other vehicles.

The initial bridgehead was small and had to be expanded to allow our armored division and its vehicles to move in. After months of shelling and bombing, Düren was a morass of fire-gutted buildings and rubble piles. Combat engineers with bulldozers cleared the areas where they thought the streets had been. An engineer officer who had been in heavy construction in civilian life said he thought it would be much cheaper for the Germans to build an entirely new city a few miles south than try to rebuild this one.

The 104th and the 8th Infantry Divisions fought hard to expand the bridgehead, and on the night of February 24–25, 3d Armored Division columns started crossing into the bridgehead.

Concentrating an armored assault force in a small bridgehead is dangerous, with so many vehicles and troops in a small area. Although we had air superiority most of the time, there was always the danger of an enemy air attack. We had just moved some elements of C Company Maintenance Battalion across the river and they had crawled off the road when the inevitable happened. All of a sudden, thousands of .50-caliber antiaircraft tracers erupted from the earth into a fiery red cone concentrated on a single object. It appeared to be a low-flying twin-engine German fighter plane the likes of which I had not seen before.

When I was stationed in Gloucester in May 1944, I had seen and heard the British Gloucester jet fighters being tested. I recognized immediately the same shrill, screaming noise. It was one of the new Me262s, and it came barreling over our columns like a bat out of hell at a very low altitude. The single bomb that it let go as it flashed by dropped on one of the columns about a hundred yards away. I heard them calling for medics, so there must have been casualties.

Just as the jet dropped its bomb, I saw one of our P47s coming in a sharp dive from several thousand feet headed directly toward the Me262. At this angle the pilot did not fire for fear of hitting our ground troops, but as soon as he leveled off, he started firing. The

German plane seemed to take off like a rocket; it appeared to have a speed at least a hundred miles per hour greater than our P47, even in the dive. In a matter of seconds, it disappeared under a low-hanging cloud bank. Our P47s didn't stand a chance of catching it.

This was a shock to all of our ground troops. We had heard that the Germans had a jet fighter, but this was the first time we saw it in actual combat. I thought immediately that if the Germans could bring several of these planes, they could wrack one of our columns from stem to stern. Unknown to us, the Germans apparently did not have the capability to bring these planes together in a mass attack.

The surprise of seeing the German jet in action generated some uneasy questions in my mind. How did they have jets in operation when we had none? I recalled, when I first arrived in England in September 1943, seeing a write-up in *Stars and Stripes* about the British development of the jet engine. In May 1944, I was at Gloucester instructing in amphibious tanks. When we road-tested our tanks, the British jets would fly over. We were impressed with their speed and grace as they came screaming across the tops of the hills, and I was glad they were on our side. I had never heard of an Me262 at the time, and I was surprised now to see one in operation.

The development of the Me262 was a perfect example of the German ability to rapidly utilize new technology. One German advantage was Hitler's supreme authority; once he made a decision to go after a new weapon or new military technology, he selected certain key people, put them in charge, and backed them to the hilt as long as they did what he said.

Hitler had a fetish for new technology, particularly if it might apply to a secret weapon. He had backed a young amateur German rocket society headed by Dr. Herman Oberth and Dr. Werner von Braun. Contrary to the advice of many of his ground force generals, he thought that military rockets had real potential. This resulted in the V1 jet-propelled pilotless bomb and the V2 rocket. Both of these weapons affected Allied military decisions to eliminate the rocket launch sites along the coast of France, Belgium, and Holland. The political situation in England put great pressure on General Eisenhower and Field Marshal Montgomery to do something about these weapons. This overemphasis on eliminating the rocket launch sites hampered the Allied campaign in northern Europe.

The 3d Armored Division attacked in strength as it broke out of the bridgehead on the morning of February 26. Although air support from medium and heavy bombers was limited by the low-hanging clouds and drizzling rain, we had massive artillery support and good close support from P47 dive-bombers. After the bitter disappointment of seeing our November offensive ground to a halt, thanks to our narrow-tracked Shermans' immobility in open country, we were now starting all over again.

The division passed through the bridgehead in five columns. The first objective was to penetrate ten to twelve miles to the Erft Canal and secure bridgeheads across it. The Germans had adequate time to prepare an extremely well-fortified defense in depth. We had hoped that, once we got through the dragons' teeth and pillboxes of the Siegfried line, the going would be much easier; however, this was not the case.

Although the Germans fought tenaciously, they were resisting our superb firepower and the full strength of a heavy American armored division in assault on a narrow front. The German infantry suffered heavy casualties, and the roadsides were littered with their dead. I was shocked to see a young German soldier sitting fully erect in his foxhole, holding his rifle. He had been struck by a single projectile, and I could see daylight through a two-inch hole in both sides of his helmet and his head. He hadn't fallen over; he just sat there passively staring out into eternity.

As Task Force Welborn on our extreme left approached the edge of the Hambach Forest to the north, it began to draw heavy small-arms and mortar fire from the woods. An infantry company dispatched toward the woods was soon pinned down. Fortunately, it had a forward observer directing fire from an 8-inch howitzer battalion on the west bank of the river. Having experience with the proximity fuse in the Ardennes, he called for the first round of HE with the fuse to mark the target. The round exploded some hundred feet in the air above the tops of the trees right at the edge of the woods. He adjusted the fire a hundred yards to the north for the second round. The proximity fuse set off the second round about two hundred feet in the air at about forty-five degrees, creating a pattern of deadly shell fragments about three hundred feet in diameter on the ground.

The effect of these shells bursting in the air decimated the German infantry on the ground, and the German commander offered to surrender. The American company commander called for a cease-fire, and the remnants of a German infantry battalion, about three hundred men, came out of the woods with their hands behind their heads. The German commander said that he had left many killed and wounded back in the woods.

Several of our task forces began to converge on Elsdorf, which they found heavily defended with log roadblocks, antitank mines, antitank guns, and assault guns, plus German infantry armed with the deadly *panzerfausts*. The Germans would try to pin down our task forces with heavy fire, then launch a counterattack with armor on the flanks. The counterattack came soon, spearheaded by four Mark VI King Tigers and two Mark IV tanks.

Fortunately, Task Force Lovelady's brand-new M26 had a good firing position on the flank and caught the Germans by surprise. It knocked out two Tigers and one Mark IV tank at a range of a thousand yards. The Germans had no idea that we had a tank that could knock out the Mark VI at this range.

To my knowledge, this was the first time that one of our M26 Pershings actually engaged the King Tiger in combat. Had the Tigers made a frontal assault, it is doubtful that the M26 could have knocked them out, because our M36 tank destroyers with the same 90mm gun had difficulty penetrating the Mark V Panther tank on the faceplate.

On the southern flank of the division, CCA ran into heavy resistance in the vicinity of Blatzheim and Kerpen. Task Force Doan alone lost four tanks in Blatzheim. The Germans fought desperately on the approaches to the canal, the last major obstacle before the flat, open Cologne Plain. The division had now penetrated ten to twelve miles from its jump-off point and had encountered almost every type of resistance. Combat Command A and CCB had gone all out and sustained considerable casualties. General Rose decided to commit CCR to establish a bridgehead across the canal, and soon the entire division was across.

In this area, between the canal and Cologne and extending north and south for several miles, was a series of large, open-pit coal mines. These "vobridge" pits were irregularly shaped, about a mile to a mile and a half across, and six hundred to seven hundred feet deep. Roads spiraled around the edges of the pits down to the bottom for access by dump trucks and power shovels. Beneath three to six feet of topsoil lay tremendous veins of brown coal (lignite) that extended downward six hundred feet or more. The power shovels would load the lignite into dump trucks, which in turn would take it to a long belt conveyor that carried it up the side of the pit to a large power plant.

These vobridge mines together with the adjacent power plants extended many miles north. The plants supplied a major part of the electric power not only for Cologne and other cities but also for the industrial Ruhr, the heart of the German steel industry. Combat Command A captured the Fortuna power plant at Bergheim. Purported to be the largest steam-generating plant in Europe, it had been relatively unscathed by any previous bombing action and was still in operation when we approached it on March 1, 1945.

The plant had several large cooling towers—reinforced concrete cylinders some 250 feet in diameter and 300 feet high. From these towers German observers were directing artillery fire. A few shots from our tanks knocked large, gaping holes in the top of the towers and eliminated these observation posts. Other than this, the plant sustained little damage. The operators had banked the furnaces and shut down the turbines when we approached.

The Fortuna power plant was equipped with American Westinghouse turbo generators. The boilers and most of the auxiliary equipment reportedly were also of American manufacture.

A large petrochemical plant that processed the brown coal was served by conveyors that carried the coal into a series of large, vertical dryers. In this state, the coal looked like a kind of wet, dark, pulverized sand. After drying, part of the material went to the burners and boilers and part to the chemical processing plant. The chemical plant pressed the material into lignite bricks for German domestic consumption. The rest of it was converted into lubricants and low-grade fuel for the German army. A number of petrochemical tank cars filled with this fuel sat on railroad sidings, ready for shipment to German army depots.

All east-west access roads and railroads had to run through narrow strips between the coal mines, which the Germans heavily fortified with roadblocks. The terrain between the vobridges—flat and open, with little vegetation for cover—offered ideal fields of fire. Because we had had a considerable number of tanks knocked out in this area, we established a major VCP at the Fortuna power plant. If the first German shot could immoblize a tank by breaking a track, the Germans would continue to fire until they set the tank on fire.

One of the new M4A3E2 tanks was brought into the VCP by the wreckers. The E2 designation indicated that the tank was experimental. We had received several of these, a hurry-up version that attempted to overcome the inadequate armor of the M4. It had an extra inch of armor welded on the front of the glacis plate and one-inch slabs of armor welded on each side of the sponsons. This gave the glacis plate an effective armor of three and a half inches and the sponsons three inches.

Although this laminated armor was not as good as solid armor, it was a lot better than what we had. The new tanks also had a heavy cast steel turret and an inch more of armor all around. This gave the turret five inches of armor on the front, tapering to three inches and down to two inches on the sides and rear. In addition, there was a heavy three- to four-inch gun mantlet mounted on the gun tube itself. We had been told that these tanks would be used for frontal assaults, but they still had the old M2 short-barreled 75mm gun. It appeared inconceivable that the army would go to the trouble of beefing up the armor but leave the gun armament the same. This extra armor added three to four tons of weight, yet the tank still had the same narrow track as the original M4A3. This limited its use in soft, muddy terrain even more.

Even with all its extra armor, the tank was penetrated twice by high-velocity German antitank projectiles. The first penetration was in the upper-right-hand corner of the tank where the reinforced glacis plate, side sponson, and top deck came together. It entered the tank directly over the head of the assistant driver and glanced down into the interior of the main fighting compartment. The next penetration struck the gun mantlet on the right side near the gunner's telescopic site. It penetrated the four-inch mantlet, then passed through five inches of armor near the gun trunnion and entered the turret. It was difficult to imagine how anyone could have survived.

The Super Pershing M26A1E2 Tank Arrives

A large steel-fabricating shop and machine shop next to the power plant apparently had made a great deal of the plant's processing equipment. Company C maintenance took over these shops for their extensive paved areas and covered work space.

Major Arrington assigned me a special project. A graduate engineer, Arrington had run his own fabricating and machine shop business in Brookhaven, Mississippi, before entering the army. As I entered his shop trailer, he was sitting at his desk with his feet propped up. I could detect a glint in his eye. He kind of half winked at Sergeant Wacowski, then addressed me in a slow drawl.

"Cooper, you've been talking big and strong about what a naval architect you are and about how you calculate the center of gravity on ships. I know damn well you're the only officer here with the audacity to keep a slide rule in your Jeep locker. Well, you're gonna have a chance to show how sharp you are."

Arrington had a perceptive mind, but he liked to generate a laid-back Southern attitude to show that he had just enough good ol' boy in him to have a good sense of humor and at the same time snap back like a steel trap to make sure you stayed on the ball. He told me to sit down, and we got into some serious talking. He explained that we were to be issued a single new Super M26 Pershing, the only tank of this type to be shipped to the European theater. The tank had a new experimental 90mm T15E1 high-velocity gun, seventy calibers (the length divided by the diameter) long. The larger the caliber, the longer the barrel, which gives the propellant charge explosion more time to expand against the base of the projectile and results in a higher velocity. With new special ammunition, this gun could produce a muzzle velocity of 3,850 feet per second, some 600 feet per second greater than the 88mm KwK43 gun mounted on the German PzKw VIb King Tiger.

Army ordnance was interested in getting the new tank into combat, hoping to match it against the King Tiger. Having already lost several of the new M26s to high-velocity German antitank guns, we knew that its armor was still inferior to that of the Mark VI Tiger. My job was to design and install additional armor on the new tank.

The well-equipped German fabricating shop contained several large pieces of inch-and-a-half boiler plate. We decided to use a laminated design for the glacis plate. We cut two pieces of the boiler plate and fashioned a V shape to fit over the V shape of the glacis plate and the lower front plate. The top glacis plate was set at thirty-eight degrees from the horizontal, which gave fifty-two degrees from the vertical and was considered to be the critical angle to generate a ricochet. This gave an air gap of zero at the top and approximately three inches at the knuckle, where the bottom front plate came in contact.

A second boiler plate was cut in a similar fashion and set at a thirty-degree angle extending out over the first plate. Where it came in contact with the bottom plate, it left a gap of seven to eight inches. We wound up with four inches of cast armor on the original glacis plate and two inch-and-a-half pieces of boiler plate with an air gap in between. We thought that even though the boiler plate was softer, the lamination and the lowered angle of incidence would help German projectiles ricochet. The new armor added about five tons to the front of the tank. A ruler was used to measure how much this would deflect the forward torsion arm bogey wheels.

We then cut a section from the faceplate of a knocked-out German Panther and trimmed it to three and a half inches thick by five feet long by two feet wide. We cut a large hole in the middle to accommodate the gun tube and two smaller holes on each side to accommodate the coaxial machine gun and the telescopic site. We slipped this plate over the gun barrel, brought it down against the mantlet, and welded it firmly all the way around. With its center of gravity fourteen inches forward of the centerline of the trunnion, this plate, which weighed fourteen hundred pounds, made the gun barrel considerably heavier on the front end.

The Super M26 Pershing already had overhead equilibrator springs attached to the turret and to the original gun mantlet, which were supposed to offset the extra length of the barrel. But the weight we had added overcame the strength of the equilibrator springs, and the gun barrel sagged forward. The mechanical gear reduction inside the turret, used to raise and lower the barrel, was insufficient to overcome this weight.

To compensate, we took two pieces of inch-and-a-half boiler plate and cut some odd-looking counterweights approximately three and a half feet long, starting one foot wide for about the first eighteen inches, then flaring to approximately two feet wide for the next twenty-four inches. We welded the narrow ends to the sides of the Panther mantlet and let them extend back horizontally and flare out slightly to miss the turret. This put the heavier section on the back side of the trunnion, thus giving a counterweight effect. These counterweights helped, although it was still difficult for the gunner to raise the gun with a mechanical elevating mechanism.

It was obvious that additional weight should be added to these counterweights, but the question was how much and where. From my limited knowledge of engineering mechanics, I knew that this would require a lengthy calculation, and the information and time were not available. This was what the major had in mind when he'd made the snide remark about my slide rule.

We decided to use an empirical method. We took some inch-and-a-half plates about one foot wide and two feet long and attached them to the rear of the large counterweights with C-clamps. By moving these weights back and forth, by trial and error we finally reached a balance point where the gun was easy to raise and lower manually. Then we welded the plates into position.

With the gun barrel rotated forward, the tank looked like a raging, charging bull elephant. The long gun stuck out like a trunk; the big, bulbous counterweights stood out like ears; and the holes in the gun mantlet for the telescopic site and the machine gun looked like eyes. We hoped it would make the same impression on the Germans.

The turret had already been modified with a counterweight on the back to compensate for the long gun. We added more counterweight to compensate. Otherwise, when the tank was on a slope, it would be difficult to traverse the turret even with a power traverse. We had noted this problem with the German Panther. If it was on a decided slope and the gun was swinging downhill, it took a long time for the German gunner to rotate the turret forward with its manual traverse.

We had now added seven tons to the tank. We checked our ground distances again and found that the bogey wheels were deflecting down an additional two inches. This caused the rear of the tank to cock up like a wild drake in heat. In spite of its odd appearance, and the fact that we had probably slowed it down about five miles an hour, the tank, with its 550-horsepower motor, still had plenty of power.

Next, we road-tested the tank, then drove it to the edge of the vobridge to test-fire the gun. We looked around for a suitable target and finally found a knocked-out German Jagdpanzer IV assault gun that had been hit by a single shot to the flank and had not burned. We hooked it up to one of our wreckers and dragged it to the other side of the vobridge, on the first level about fifty feet below the crest. The Jagdpanzer was positioned with the forward glacis plate facing us. The distance to our target was approximately a mile and a half.

The ammunition for the 90mm T15E1 gun was a standard 90mm round, but the cartridge case was longer to accommodate a larger propellant charge. Initially, we used two men to load the round into the tube. However, after a little more experience, one man could do it, albeit with some difficulty. There were bound to be some problems with an experimental tank.

Major Dick Johnson sent over the crew from the 33d Armored Regiment to operate this tank. We wound up instructing them at the same time we were learning ourselves. An artillery maintenance sergeant in charge of the firing had previously bore-sighted the gun, so we were ready to fire. I made sure that everybody stood back to the sides and rear of the tank to give the blast cone adequate clearance.

Anyone standing behind an M4 Sherman could see the projectile go out and curve down slightly as it sped toward the target. This new high-velocity gun was entirely different. When we fired the first round, we could barely see the projectile. It appeared to rise slightly as it struck the target. This was an optical illusion, but the effect was awesome. When it hit the target, sparks shot about sixty feet into the air, as though a giant grinding wheel had hit a piece of metal.

When we looked at the target, I was dumbfounded. The 90mm projectile penetrated four inches of armor; went through a five-inch final drive differential shaft, the fighting compartment, and the rear partition of the fighting compartment; penetrated the four-and-a-half-inch crankshaft of the Maybach engine and the one-inch rear armor plate; and dug itself into the ground so deep that we could not locate it. Although we had been told by the ordnance officers from Aberdeen that the tank gun could penetrate thirteen inches of armor at a hundred yards, it was still difficult to believe this awesome power. We all realized that we had a weapon that could blast the hell out of even the most powerful German Mark VI Tiger.

We instructed the new crew on the use of the gun and let each man fire it. We explained that the special ammunition was longer and more difficult to load and that the extra armor would make the tank more difficult to steer; however, with a little experience they could work this out. Although the tank had extra armor, they were not to expose it foolishly. The objective was to get into combat under the best conditions and see what it could do against German armor.

The crew was so glad to get this tank that the men were willing to suffer any inconvenience. I'm sure they felt that the tank, supposedly the most powerful of any in the American, German, or Russian armies, increased their chances of survival.

I told Major Johnson that he ought to have his crew watch this tank closely, particularly the final drive and track system and the engine, because the seven extra tons of armor might eventually cause some maintenance problems. In spite of this, I felt that the tank should be able to perform its mission.

The Assault on Cologne

On March 2, the VII Corps had established a small but fairly firm bridgehead on the east bank of the Erft Canal. General "Lightning Joe" Collins and General Rose thoroughly understood each other, and Collins had great confidence in Rose, who was extremely aggressive and strongly believed in exercising command from the forwardmost elements.

The 3d Armored Division moved out of the bridgehead with two combat commands abreast and one in reserve. Each of the combat commands was heavily reinforced from the infantry divisions. Before daybreak on March 3, the division launched an all-out assault against Cologne.

Combat Command R ran into heavy resistance at Stommeln. The Germans were heavily dug in with armor and infantry. Although P47s worked the town over and inflicted severe damage on the Germans, they still held on. General Rose committed CCB in a flank attack; after heavy fighting, the defense of the town collapsed and the division regrouped and proceeded. This textbook-style armored movement not only overcame German resistance in the heavily fortified town but prevented the Germans from escaping to the next town to set up another defense in depth. This same tactic was successfully used over and over in the battle of Cologne.

While CCB was outflanking Stommeln, the 83d Reconnaissance Battalion bypassed Sinnersdorf and headed straight toward the Rhine River at Worringen. There they ran into a hornet's nest. The Ninth Army had reached the Rhine north of us, and German troops pinned between the Ninth and First Armies were streaming south toward the bridges at Worringen and Cologne. The 83d was greatly outnumbered and had to withdraw slightly; however, they were immediately reinforced by CCB, which finally cut off the Germans coming from the north. Large numbers of prisoners were taken in this area.

Although the 3d Armored Division had experience in city fighting, Cologne was by far the largest city we had encountered. From the air it looks like a giant half circle stretching along the west bank of the Rhine River. The heart of the city, which in peacetime had a population of 800,000, had been heavily damaged by aerial bombing. The German army made good use of the skeletal walls of burned-out buildings, and intact buildings were also heavily fortified.

At dawn on March 4, the entire VII Corps advanced on Cologne and areas south toward Bonn to try to destroy and capture all German units west of the Rhine. The 3d Armored Division attacked with CCB on the left from the north road to the river farther southwest, where it linked up with CCA, whose sector ended south of Sinnersdorf. The 1st Infantry Division with CCR attached covered the area south of the city and advanced toward Bonn.

The greatest threat to a tank entering narrow city streets is attack from above; the lightest armor is on its top deck. Because a tank is relatively blind when buttoned up, it becomes heavily exposed when under observation from the upper floors of buildings. Early in the war, the Germans had learned the danger of a bottle filled with gasoline, wrapped in a gasoline-soaked cloth, ignited, and thrown on top of a tank. This "Molotov cocktail" turned the tank into a blazing inferno. The light top deck armor could also be easily penetrated by a *panzerfaust*.

The greatest dangers to infantry were sniper and automatic weapons fire from well-protected positions in the buildings, plus mortar and artillery fire directed by forward observers on the upper floors. Nothing was more effective than the direct fire of a tank at close range against a fortified position.

As the infantry started down the block, they would fan out and crouch down low against the edge of the buildings on both sides. The first tank would echelon to the right, the second tank to the left some twenty-five to fifty yards to the rear. The first tank would fire down the street at the building on the left in the next block, concentrating on the upper floors. Generally it would fire both HE and white phosphorus to set the tops of the buildings on fire. Any Germans not killed by these immediate blasts would run into the basements, but the infantry would toss grenades in the basement windows and kill any men caught down there. The second tank would concentrate on the right side of the street, using the same tactics. Any survivors would come screaming out of the building with their hands over their heads.

Combat Command A was making good progress through the center of the city when Task Force Kane ran upon the airfield. The field was protected by sixteen dual-purpose 88mm guns. To approach them, the tanks had to cross the open airport runways. They called for an artillery barrage of white phosphorus smoke shells. Under the cover of the smoke screen, the tanks advanced across the open field with infantry riding on their backs and soon overran the 88s and the infantry surrounding them. This was a good example of the close cooperation between the tanks and the self-propelled artillery. Had the tanks made a frontal assault across the open airport, they could have been slaughtered by the 88s. Spearhead had learned its lesson well, having paid for it dearly in blood and tank losses in previous engagements.

Meanwhile, CCB on the north met extremely heavy resistance. The Hohenzollern bridge, in the heart of the city just opposite the Domplatz, was the last remaining bridge across the Rhine at Cologne. As CCA and the 104th Infantry Division began to close in, the Germans blew the bridge, and the remaining German troops tried to escape north on the river road, apparently hoping that the bridge at Düsseldorf might still be open.

Combat Command B had to bear the full brunt of this advance. As CCB traveled along the river road and other streets parallel to it, it came in contact with several batteries of dual-purpose 88s supported by tanks and assault guns. At the same time, CCB was being harassed by flanking fire from German batteries dug in across the river. The ensuing engagement was extremely heavy, especially for CCB's Task Force Lovelady.

The two combat commanders, General Hickey of CCA and General Boudinot of CCB, didn't hesitate to use the natural rivalry between the commands to spur their troops to greater efforts. Although all American soldiers realized that the Germans were the enemy, friendly rivalry promoted esprit de corps. It was with such thoughts that General Boudinot called Colonel Lovelady on the radio.

"Lovelady. Boudinot here. Where are you?"

"General, we're at phase line B and stopped cold in our tracks," Lovelady responded, "but we're holding on as best we can."

"Task Force Doan is all the way down to phase line K," Boudinot replied, "and they're going to capture the center of the city before we even get inside the city limits."

After ducking a few more rounds of incoming 88 shells, Lovelady pressed the button on the radio phone. "General, it's not competition I'm worried about at this point, it's opposition," and he hung up.

Task Force Lovelady finally overcame this heavy opposition and continued south down the river road into the factory area, where it encountered more resistance. The Ford Motor Company had a large assembly plant in this area that made trucks for the German army. The plant had sustained little damage and was captured largely intact. On the roof of the main administrative building was a large executive boardroom, beautifully paneled on one side and with large plateglass windows with heavy draperies on the side facing the river. A long oak table surrounded by a dozen or more stuffed leather chairs occupied the center of the room. The walls were festooned with swastika symbols, and on the end wall was a life-sized portrait of Adolf Hitler.

Standing in this handsome room and looking out over the broad vista of the river, I couldn't help but wonder why this plant had such little damage whereas the surrounding area had been devastated by bombing. From the large windows we could clearly see the German positions across the river, and I'm sure the Germans could see us. It occurred to me that this wasn't a safe place to be; however, the Germans didn't fire across the river at the plant while I was there.

Combat Command B and CCA eventually converged at the cathedral. Although sporadic sniper fire continued, German resistance in the city had collapsed. As a last act of defiance, a German Panther engaged one of our Shermans in front of the cathedral and knocked it out, killing three of the crew. One of the new M26 Pershing tanks came up from around the corner (into the main square in front of the cathedral) taking the German Panther completely by surprise. The M26, commanded by Ssgt. Bob Early with Cpl. Clarence Smoyer, gunner, headed straight toward the flank of the Panther. Corporal Smoyer had engaged the gyrostabilizer gun control, which allowed the 90mm gun to maintain its level position while the tank was still in motion. All American tanks were equiped with the gun stabilizer, but it was seldom used in combat as most gunners still preferred to fire from a stationary position. The Panther crew expected the Pershing to stop before firing. As the Panther was swinging its gun around, the Pershing bore down at top speed and Smoyer let go with the first round, which struck just the Panther gun shield deflecting down through the thin top deck armor, severing the German gunner's leg and killing him. Corporal Smoyer fired two more rounds through the side of the Panther, setting it on fire. Three of the crew were burned to death while the other two bailed out. This was the last armored engagement in the city. The battle of Cologne was over.

The heart of Cologne was devastated by heavy aerial bombing. The main railway station in the heart of town was destroyed. However, eight hundred railroad cars were still intact in the marshaling yard, which extended radially northwestward for more than a mile. Many of the cars were loaded with German ordnance equipment and other supplies. Although the bombing around the cathedral was heavy, it was obvious that both our air force and the RAF had deliberately refrained from bombing the cathedral itself.

On entering the cathedral through the main front doors, we immediately encountered a tremendous amount of rubble: wooden pews, benches, and chairs plus gargoyles and statuettes that had fallen to the floor. Many of the windows had shattered, although the Germans had long since removed the beautiful stained-glass windows. At least one 500-pound bomb had penetrated the transept on the south side of the cathedral. The explosion blew off a large section of the roof and destroyed all the windows in this section of the structure, but the main stone buttresses did not appear to be structurally damaged. Ernie Nibbelink had his camera and took several pictures, probably the first taken inside the cathedral after the city fell.

By March 7 the city was completely occupied, and the 3d Armored Division took a well-deserved rest. Combat replacements came up, the ordnance ammunition unit resupplied all units, and our maintenance crews concentrated on much-needed repairs.

We occupied Cologne for the next few days. Other than an occasional incoming artillery or mortar round, the city was relatively calm. Many of the buildings, particularly the hotels, had basements that were three or four levels deep that had been converted into bomb shelters. Our troops moved in and made themselves comfortable while awaiting orders. It did not take the soldiers long to find the elaborate wine cellars in some of the hotels; GIs seem to have an almost radarlike sense for locating any form of alcohol. In one hotel alone, our troops found 750,000 bottles of wine, Cognac, champagne, and schnapps. That in itself was enough for every man in First Army to have at least two bottles.

First Army, which had taken the major brunt of the fighting in Western Europe since D day, was rumored to be replaced by the newly formed Fifteenth Army. First Army would continue to hold its positions on the west bank of the Rhine; after the river was crossed we would be phased out of the European theater entirely. We planned to go down to Marseilles for a few days of rest and relaxation, then get ready to be shipped to the Pacific for the invasion of Japan.

Our corps commander, General Collins, addressed the troops in a special formation in the Cologne sports plaza. VII Corps had made the breakthrough in Normandy, blocked the German counterattack at Mortain, closed the Falaise Pocket, enveloped Paris, and driven through Namur and Liège into Germany. General Collins, who noted that he'd had the privilege of commanding many fine divisions and some truly great ones, classified the 3d Armored among the great ones; it was the first unit to break completely through the Siegfried line and capture a German town, which earned it the well-deserved nickname of Spearhead. All of our soldiers were issued a little yellow patch with a black border and a red spearhead in the middle with "Spearhead" written around the bottom. This was to be worn on the right upper sleeve of the blouse opposite the 3d Armored Division patch on the left sleeve. In addition, the division patch was redesigned, and the notation "Spearhead" was added to the bottom. We were also issued little yellow spearhead medallions to paste on the right side of our helmet liners. The men were proud of this nickname.

We were finally briefed that the main Allied effort was going to come from the 21st Army Group, north of us. This was to be a major amphibious assault and perhaps the largest single buildup since D day. The assault would be preceded by a massive air and artillery bombardment. The navy had been ordered to operate assault landing craft on the river. The quartermaster truck groups included several battalions of DUKW amphibious trucks. There were also several battalions of tracked landing vehicles (LVTs). In April 1944, I had helped train the quartermaster truck group at Gloucester to maintain and operate the new LVTs. We had apparently done a good job, because they were reported to have operated effectively in the low, swampy marshes around Carentan during the Normandy invasion.

On March 7, while we were in Cologne awaiting the grand finale,

Combat Command B of the 9th Armored Division captured intact the Ludendorff bridge at Remagen. The sudden, unexpected capture of a bridge across the Rhine River took SHAEF completely by surprise and sent shock waves through the high echelons of command. Although the 21st Army Group was still to make its major crossing of the Rhine, the capture of the Remagen bridgehead brought the major thrust into the heart of Germany back to the 12th Army Group and particularly to the First Army. The battle of the Rhineland was rapidly drawing to an end, and the battle of central Germany was about to begin.

11

The Battle of Central Germany

The Western Front, March 23, 1945

In war, the farther forward you are, the more you know about the immediate situation but the less you know about the overall situation. The farther to the rear you are, just the opposite is true. When these views conflict, the American soldier is trained to use his own initiative and judgment.

This was the case when CCB of the 9th Armored Division suddenly encountered the Ludendorff bridge intact. They immediately tried to capture the bridgehead and depended on the rest of their division and corps to back them up later. When General Milliken, III Corps commander, reported the seizing of the bridgehead to General Hodges, Hodges told him to put the troops necessary to secure the bridgehead across and await further orders. When Hodges called General Bradley to report the successful coup, Bradley was elated; however, his excitement was toned down somewhat when Gen. Harold R. Bull, a British staff officer from SHAEF, told him he must release four divisions of the 12th Army Group.

There has been some disagreement among historians as to exactly what happened, but it was obvious that General Bull was not interested in doing anything that would de-emphasize the role of the 21st Army Group. Bradley disagreed with losing four divisions at this time and called Eisenhower directly. After Bradley explained the situation, Eisenhower approved a limited buildup in the bridgehead. Bradley passed this information to Hodges, who in turn decided to order General Collins to bring VII Corps to shore up the northern flank of the bridgehead.

During the early planning of Operation Overlord, the feeling existed in SHAEF headquarters that the British had taken the brunt of the war for many years and should therefore have a major role in the final destruction of Germany. Eisenhower faced subtle pressure from Churchill on down to give the British a more important part in the battle of western Europe. During the Normandy landings, the 21st Army Group under Montgomery played a major part. Montgomery realized that the British did not have sufficient replacements to sustain heavy losses, as the Americans could because of their larger pool of replacements. Even allowing for this, the British Second Army and the Canadian First Army put up a powerful fight in Normandy. Montgomery, due to his inane ultraconservativeness, failed to exploit his opportunities in the eastern sector of the Normandy bridgehead, and as a result, the British and Canadian role was soon eclipsed by the brilliant exploitation of the Saint-Lô breakthrough by the newly formed 12th Army Group under General Bradley.

Since the First Army's arrival on the German border, Eisenhower had encouraged a broad front strategy. He apparently felt that as long as the Germans put up a defense, it was very important to prevent any salient developing that could be cut off by the enemy. Many disagreed with this strategy, although it seemed to work.

Now that all of the Allied armies were drawn up along the Rhine, the situation changed drastically. As of February 23, when the major offensive in the Rhineland started, the Germans had seventy-three divisions opposing seventy Allied divisions. Although the German divisions were greatly weakened, they still held a large portion of the Siegfried line to the south and were still capable of putting up a great fight. Since the later stages of the Battle of the Bulge, practically all production of Panther and Tiger tanks had been committed to the western armies. The Germans were now desperately defending their homeland, and many were determined to carry out Hitler's orders to yield no ground and fight to the last man.

In the early planning for the Rhine crossings, there appeared to be little advantage in attempting a crossing in the Bonn-Remagen area. The hills on the east bank were high, and observers on them could completely dominate the flat, rolling plains on the west bank. The terrain was similar to that in the Ardennes. The limited road nets required penetration of some fifty miles before the troops could swing north and east.

In spite of the Remagen bridgehead, Field Marshal Montgomery insisted on even more control and urged Eisenhower to transfer Hodges's First Army to the 21st Army Group. Although Eisenhower believed that the main effort should come north of the Ruhr in the 21st Army Group area, he was reluctant to take the First Army from Bradley.

Although Eisenhower's head may have been with the logic of a strong offensive north of the Ruhr, his heart remained with the 12th Army Group and his American troops. He suspected, according to many historians, that by turning the First Army over to Montgomery, he would have held it back, and the 21st Army Group would have advanced beyond them toward Berlin to gain more glory for the British.

General Marshall, back in Washington, also opposed this move. Eisenhower finally told Montgomery that he would consider giving the First Army a more northern role in the final offensive, provided it remained under the 12th Army Group. Montgomery said he would rather go without the First Army under those circumstances.

March 23 was the date for the 21st Army Group's massive assault across the Rhine River. While all of the big preparations were to assist the 21st Army Group, Patton's Third Army made a quick, unexpected crossing at Oppenheim. This undoubtedly miffed Montgomery as the Third Army had stolen his thunder a few hours prior to his gigantic crossing.

Bradley had two armies across the Rhine, the First at the Remagen bridgehead and the Third in the area of Oppenheim. Eisenhower now unleashed the 12th Army Group with priority equal to that of the 21st Army Group. This was all Hodges and Patton were looking for. The SHAEF plan for the final assault on Germany called for the 21st Army Group to cross the Rhine north of the Ruhr. The American First Army was to break out of the Remagen bridgehead south of the Segan River. The VII Corps, on the northern flank of the First Army, was to drive due east across the Dure River, continue until it could swing north and envelop the southern flank of the Ruhr Pocket, and eventually meet up with the Ninth Army coming from the north. The Third Army, breaking out of its bridgehead at Oppenheim, would swing north and east to secure bridgeheads across the Main River. The First and Third Armies would then proceed from Frankfurt and Kassel to the north and east. From this point on, the objective of the 12th Army Group was to seek out and destroy all German forces.

The Remagen Bridgehead

The 3d Armored Division left Cologne on March 20 to assemble near Honnef, preparatory to crossing the Remagen bridge. Our division artillery had accumulated considerable ammunition, because it was normal practice when a division was in a holding position to fire at German targets of opportunity. Not wanting to exhaust the combat load of ammunition in the ready racks, we stored the extra ammunition on the ground. When the division was ordered to move, the division artillery commander was not about to leave this ammunition there, because 105mm ammunition was hard to come by. A quartermaster truck company was ordered up from COMZ to haul the additional ammunition.

The main road to Remagen ran down the west bank of the Rhine, an area of mostly flat plains, a few low-lying hills, and numerous villages. The column sometimes had to proceed under direct observation of German artillery observers across the river. Where the road was exposed, engineers had improvised camouflage nets hung from telephone lines.

After our columns passed down this road, they were followed by the quartermaster truck company bringing the ammunition. About halfway between Cologne and Bonn, the German artillery had knocked down a telephone pole and brought the camouflage net down for a distance of some two hundred yards. When this happened, the infantry captain in charge of the area told the lieutenant in charge of the village just north of him to send the trucks. They waited until just after the German shells landed, then released the trucks one at a time, hoping they could get across the open area before the next round came in. This procedure worked well for a while, but their luck soon ran out.

As one particularly slow truck reached the halfway point, a German shell exploded directly in front of it. The driver panicked and slammed on the brakes, and the crew hit the ditch on the side away from the river. From his position a hundred yards to the south, the captain called for the crew to come down the ditch toward him. The crew panicked and froze in place. The captain realized that if they stayed there, the truck would be hit, and if the ammunition exploded they would be killed instantly.

The captain crawled down the ditch himself and told the men to follow him. At the same time, a second round hit to the rear of the truck, and the explosion set the tarp on fire. Just as they got back to the village, the truck exploded. Fortunately, the captain and the truck crew had reached a safe position, and no one was injured.

The truck crew was really shaken; this was the first time they had encountered direct enemy fire. As COMZ troops, they were used to working in relative safety, and it never occurred to them that they would be exposed to this type of danger. Not until they were in the relative safety of a basement in the village did they feel secure.

The 3d Armored Division moved into an assembly area southwest of Bonn near Königswinter. Although First Army had attempted to expand the bridgehead, the bridge was struck numerous times by direct fire from German 88s and by indirect fire from larger artillery. Many air attacks had been made, although the antiaircraft battalions discouraged German planes from making a pass at the bridge itself. The Germans even fired a V2 rocket from the Netherlands and struck a house in the village nearby. Although engineers erected several pontoon bridges, they made a valiant attempt to save the Ludendorff bridge. The full span on the upstream side was still intact, and the signalmen had run numerous communication wires across the bridge. In spite of these efforts, the weakened bridge collapsed on March 15, carrying a number of engineers and signalmen to their deaths.

We crossed into the bridgehead on the morning of March 23 on a pontoon bridge at Honnef. The engineers lashed large pontoons close together with treadways to make rafts to carry the heavy M26 tanks. Our Super M26 made the crossing in good shape. The division joined the VII Corps, which was massing its strength on the north side of the bridgehead.

Envelopment of the Ruhr Pocket

With the Ninth Army bridgehead north of the Ruhr and the First Army bridgehead south of the Ruhr at Remagen, the Allies were now prepared to launch a massive double envelopment. The 2d Armored Division (Hell on Wheels) would lead the assault on the north. The VII Corps of First Army led by the 3d Armored Division (Spearhead) would lead the assault on the south.

The 2d and 3d Armored Divisions were the only heavy armored divisions left after the 1943 reorganization converted the remaining divisions into light armored divisions. The heavy armored divisions had 232 medium tanks compared to 168 medium tanks for the light armored divisions. The tanks plus the accompanying maintenance and supply organizations gave the heavy armored division much greater staying power.

Since Normandy, these two divisions had worked closely in every major operation. The men of these divisions knew that they were part of the first team and were destined to become the main effort of the Allied armies in the west until the end of the war in Europe.

Plans for enveloping the Ruhr Pocket were highly innovative and brilliantly carried out. Normally, the flank penetration would be limited to ten to twelve miles. In the envelopment of the Ruhr Pocket, we were planning an entirely different ball game. The armored columns would move out rapidly and make extremely deep penetrations along relatively narrow fronts. Air cover would let them know what was ahead and alert them to any serious threats to their flanks.

The First Army assault from the Remagen bridgehead, with VII Corps in the lead, started on March 25. The attack concentrated on a narrow area between the Segan River and the Land River. The Germans opposed our corps with elements of three *volksgrenadier* divisions, one parachute division, and three panzer divisions plus separate armored groups and combat engineers. The German units had been decimated, and few were anywhere near full combat strength.

The 3d Armored Division, leading the VII Corps, moved out at dawn on March 25 in four columns. Combat Command B took the two northern columns and CCA took the two southern columns. Combat Command R followed the two middle columns, and the 83d Recon Battalion followed the north column of CCB. The division was virtually back to full strength in tanks and other equipment. The older men who had survived combat felt like veterans and took great pride in imbuing the new replacements with the accomplishments of the Spearhead Division. Morale was good, but we knew we had a tough fight ahead of us.

Although the Germans had been greatly weakened, they were now fighting desperately for their homeland. The rugged terrain afforded them excellent defensive possibilities. The division had been heavily bloodied so far, which humbled the survivors. We had also sustained great losses in tanks and other combat equipment. The battle-hardening experience of recovery, evacuation, repair, maintenance, and replacement had developed a strong mutual respect between the combat soldiers and the maintenance soldiers, who depended on one another for their survival.

The division's new objective was Altenkirchen, headquarters of the 15th German Army. Combat Command A immediately ran into heavy tank and antitank fire on the southern flank. Combat Command B, on the north, ran into even heavier resistance from a *kampfgruppe* of Panther and Tiger tanks, which outgunned our M4 Shermans. Although CCB had three of the new M26 Pershings spread out between the two columns, they did not begin to match the twenty to thirty Panthers and Tigers.

The M26 Super Pershing was in this group, but the maintenance crew had to nurse it along because it was overheating. The extra weight of the armor and the extremely rugged terrain put a much heavier load on the engine. The maintenance crew constantly adjusted the V belts on the coolant fans to try to rectify the problem. This helped somewhat, but it was not until we got into open country that the tank became fairly reliable.

Late on the afternoon of March 25, I left CCB in the Altenkirchen Woods, north of the city, and headed back to the maintenance battalion near Honnef. We had had considerable losses that day, and I wanted to submit my combat loss report in order to get replacements as quickly as possible.

I was traveling with CCB on the northern route just south of the Sieg River. The 78th Infantry Division was deployed along the south bank of the river. A regimental combat team of the 1st Infantry Division was traveling eastward in a truck convoy along the same route as I tried to head west. At one point, the road crested the top of a hill where the trucks were exposed to observation from the Germans across the river to the north. The Germans started interdictory fire.

Normally, the trucks would slow down in the defiladed position, then race rapidly across the open space one at a time. Due to the traffic jam farther down the road, the trucks were bumper to bumper on top of the hill. The infantrymen bailed out and took cover on the south side of the road. One of the trucks had already been hit and the top was blasted off.

I reasoned that sooner or later the Germans would score a direct hit on the trucks and set them on fire, and I would not be able to get across the road. I figured that the Germans were firing a single 155mm howitzer because of the size of the explosion and time interval between rounds—approximately twenty to twenty-five seconds, which was all the time I had to get across the four-hundred-yard opening. I looked at the sweep second hand on my watch, gave Wrayford the countdown, and sure enough the next round came in right on time.

Wrayford already had the Jeep in four-wheel drive in low gear. We took off in a cloud of dust and screamed across the top of the hill. We crouched down in the Jeep to where we could barely see over the windshield. After a lot of skidding on the soft, loose dirt on the shoulder, we reached the crest in about eighteen seconds. We heard the next round coming in and ducked as low as we could. As we passed through a slight depression, with our heads just below the level of the edge of the embankment, the shell exploded about fifteen feet from the edge of the embankment, and the blast went over our heads. Wrayford was driving like a runaway racehorse and never veered off his course for a second. The concussion seemed to move the Jeep to the side, but we screamed along amid a cloud of flying fragments and falling clods of dirt. When we reached the other side, we kept on going.

By this time, VII Corps had shattered the northern flank of the German 15th Army, and the division started moving much faster. The situation now became highly fluid, similar to that after the breakout in Normandy, but the conditions were different. The terrain was still rugged, and it was difficult to maintain contact among columns. German communications were still somewhat intact, and they continued to put up numerous roadblocks and counterattack from the flanks.

First Army's overall tactical plan called for a deep penetration so rapid that we would get completely through their advance communication zone. By the early morning of March 28, the division had slashed through Herborn and Marburg and was ready to swing north. In less than three days, it had driven seventy miles (more than a hundred miles by road), which was farther than the Germans had driven in the first three weeks of the Battle of the Bulge.

The division was ordered to move rapidly to the north to meet up with the Ninth Army in the vicinity of Paderborn. The 2d Armored Division was driving hard across the northern border of the Ruhr. We knew that if we could connect with the Ninth Army, we would completely cut off major elements of the German army in the Ruhr Pocket. The division fanned out, each of its six columns with four P47 dive-bombers over it during the daylight hours.

Even though we were deep inside German territory, our complete domination of the air gave us tremendous superiority. All opposition was bypassed where possible, and if a column became bogged down another would outflank the roadblock. Additional battalions from the 1st and the 104th Infantry Divisions were assigned to the task forces.

On the night of March 28, I left CCB with my combat loss report. On the morning of the twenty-ninth, I returned to Marburg and headed north, traveling alone, to try to catch up with the division. Whenever I left the combat command in the evenings, I always made it a practice to go by headquarters and look at the G2 map. It was important to know the next day's objectives and the routes the columns would follow. When I made the return trip, I wanted to follow the road the combat command had been on. In a fast-moving situation such as this, the Germans were cleared only to the hedgerows. As a liaison officer traveling alone, I knew I was particularly vulnerable.

About ten miles north of Marburg, with the windshield down and Wrayford driving at our top speed of sixty-five miles an hour, we suddenly came to a Y in the road. For a moment I was not sure which was the main road and which was the secondary road. I took a guess and told Wrayford to turn to the right. We had gone about a hundred yards when it hit me and I screamed, "Stop! dammit let's get the hell out of here fast!"

Wrayford slammed on the brakes, turned so fast that he nearly flipped the Jeep, then headed back at top speed in the opposite direction. When we got back to the road junction, we stopped to look at the map again.

I heard a voice call out, "Are you from the Third Armored?"

I looked in the direction of the voice, and on a knoll about fifteen feet above the road to my right I saw a couple of GIs in their armored car. They were too well camouflaged to be seen when we came down the road the first time.

"Yes, we're with CCB and we're trying to catch up with the column," I replied.

The sergeant, from the 83d Recon, told me I was on the right road but had taken the wrong fork. The road to the left was the main road, and the column was somewhere between this point and Paderborn. Had we continued down the road to the right another hundred yards, we would have met a German roadblock that faced our roadblock back at the Y. They were sweating each other out.

As we headed north up the main road, I contemplated what had just happened. Why had I suddenly decided to tell Wrayford to stop and turn around? It finally dawned on me. The road that we had taken was covered with dust. A main paved highway would never be covered with dust unless no traffic had been on it for some period. Had our tank columns taken this road, the dust would have been blown to one side and we would have seen evidence of tank tracks. I was so used to this that I had taken it for granted. My thoughts had undoubtedly saved our lives. Many times, God, in his infinite mercy, has strange ways of communicating with us.

The division launched its attack at 0600 from Marburg on the morning of March 29 and continued to attack relentlessly until 2200 that evening. The division traveled in four roughly parallel columns from three to five miles apart. By 2200, elements of the division had driven 90 miles north (118 miles by road). In the history of land warfare this was the longest armored advance against an enemy in a twenty-four hour period. Even Desert Storm could not equal this record.

Taking advantage of the rugged country, the Germans put heavy roadblocks in the narrow defiles between the hills. Combat Command B, on the extreme right, was alert to possible counterattack from a German *volksgrenadier* division reported somewhere to our east. One CCB column suddenly found itself in a narrow defile under heavy fire from German automatic weapons and *panzerfausts*.

The Germans fired the *panzerfausts* directly down from a rock ledge some thirty feet above the highway and struck the tanks on their thin deck armor. The column was stopped cold. When our infantry tried to infiltrate around them, the Germans moved to another position and continued firing. Here was another example of how a small group of determined soldiers with small arms and *panzerfausts* could hold up a major column. The Germans held the column up until they were reinforced and a major engagement developed. The 104th Infantry Division finally sent reinforcements, and CCB bypassed the area. By using infantry to take over and allow the armor to leapfrog around, the advance could continue unabated. This type of maneuver went on continuously throughout the entire division area.

Combat Command B headed toward Paderborn. It was the site of the German panzer training center, which was comparable to Fort Knox in the United States, and reportedly had two training battalions of thirty to forty Panther and Tiger tanks each. There were also numerous miscellaneous units of antiaircraft troops and air force personnel who had been inducted into the infantry. This made a formidable defending force.

Major General Maurice Rose Is Killed in Action

As the battle grew closer to Paderborn, the concentration of American and German troops in a small area became more dense. Our columns constantly crossed over German columns, and in some instances our columns crossed over one another.

During one such incident, Gen. Maurice Rose was trying to pass up to the task force commander's half-track when a German tank column cut into our column. General Rose's driver slammed on the brakes and brought the Jeep to a quick halt as it came up against the rear of a King Tiger. Suddenly, the young German tank commander, armed with a burp gun, opened his turret hatch and started screaming at the American general. The general, his driver, and his aide got out of the Jeep and held up their hands. For some reason, the German tank commander became extremely agitated and kept pointing to Rose and hollering at him, all the while gesturing toward the general's pistol.

In the armored force, officers carried their pistols in shoulder holsters. It was reported that Rose carried a second pistol in a hip holster on his web belt around his waist.

What happened is a matter of conjecture; however, we believe that the general thought that the tank commander wanted him to surrender his pistol. When he lowered his arms to release his belt, the German tank commander thought Rose was going to draw his pistol. In a screaming rage he fired his burp gun and struck Rose in the head, killing him instantly. As the general's body pitched forward, Major Bellinger, his aide, and Technician Fifth Grade Shaunch, his driver, took off and under cover of darkness escaped into the woods. Major General Maurice Rose was the first and only division commander killed in World War II in the European theater.

Right after the Battle of the Bulge, in early February, Generals Rose and Patton reportedly had a conversation. Rose had served under Patton in the 2d Armored Division. Patton said that when his time came, he would like to die in battle leading his troops. Rose had replied that he did not think anything this glamorous would happen to him, that he probably would be killed in an automobile accident after the war was over. Two months later, General Rose had been killed in action leading his troops. Several months after the war was over, General Patton died as the result of an automobile accident. Such a twist of fate was one of the great ironies of war.

The news of General Rose's death shocked the men in the division. Although few knew him personally, those who had survived since Normandy, when he became our division commander, knew him by reputation. My closest contact was when I had the honor of receiving a Bronze Star from him during a decoration ceremony in Werbomont, Belgium, right after the Battle of the Bulge. We stood at attention as the general passed down the line to each man. When he got to me, he stepped forward, pinned the medal on my combat jacket, stepped back, and said, "Congratulations, Lieutenant."

"Thank you, sir," I said, and threw him one of my smartest VMI salutes. He returned the salute and stepped to the next man. For a brief moment he looked me straight in the eye, and I returned the look. I felt as though I had just been knighted by a king.

To a soldier, a general was surrounded by an aura of mystique. Although from time to time a soldier may have felt that the orders coming down to him were stupid, he still had to believe that, when the chips were down, his general was looking after him and would make the right decisions. A healthy respect for one's general was an essential part of esprit de corps, which was an important part of morale. The higher the morale, the better the chances for survival. At the time of his death, General Rose had been key to the division's survival.

Annihilation of a Task Force

Following General Rose's death, confusion was rampant among our leading elements. The general was trying to get Task Force Doan to secure our left flank when he was struck down. German groups of tanks and infantry counterattacked our task forces whenever possible. One major engagement just south of the Paderborn airport exemplified the tragic inferiority of our tanks.

One of our columns proceeded up a slightly inclined straight road. A narrow, winding road met the straight road about half a mile from the point where our column entered it. Heavily wooded, rolling hills lay on the right side of the road, and a level, open field was on the left with woods set back about three hundred yards. The column consisted of a company of M4 Sherman tanks followed by a company of armored infantry in half-tracks. These were followed by several GMC trucks and Jeeps and three M36 tank destroyers.

Suddenly, seven King Tiger tanks appeared along the crest of the forward slope on the left side. As the tanks advanced toward our column, they turned to the right into a column formation and opened fire. We had no time or room to maneuver, and the Shermans could not utilize the advantage of our gyrostabilizers. Three more King Tigers emerged from the hilly woods road to the right. Our tankers and infantrymen were faced with their worst fear: to be caught in the open by King Tiger tanks at close range, without the ability to maneuver or seek cover.

The seven King Tiger tanks on the left proceeded down the entire length of the column, then turned around and came back. At extremely close range, a hundred yards or less, they raked the column from stem to stern. Some observers said it was more like a naval engagement than land warfare.

The infantry immediately took cover in the ditches on both sides of the road. One of the Sherman tanks, with a 76mm gun, broke out of the column and took cover behind a small stucco farm building to the left, just off the road in about the middle of the column. As the Tigers came down on their first pass, the Sherman crew swung their 76mm gun 180 degrees to the rear and let go at close range. The Tiger's thinner armor over the engine compartment was penetrated, and the tank started to burn. The victory for this brave crew was short-lived, however, because the Sherman was knocked out by another Tiger on its return pass.

Although the entire column was trapped, some of the veteran crews stayed cool and utilized their advantages. One of the crews of an M4 Sherman with a short-barreled 75mm M2 gun was near the middle of the column when the three King Tigers appeared on the right side. The alert tank commander immediately saw two possibilities. First, he knew that the King Tiger had a manual traverse, and it would be extremely difficult and time-consuming for him to swing the turret and elevate the gun to zero in on him. Next, our tank commander knew that an armor-piercing shot from his low-velocity 75mm would just bounce off the King Tiger.

In a split second he told his gunner to load a white phosphorus round. It struck the glacis plate right above the driver's compartment with a blaze of flames and smoke. Although there was no possibility of penetration, the shock in the tank must have been terrific. The entire faceplate in front of the turret was covered with burning particles of white phosphorus which stuck to the sides of the tank. The smoke engulfed the tank, and the fan in the engine compartment sucked the smoke inside the fighting compartment. The German crew must have thought the tank was on fire and immediately abandoned it. Although the tank suffered little damage, had the crew stayed inside they would have been overcome by the deadly fumes.

The Sherman immediately turned its gun on the second tank in the column and fired white phosphorus, with the same result. Although the ingenious tank commander knocked out two King Tiger tanks (without ever getting a penetration), his tank was then knocked out by another Tiger.

The King Tigers on the left proceeded all the way to the end of the column, where they knocked out one of our M36 tank destroyers, which blocked the rear of the column. The lead tank in the column had already been knocked out and trapped the entire column. As the German tanks returned to the front of the column, they swung their guns around to the other side and picked off the remaining tanks and half-tracks. It was like shooting ducks in a pond. The remaining King Tigers withdrew, leaving our entire column bleeding and burning.*

When our maintenance crews arrived on the scene, we found a catastrophe. The Germans had knocked out seventeen M4 Sherman tanks, seventeen half-tracks, three GMC trucks, two Jeeps, and one M36 tank destroyer. The column had been annihilated. Fortunately, the personnel casualties had not been as high as the appearance of the wrecked column indicated. The German tanks were so close that the machine guns in the turrets would not depress low enough to reach the men in the ditches. We immediately started dragging back those vehicles that had not been totally burned. The burned-out vehicles were pushed off to one side of the road and abandoned.

I was shocked to see the devastation. It was obvious that our tankers did not have a chance against the Tigers. Unfortunately, for us, there were no M26 Pershing tanks in this column. I couldn't help

*Such was the awesome power of the Tiger against the vastly inferior M4 Sherman.

but think that if we'd had them, the outcome would have been far different.

We got the "W" numbers off all the vehicles that had been damaged beyond repair. These numbers plus the map coordinates were all I needed for my combat loss report in order to get replacement vehicles. While the maintenance crews worked, I examined the three King Tigers that had been knocked out. The upper left side of the rear armor on one of them had been penetrated by a 76mm, which had gone directly into the fuel tank and set the tank on fire. The projectile had been fired at such an angle that it went through the fuel tanks into the fighting compartment and struck the inside of the six-inch faceplate. Because it did not have enough energy to penetrate the faceplate, the projectile ricocheted inside the tank and created havoc with the crew. The tank was completely gutted by fire, so it was impossible to tell which had been worse for the crew. I had always been curious about the actual penetrating power of a *panzerfaust* and also about the strength of the armor on a King Tiger. I felt it was a good time to test out both. I told Wrayford to give me one of the 100-meter *panzerfaust*s.

I took the *panzerfaust* and paced off approximately thirty yards directly in front of the tank. I set the sight for thirty yards and aimed directly at a ten-inch-square patch of the forward turret faceplate just to one side of the gun mantlet. I fired, and the *panzerfaust* struck it dead center. There was a tremendous explosion, and we were showered with small cement particles. (The Germans covered their tanks with a thin layer of cement to protect them from magnetic mines.)

The blast center was about four inches to the right of the aperture where the machine gun came through the faceplate. Upon closer examination, I could see a distinct penetration about a half inch to three-quarters of an inch in diameter on the outside that went all the way through the faceplate of the turret and opened out about half an inch in diameter on the inside. The hole was complete all the way through the eight-and-a-half-inch turret faceplate. The particles from the blast that showered inside would have killed any of the crew who was still alive.

I examined the two Tigers that had been knocked out by white phosphorus. To save time, the Germans used an unusual technique in welding the six-and-a-half-inch faceplate to the three and a half inches of armor on the upper sponsons. Normally, the edge of the faceplate and the sponson plate would be V grooved approximately three inches deep, then filled with weld metal to the surface. They would have then been welded inside so that the inside bead met the outside bead to produce a solid weld throughout the entire thickness of the plate. Because this welding process would have been extremely time-consuming, the Germans used a substitute method. They notched both plates in a tongue-and-groove castle-head fashion. The notches were trimmed to a tight tolerance and the plates were brought together in a trilock type of construction, similar to one's hands brought together with the fingers overlapping. In this manner they got a very close fit. Then they welded a zigzag bead into the castle-head sections, which penetrated to only about half an inch. They did this both inside and out to complete the joint.

The point of impact of the white phosphorus shell was similar on both Tigers. It struck the upper-right-hand corner of the front glacis plate about a foot and a half from each edge. The detonation probably deafened the driver, and the blast opened up cracks in the welds. These cracks let even more of the white phosphorus gas into the tank and apparently contributed to the crew's horror that their tank was on fire. There was no other apparent damage to either of the tanks.

Three companies of the maintenance battalion established a VCP south of Korbach and started collecting the many tanks and other armored vehicles that had been shot up. I headed south about fifty miles to battalion headquarters, which was just north of Marburg. We had bypassed many isolated units, and the Germans constantly crossed our communication lines. Armored vehicles escorted supply columns; our liaison officer to 1st Infantry, on our left flank, had to be escorted there by light tanks. I finally realized that "running the gauntlet" had taken on an entirely new meaning, and I had to exercise every precaution.

Major Arrington was shocked when I told him about the annihilation of the task force south of Paderborn. Word about General Rose's death had gotten back and everyone was keyed up. The antitank platoon and outer perimeter defenses were beefed up accordingly, and everyone was on constant alert for an encounter with a roaming German unit. Major Arrington told me I would have to take several replacement medium tanks and half-tracks back to C Company. As I went out the door, he hollered, "Cooper, watch your butt and don't take any unnecessary chances."

I instructed the tank and half-track crews to be extremely alert, and we proceeded north back to C Company without further incident.

On arrival, it was obvious that C Company had its hands full. Replacement tanks and other vehicles were immediately issued. One of the damaged tanks brought into C Company had its 76mm gun barrel completely missing six feet from the tip. Our first thought was that it had been hit from the side by a lucky German armor-piercing shot. Further examination indicated a long, jagged sliver type of break that did not look like one caused by a single armor-piercing shot. The fracture appeared to be caused by an internal explosion.

Had the crew been firing a 76mm HE that exploded in the tube, the projectile would have never left the tube; as a result, the tube would not have retracted to its full recoil position, thus opening the block. In this case, the breechblock was open, with the resulting severe blast damage back inside the tank. We concluded that a rare event, perhaps a one-in-a-million chance, had occurred. It was assumed that the American tank crew had just fired a round and the tube had recoiled, opened the breech, and ejected the shell case into the turret. At the same moment, a German 75 HE struck the end of the American gun tube dead center. The 75mm projectile went down the 76mm tube approximately six feet before it exploded and blew off the end of the gun barrel. The nose of the German projectile proceeded down the barrel, through the open breech, and into the turret, killing two of the crew.

The two bodies still inside the tank had been dismembered by the blast. When two of our tank mechanics got inside the turret to remove the bodies, they were both overcome by the horror of the blood and gore. Sergeant Fox immediately called for volunteers to remove the bodies. This turned out to be one of those instances, often repeated in combat, that separates the men from the boys. There were several big, rough men in the group, the boisterous, heavy-

drinking, cussing type who constantly tried to convey the impression
of extreme masculinity. You might have expected several of them to
step forward, but there was dead silence. Everybody looked around
at everybody else, and nobody moved.

Finally, a high-pitched voice from the edge of the group called out,
"I volunteer, Sergeant."

Out stepped a tall, young soldier who was pale and thin to the
point of looking emaciated; I wondered how he had passed the physical exam to get into the army. He was Technician Fifth Grade Smith,
a fire control instrument repair mechanic in the headquarters section. He was a hard-working, low-key individual who kept more or
less to himself. A skilled watchmaker in civilian life, he had long, del-
icate fingers. He normally worked in an enclosed, well-heated shop
truck; because there was a shortage of skilled instrument mechanics, he had only a few men to help him. Indeed, there were plenty
of other men with less precise skills who could have been spared for
the time-consuming job of removing the dismembered bodies.

Two other men volunteered to help Smith. Care had to be taken
to make sure that the dog tags were kept with the correct body and
all the connecting parts were put in the same shelter half. The shelter halves were then closed, placed on the ground, and marked for
the graves registration people to pick up. The interior of the tank
compartment then had to be thoroughly scrubbed with disinfectant.
The artillery mechanics replaced the gun barrel and the electricians
repaired all the wiring. Finally the paint crew painted the entire interior with a heavy coat of thick white lead. This covered up all the
blemishes and pockmarks inside the tank and at the same time the
persistent odor of the drying paint tended to offset the pungent
stench left by the mutilated bodies. Some said the odor never completely left the tanks; however, by this time the new crew would have
gotten used to the tank.

The new tank crew were always reluctant to accept a tank in which
crew members had been killed. We often painted the numbers on
the transmission and changed the company and battalion designation of a particular tank. The tank was issued to another company
so the new crew never knew its history, and we never told them.

After Smith had done his job, one of the officers asked him why
he volunteered to help with the cleanup.

"I figured someone had to do it," he replied. "I have a younger brother who's a rifleman in the 1st Infantry Division somewhere forward of us. If he was killed, I would like someone to recover his body so he could be given a decent Christian burial. All soldiers should be entitled to this, at the very least."

Great courage was not limited to the battlefront but was often found in quiet and unexpected places.

After the debacle south of the Paderborn airport, the remainder of CCA came in and cleaned up the situation. The remaining elements of Task Force Welborn regrouped and started moving north. Combat Command A was moving in the middle and CCR was coming up on the left. The VII Corps, with the 3d Armored Division leading, was now in position to make the final assault on Paderborn.

Roving bands of Panther and Tiger tanks with infantry were withdrawing from the city and concentrating around the airport and north of there. As our task forces proceeded to the airport, they encountered heavy fire from 88mm dual-purpose guns. Although these guns could be lowered from vertical to horizontal for use as antitank fire, their high profile made them difficult to protect. The Germans would stack sandbags about five feet high in a ring around each gun, but the tops were completely open and they were vulnerable to artillery fire. By rapid deployment of our M7s, we put a few rounds with proximity fuses over each gun emplacement. The downward blast killed the crew and neutralized the gun. With the 88mms neutralized, our tank columns enveloped the airport and proceeded into the city.

The youthful zeal of the cadets who had successfully crewed the Tiger and Panther tanks against our armored columns was contagious and filtered down to the lower ranks of the preteen Hitler *Jugend*. Some actually took up arms. One eight-year-old Hitler *Jugend* boy stepped out from a building with a *panzerfaust* and knocked out one of our Sherman tanks. He was immediately gunned down by the tank commander. The tragedy of war puts no limits on age.

The hangars around the airport had plenty of paved areas and appeared to be a good place to establish a forward VCP. As we examined this area, I noticed three German aircraft next to one of the hangars. Because we had been trained to be on constant alert for new types of enemy weapons, I was curious to examine these planes further. Low slung and streamlined, they had a two-man cockpit and twin engines. Slung low under each wing, the engines were long with a tubular exhaust going out the rear; however, they had no propellers. As I got closer, I realized that they were jets. These were the Me262s, the same type of aircraft that had bombed us so successfully when we were crossing the bridge at Düren. The planes appeared to be in good condition, although there had been a crude attempt to smash the instrument panels. I took brief notes describing the type and condition of the planes and also the map coordinates, and turned in the notes with my combat loss report that night. As far as I know, this was the first ordnance report made of an ME262 captured intact.

Closing the Ruhr (Rose) Pocket

Early on the morning of April 1, an order from VII Corps headquarters changed the division's disposition slightly. The division was ordered to continue its assault on Paderborn and at the same time dispatch a task force to Lippstadt, about twenty miles to the west.

At 0300, Task Force Kane started toward Lippstadt. The 2d Armored Division had broken out of the bridgehead north of Wesel on the Rhine, about sixty miles to the west, and was proceeding rapidly across the northern flank of the Ruhr toward Lippstadt. The two units were to meet in that vicinity and close the pocket.

Both Task Force Kane of the 3d Armored Division and the 2d Armored Division task force had been driving relentlessly for several days. They had overcome mines and roadblocks and seen their lead tanks constantly knocked out. Their mission had been to plunge rapidly forward, bypassing any resistance and leaving their flanks exposed, hoping that high speed and rapid maneuver would protect them. They did have the advantage of air cover during daylight, weather permitting.

Both columns approached with considerable trepidation. The men were physically and mentally exhausted but at the same time so keyed up that they would fire at anything and ask questions later. They had each other's radio frequencies and constantly tried to call each other; however, the combat radios had limited range, which was reduced further by the rugged terrain. To offset this, each task force commander sent his L5 Cub artillery spotter to try to make radio contact. Although the L5s had to dodge ground fire, they were able to make radio contact at 1520. About ten minutes later, the task forces met at Lippstadt.

The key to logistic support of a rapidly moving armored corps, rarely understood by military historians, was the capability of the lead armored division's forward maintenance elements to assist the forward elements of the motorized infantry divisions. When VII Corps moved two hundred miles to form the pocket, it required not only the 4,200 vehicles of the 3d Armored Division but also another 10,000 vehicles to transport and support the motorized infantry divisions. A task force with fifty tanks moving thirty to forty miles a day will have between fifteen and twenty tanks drop out during the day just for maintenance and repair. These repairs could include everything from the minor changing of spark plugs and V belts to the actual replacement of a transmission or track suspension element. Tanks, half-tracks, and other armored vehicles are subject to extremely heavy wear and tear in normal, everyday operations.

The maintenance on the four-wheel- and six-wheel-drive vehicles is also extremely high. The demand for tires was unending, because they were constantly damaged by battle debris on the highways plus shrapnel fragments from mortar and artillery explosions. A two-and-a-half-ton GMC truck, moving over a combination of highways and cross-country in six-wheel-drive, would have to have a new engine approximately every ten thousand miles. Although two and half tons was the load rating, they normally carried anywhere from five to eight tons.

The maintenance problems on German tanks and armored vehicles were even greater than on ours. The metal-to-metal connection on their tanks was a high-wear item. With the rubber doughnuts and rubber tracks on our tanks, we could get about five times the track life of a comparable German part. With little or no maintenance support, the German units were at an extreme disadvantage.

The meeting of the 2d and 3d Armored Divisions in Lippstadt sealed the trap around the German troops in the Ruhr Pocket. The

G2 grossly underestimated the number of prisoners caught in this trap. It was believed that the bulk of the German armies would withdraw and join a new army group in the Harz Mountains. Early estimates said there were 35,000 to 40,000 Germans in the entire Ruhr area. It turned out that the major elements of the German 5th and 15th Armies, including the headquarters of Army Group B under Field Marshal Model, were cut off in this pocket. When Model requested permission to withdraw, Hitler ordered him to stand and fight under penalty of death.

Model, true to the Prussian tradition that a German field marshal never surrendered, was determined not to breach this honor. After being driven to a wooded area, he got out of his Volkswagen, walked a few yards, and shot himself. The disintegrating German units eventually surrendered and yielded about 380,000 prisoners, the largest single group of prisoners ever taken. This site would later be known as the "Rose Pocket," in honor of our division commander.

12
Final Thrust Across Germany

After the envelopment at Lippstadt, the 3d Armored Division withdrew. The 8th Armored Division and some infantry units cleaned up at Paderborn, and the 3d Armored Division headed eastward. On April 4, the division advanced rapidly in four columns to secure bridgeheads across the Weser River, about thirty miles to the east. The river appeared to be the next great natural land barrier.

As we approached the foothills of the Harz Mountains, the terrain was still rolling, with many patches of dense woods. When the division encountered small pockets of resistance in an operation of this type, it would become stretched out. A tank platoon would drop off to take care of this, and the others would bypass. Whenever these voids occurred, the Germans would infiltrate across the columns and sometimes try to block the road again.

This situation was extremely risky for our liaison group. One of the division liaison officers and his driver had disappeared while following one of these columns. The next day his wrecked Jeep was discovered alongside one of the secondary roads and both bodies were in the ditch, their skulls crushed and their faces beaten to an unrecognizable pulp. When news of such atrocities filtered down to our troops, it created no incentive for compassion when our men captured German soldiers.

I told Wrayford that we had to stay on the ball. That afternoon we passed a scout car that had stopped along the road. A couple of men with rifles were apparently trying to spot a sniper in the woods. About half a mile farther down the road, we had a flat tire. I realized that we were in the middle of one of those voids, and we both jumped out of the Jeep and began to change the tire. We had just finished, and Wrayford was tightening the lugs, when we heard loud German voices coming from the woods. Then we saw that the Germans were coming out of a firebreak and were headed in the same direction we were. If they got to the intersection first, they would either shoot us or take us prisoner. We were determined to get there first.

The Jeep was in a defiladed position, so I didn't think the Germans could see us. I got one of the M1 rifles out of the Jeep and sighted along the hood as Wrayford spun the lug wrench as though it was motorized. When he finished, we jumped into the Jeep and hightailed it down the road. As we screamed past the intersection, the Germans were about fifty feet back in the firebreak. I pointed my M1 rifle dead at them. They hollered something; I wasn't sure whether they wanted to surrender to us or shoot us. We didn't stop to find out. I assumed that the recon outfit behind us would soon clean them out.

The Germans had blown most of the bridges across the Weser. However, CCB, after a considerable firefight, managed to get a bridgehead across the lower section of the river. They made multiple crossings and either killed or captured those in the bridgehead, then proceeded rapidly eastward toward Northeim.

It was on this stretch between the Weser River and Northeim that our Super M26 tank finally got into action. Some of the German units that had fallen back from the bridgehead set up a few isolated strongpoints along our route.

One such position, on a wooded hill south of CCB, opened fire as the column passed. The Super M26, in the forward part of the column, immediately swung its turret to the right and fired an armor-piercing shot toward an object on the forward slope of a wooded hill about fifteen hundred yards away. A blinding flash of sparks accompanied a tremendous explosion as debris shot fifty feet into the air.

The unknown object was a tank or self-propelled gun; had it been a half-track or other vehicle, the flash would not have been as large. The rest of the column let go with a deluge of tank and automatic weapons fire, and the Germans soon broke off the action. Although we didn't know what the Super M26 hit, we did know that a Panther or a Tiger would not have been knocked out by an M4's 76mm at this range. No one was anxious to go over and check it out. The Super M26 had finally won its combat plaudit and as far as I know was never again engaged in any action.

The Tragedy at Nordhausen

Combat Command B entered Nordhausen early on the morning of April 11. The British had bombed the city the night before, and a large contingent of German troops had already withdrawn. Our tank columns wound their way slowly through the town, occasionally neutralizing a roadblock or flushing out snipers. City fighting was always a start-and-stop operation, but by this time our men had developed considerable experience and we were making progress through the city, block by block.

During one of these stops, Maj. Dick Johnson came up to my Jeep. "Cooper, we've seen a lot of grim things in this war together," he said, "but there's something in the next block that you won't believe until you see it."

I tried to find out more, but he just shook his head and went back to the T2 recovery tank to our rear.

The small-arms fire up ahead subsided and the column moved forward again. As we approached the corner of the next block, we saw a tall, frail-looking creature with striped pants and a white towel draped over the head. The exposed skin of his naked torso looked like translucent plastic stretched over the rib cage and sucked with a powerful vacuum until it impinged to the backbone. There were no breasts, but the height indicated a male. There was no face, merely a gaunt human skull staring out from beneath the towel. The teeth were exposed in a broad, tragic grin, and in place of eyes were merely dark sockets.

"I never thought I'd see a live walking ghost," remarked Wrayford.

As we proceeded down the road, we encountered several more of these gaunt figures standing or sitting, but most of them were sprawled on the road and sidewalk where they had collapsed. In their last struggle to survive, these tragic figures of skin and bone had attempted to walk as far as possible and when the last bit of energy had been wrung from their feeble bodies, they simply dropped dead.

Farther down the block, I noticed two warehouse-type buildings three to four stories high, separated by a vacant lot about a hundred yards wide. The doors and windows of the first building had been broken open, and German civilians were looting the warehouse. There must have been sixty people going in and coming out, mostly children and old men and women, each with armloads of bags or boxes filled with food. Several were pulling small sleds that dripped a red substance, which I later realized was frozen strawberry jam. The crowd was ravenous; they were pushing and shoving one another to get as much food as possible. They paid no attention to the pitiful wretches lying in the streets and gutters.

In the vacant lot between the two warehouse buildings was a barbed-wire enclosure that was split in the middle to form a partial gate. What appeared to be garbage was piled in three rows about six feet high and four hundred feet long. To my abject horror I noticed that parts of the stacks were moving. Suddenly, I realized that these stacks were naked human beings, writhing in their excrement and left in the open to die. The stench was overwhelming.

According to our medical officers, these slave workers could survive perhaps thirty to forty days without food under these conditions. They would lose 30 to 40 percent of their body weight, and their stomachs would be grossly bloated and distended due to the gases and the acid in their digestive systems. These people showed no such distended stomachs; they were nothing but skin and bones. They had been deliberatetly, painfully starved to death. Even our combat tankers, who had experienced much of the death and destruction of war, were horrified at the barbaric treatment that these people endured.

General Hickey was ordered by General Collins, the corps commander, to assemble every able-bodied man, woman, and child in the city to bury the dead bodies. Collins also called First Army headquarters and requested a field hospital be sent immediately to take care of any survivors who might be rescued from the piles. Engineers with bulldozers dug large mass graves about ten feet deep and three hundred feet long. German civilians made small wooden stretchers out of scrap lumber, picked up the bodies, and took them to the burial sites.

When I came back through Nordhausen on my way to maintenance battalion headquarters, I saw a steady stream of Germans carrying these lifeless skeletons, arms and legs dangling over the sides of the stretchers, to the burial sites. The whole scene reminded me of ghouls in a grave robbery scene from an old horror movie. The bodies were laid side by side in the mass graves. The army sent a Protestant and a Catholic chaplain and a Jewish rabbi to perform ceremonies as these people were finally laid to rest.

General Sherman once said, "War is hell." The Nordhausen tragedy made one think there must be different degrees of hell. Although the terror and violence of war can harden a person to new terrors, an unusually traumatic event can still shatter this external protective shell.

The 3d Armored Division medical officers cared for the survivors of the death camp until they could be relieved by the army field hospital. Of the approximately three thousand bodies stacked in the piles in the open field, about 10 percent were alive. Captain Comar, our battalion surgeon, said that some would survive but that malnutrition had probably already caused severe brain damage.

The V2 Rocket Factory

One of the columns of CCB discovered the entrance to an underground factory in nearby Robla. It was located in an old, abandoned mine that had been extended considerably for the production of the V1 buzz bomb and V2 rockets. The Germans had also been working on a new secret rocket motor for an interceptor.

The factory was staffed by slave workers, primarily from eastern Europe. They lived in wire-enclosed concentration camps and survived under the most primitive conditions. Those who were recalcitrant or failed to do their masters' bidding were transferred to another enclosure, where they were slowly and deliberately starved to death. This was the enclosure we had found in Nordhausen.

The underground factory was elaborate, with some tunnels up to two miles in length. The Germans, highly ingenious engineers and inventors, had organized and built this factory in spite of day-and-night bombardments by the American and British air forces. After examining this system, I could understand how the Germans produced the V2s in such mass quantity. After the parts were fabricated underground, they were taken to the surface and sent to small towns in the vicinity of Nordhausen for the final assembly, which took more space than was available in the narrow underground passageways.

On the western edge of Robla was a schoolhouse with fruit trees planted in a geometric pattern behind the playground. Among the rows of trees were pyramid-shaped stacks of aluminum fuel tanks covered with camouflage nets. They were apparently meant to appear from the air as just more trees. This careful camouflage must have been effective, because there were no signs of bombing.

We broke into the schoolhouse and discovered a small but self-sufficient assembly plant with workbenches, cabinets, and parts for V2 rocket motors. In the larger rooms, the parts were being assembled and tested.

There were three subassemblies, each approximately five feet in diameter and ten feet long. The forward section contained a pointed nose cone, which flared to a bulletlike shape that contained the warhead and inertial guidance section. The midsection contained the large tanks for the fuel and the oxidizer. The rear section contained the rocket motor, piping, and pumps for the fuel and the oxidizer, and the controls for the rocket motor. The rear section was tapered from the main diameter and sloped back in the tail section, which included large fins to guide the missile.

Each section was assembled and mounted on heavy wooden pallets made from six-by-six rough-cut timbers. After the motors were tested, the pallets were enclosed in large eight-by-eight frames covered with black tar paper. The doors at the end of each pallet were hinged at the bottom and held in the upright position with simple screen-door-type hooks.

The boxes were taken to a mobile launch site on three separate trucks. A crane was used to set the sections on the ground and line them up properly. The end doors were lowered and removed, and the three boxes were joined with additional hooks. A missile crew could thereby assemble the sections completely under cover. The boxes also provided some camouflage from the air.

Once the assembly was completed, the crews released the hooks, and the tops and sides of the boxes folded back. A crane then erected the missile on a launching tripod. Fuel trucks pumped the fuel and oxidizer into the tanks and the missile was ready to be launched. Once the launch was completed, another missile could be launched from the same position, or the tripod could be moved to a new location. The ability to use mobile launch sites was one advantage that the V2 had over the V1. The V1 required a long track at a fixed launch site, which was vulnerable to air attack.

Our ordnance reports came to the attention of Col. John Medaris, First Army's chief of ordnance. Medaris sent a group to study the V2 installations. They found the Germans had developed a truly amazing organization, and that the underground plant was a lot more extensive than we had thought. Not only were some of these tunnels more than two miles long, but they extended in layers some 600 feet below the surface, completely impervious to bombing.

When we captured this plant, the V2 was in full production and they had turned out thousands of rockets. Although there were many of these rockets in the distribution pipeline, all the launching sites in France, Belgium, and Holland had been taken. Prior to this, London and the south coast of England had suffered devastating damage from the rockets. Colonel Medaris became extremely interested in the V2 rocket system. After WWII he was promoted to major general and commanded the German rocket team who established the Army Ballistics Center at Huntsville, Alabama.

That evening I returned to battalion headquarters to deliver my combat loss report. It was during breakfast the next morning, April 12, that we heard a BBC broadcast that President Roosevelt had died and Vice President Truman had been sworn in as our new president.

Although I never agreed with much of Roosevelt's domestic policy, I always felt that we had been extremely fortunate to have a president who clearly saw the danger of Nazi and Japanese aggression long before we got into the war. I sensed that the troops felt that Roosevelt's death was a great loss. He had been president throughout this worldwide crisis and had experience dealing with our allies. Truman, on the other hand, was relatively unknown.

Later that day, Truman spoke to the American people and particularly to the armed forces overseas. His speech was rebroadcast over BBC. I was impressed with his humility, especially when he asked for our prayers to guide him during his hours of great decision. I instinctively felt that anyone with such basic simple faith would be guided in the choices he would make.

Some of the German troops who escaped the Ruhr Pocket headed eastward and established themselves in the heavily wooded Harz Mountains north of Nordhausen. This posed a serious threat to the northern flank of VII Corps. General Collins dispatched troops northward to join with troops from XIX Corps and the Ninth Army coming southward. They surrounded the Harz Mountain Redoubt and penetrated its outer defenses. In certain local areas, the fighting became extremely heavy; however, we gradually isolated the German troops into smaller pockets. Here again the original estimates of some 20,000 to 30,000 Germans in the pocket turned out to be in gross error. The final count was 84,000 Germans.

With this threat to our northern flank neutralized, we proceeded eastward toward Sangerhausen, twenty miles away, to join the column; the division trains moved forward to Duderstadt. As we came downhill into the small village, we saw a Panther tank that had just been knocked out. We stopped a moment to check it out, and Wrayford climbed on the glacis plate to look into the turret. There were no bodies in the tank or lying on the ground, so we assumed that the crew had survived. Before I could stop Wrayford, he crawled inside the turret through the cupola hatch. I was leery of getting inside German tanks because of the possibility of booby traps; however, the crew apparently had abandoned the tank too rapidly to think about this.

Wrayford soon poked his head above the cupola. I knew from the broad grin on his face that he had found something interesting. When he was back on the ground, I noticed a bulge beneath the hand-warming slot in his combat jacket. He pulled back the edge of the slot.

Out poked the head of a small hound puppy, no more than two to three weeks old. He had found her in a shoe box in the sponson. He had also found a complete set of electric train equipment. It appeared that some German tanker had picked this up and was taking it home to his young son.

There wasn't room in the Jeep for the trains, but Wrayford put the puppy in his pocket and away we went. He named the dog Jeannie, and she immediately became a full-fledged member of our crew. Wrayford thought of her as Private Jeannie; he wanted to outrank at least one member of the crew.

I couldn't help but think that somewhere in Germany a small boy was going to miss getting a puppy and an electric train from his daddy. In fact, there was a strong possibility he might not get his daddy back. I was sad for the child, in spite of being hardened by stories of children in the Hitler *Jugend* who killed American soldiers. They were no longer innocent children; they had become pawns of a vicious despot.

We were now approaching the heart of Germany. Within sixty miles there were three major metropolitan areas: Berlin, Dresden, and Halle. Once the heavy bombing of German cities started, the Germans began to develop a highly concentrated and well-organized antiaircraft defense system. In addition to the numerous fighter fields in this area, there were also antiaircraft guns. The key weapon was the dual-purpose 88, which was located in large clusters along the bombers' approach routes.

One of these 88mm gun clusters was on a hill just north of Sangerhausen. The division's main line of advance was now northeast toward Eisleben. The main tank elements of the lead column passed this point without noticing it, but as soon as the half-tracks and trucks loaded with infantry started passing, the German guns suddenly opened fire.

Several trucks and half-tracks were hit and set on fire, which resulted in heavy casualties. Fortunately, our 391st Armored Field Artillery Battalion had not passed this point. Within a matter of minutes, the entire eighteen-gun battalion went into position and started firing for effect. Using proximity fuses, and firing at a rate of ten rounds per minute per gun, they laid three thousand 105mm shells on the target before a cease-fire was ordered. The entire cluster of twelve to eighteen 88s was devastated. This was actually overkill, but we did not realize the true nature of the target.

The next town we came to was Polleben. It was declared an open city, and we captured it without further ado. We found a British POW camp there and liberated 450 British soldiers, some of whom had been there since Dunkirk. One British major reportedly broke down and cried when he saw the first Sherman tank come into view.

The next town of Koethen had a large German air base, which was also a Luftwaffe training ground. There were hundreds of fighter planes and light bombers there and at other nearby airfields. The Germans not only faced a severe aircraft fuel shortage, but pilots were virtually nonexistent; air force ground crews, along with officer candidates and naval personnel, had been combined to form infantry divisions.

For the 3d Armored Division, the war was now reaching a critical and final stage. The division had advanced rapidly and was now spread over a front of some forty miles. We had bypassed numerous small towns where enemy troops were dug in, and our infantry divisions had not had time to come forward and clean out these pockets of resistance. The supply convoys and liaison officers had to be on constant alert; even though townspeople may have put out white flags and surrendered when the troops came through the first time, there was no assurance that German soldiers hadn't reoccupied the town and blocked the entrances to it again.

In anticipation of such moves, SHAEF had printed a bulletin in German, English, French, and Russian and posted it on the door of the *burgermeister*'s office of each small town that surrendered. The bulletin stated that once a town surrendered, it came under the protection of the Allied occupation forces, and all weapons, including firearms, swords, daggers, and any other military paraphernalia were to be turned in within twenty-four hours. Once the white flags had been put out, any attempts to rearm or generate further resistance either by civilians or military would be dealt with severely.

Just east of Koethen, I stopped at a task force headquarters, and a messenger on a motorcycle came in. He had just returned from a column on the other side of the next village. He excitedly reported that the village, which had put out white flags and surrendered, had opened fire on him.

The task force commander called a light tank company commander and told him to send a platoon to retake the town. The platoon leader had new M24 light tanks with 75mm guns and took along a platoon of armored infantry. He moved the tanks five hundred yards south of town. Although there were several white flags still hanging from the upper windows of the farm buildings, the troops started receiving fire immediately. German soldiers came out of the basements and fired some *panzerfausts,* but they were out of range.

The platoon fired a salvo of white phosphorus into the village. Several of the buildings and some of the adjacent haystacks caught fire, and the civilian men, women, and children together with some German soldiers came screaming out of the village with their hands up. That ended the resistance there, and I'm sure the word got around to other villages.

This highly fluid situation presented opposing contrasts. When a major German combat group was defeated, some of the soldiers would surrender and others would break into small task groups. At the same time, we had overrun many POW camps with Russian, Polish, and other east European prisoners of war. After suffering years of deprivation in these German camps, the men readily vented their spleen against all things German, both military and civilian.

We were traveling east on the road from Koethen. The countryside was flat, open farmland, and the road was straight as an arrow with a few occasional trees on either side. As we approached a clump of trees, I noticed two figures; one appeared to be jumping up and down, raising his hands, and hollering. I told Wrayford to slow down. The man yelled for us to halt. He was dressed in heavy gray German infantrymen's trousers and heavy black infantry combat boots. He had on an old, worn farmer's coat and a farmer's hat. The other man, who was much larger, wore a tattered Russian uniform.

The Russian had the German by the scruff of his neck and was shaking him violently. The Russian had a bayonet in his hand and threatened to kill the German. As we approached, the Russian lowered the bayonet but maintained his grip on the German's collar. The conversation that ensued was a mixture of English, German, and

Russian. It did not require expert knowledge of the languages to grasp what was going on.

The German had apparently disguised his identity with a farmer's coat and hat. Not willing to parade around without pants or shoes, he had kept on his soldier's pants and combat boots. He realized that any German soldier captured behind American lines in civilian clothes could theoretically be shot as a spy, but at the same time, if he continued to insist that he was a civilian, the Russian was going to kill him. The German kept repeating, *"Nein, nein, me no soldat, me civil, me civil."* This infuriated the Russian, who raised his bayonet and seemed ready to cut the man's throat.

The young German panicked and in a violent surge broke loose from the Russian's grip and jumped on the back of my Jeep, screaming and hollering, *"Ya, ya, me soldat, me soldat, me Deutsch soldat."* He evidently figured that he would have a better chance with the Americans than the enraged Russian.

I hollered halt and the Russian stopped his advance toward the Jeep. The young German soldier was trembling all over and burst into tears. In my best German, I told him that the Americans would not kill him. We drove him about a mile down the road, where I turned him over to the MP guards at a POW camp. He seemed relieved when he saw his fellow prisoners and realized that some of them had on all types of clothing, both civilian and military. He had a wan half smile on his face as he departed with the MP, and he raised his hand slightly as if to say *danke schön.* He realized that his life had been spared and he had now become a survivor.

The division had moved about three hundred miles in continuous combat since jumping off from the Remagen bridgehead. The men were thoroughly exhausted. There seemed to be no letup, and it appeared that the enemy was determined to fight until every square foot of Germany had been conquered.

The strain of the long march also had a telling effect on the equipment. Any M4 tanks that had survived since Normandy (and there were very few) were badly in need of track changes. Because there had been no chance to do routine heavy maintenance, many crews and maintenance mechanics did their best to keep everything patched up and going.

To make matters worse, we faced a severe shortage of fifty-weight engine oil for the tanks. Both the R975 Wright engine and the V8 Ford engine used this oil in their crankcases; they also required five gallons of it for the oil bath air cleaners. This was primarily a logistic problem; we had moved so rapidly that it was becoming increasingly difficult for the supply truck convoys to get to us. We had to let the air cleaners go and do the best we could to ration what oil we had. By this time, the maintenance people had learned how to improvise in the field under difficult conditions and had become an extremely efficient, well-coordinated organization.

It was difficult to determine whether the small villages were occupied by our troops or the Germans. The situation could change several times in a single day. In one incident, Maj. Bill Derner, division headquarters liaison officer to the maintenance battalion, and Capt. Bob Grindatti of the maintenance battalion were proceeding back to division trains at Sangerhausen. They came to a fork in the road where the paved road led north to Quellendorf and the dirt road led west. They decided to take the road to Quellendorf and proceeded with caution.

As they went up the road, they encountered a detachment of American engineers with a bulldozer removing a German roadblock. They asked if the road was cleared to Quellendorf and were told yes, that the company commander had just proceeded up that road a few minutes ago.

Thinking that Quellendorf was in American hands, they headed out, with Captain Grindatti's Jeep in the lead. Just as they approached the outskirts of the town, they encountered heavy small-arms fire. The major realized that they were surrounded and ordered his group to surrender. Captain Grindatti had been hit several times in the stomach and was bleeding severely.

The Germans apparently were just going to walk away and leave him there; however, Major Derner insisted that his captors take care of the wounded man. They reluctantly agreed and took Grindatti into the village, where a German medical officer attended to his wounds. One of the division's task forces overran Quellendorf that afternoon; Captain Grindatti was liberated and sent back to an army base hospital. In the meantime, Major Derner and several other prisoners, including the captain who had commanded the engineers south of Quellendorf, were imprisoned at Alten-Grabow until May 3, when the British captured the town.

The division's next objective was Dessau, a medium-sized city on the Elbe River near the confluence of the Mulde and the Elbe. The end of the war in Europe was rapidly approaching, and rumors abounded. There was considerable speculation that Hitler and some of his staff would withdraw into the Berchtesgaden area in the Alps and set up a strong defensive position there.

A move in this direction, however, had been frustrated by the rapid movements of the Third Army and the Seventh Army to the south, which isolated this area. The next question was, would we go into Berlin? The XIX Corps of Ninth Army, north of us, had already established bridgeheads across the Elbe River. The answer to this question appeared to be yes, and the VII Corps received its final field order. Our objective was to establish bridges across the Mulde and the Elbe and attack Wittenberg, forty miles southeast of Berlin.

German resistance had apparently stiffened considerably in these last few days, and the Germans reacted furiously with heavy artillery barrages when our engineers started to put a bridge across the Mulde. The engineers sustained a number of casualties. My friend Lieutenant Frost was killed during one of these barrages. He was one of my liaison buddies with CCB, and was with me when we got lost going into Airel our first night in Normandy. The loss of any life is tragic, but to lose one's life after making it all the way through the war up until these last few days seemed almost incomprehensible.

Although it would seem natural for a soldier to hesitate taking risks as the war drew to an end, by this time we had learned to take things one day at a time. For a man living between life and death, there is no tomorrow. Living in the present helps a soldier survive emotionally.

The division now found itself stretched somewhat precariously. At the leading edge of the VII Corps, it occupied a forty-mile front from just southeast of the Harz Mountains to where the autobahn crossed the Mulde River. The 1st and 9th Divisions were still cleaning up the Harz Mountains, although a couple of battalions of the 1st Infantry had been assigned to CCA and CCR. The 104th Division, to our south, was committed to capture Halle, and one battalion had been assigned to CCB.

The Germans had organized three new divisions to oppose us: the Potsdam, Scharnhorst, and Ulrich von Hutten Divisions. Personnel were mostly the remnants of shattered units plus air force ground and flight personnel, although the Germans did bring in a number of veteran officers and noncoms with combat experience. These three divisions were the outer defense line against an assault on Berlin from the southwest. Hitler reportedly visited these units on April 13 and told them they would soon be the focus of a major German counteroffensive.

With our division spread out and opposed by three new divisions, our situation was critical.

The Final Assault

The battle of central Germany now reached its final stage, although the situation was vague as far as we were concerned. We understood that the Allied powers had agreed at Yalta on the final occupation of Germany, but we knew nothing of the details. We assumed that the Russians would occupy eastern Germany, which probably would include Berlin. Because the VII Corps had been ordered to put a bridgehead across the Elbe and advance to Wittenberg on the main road to Berlin from the southeast, and because the Ninth Army already had bridgeheads across the Elbe south of Magdeburg, it was assumed that we would advance on Berlin and meet the Russians in that vicinity.

I went to CCB headquarters, just south of Dessau, to look at the situation map in the G2 trailer. It was covered with a sheet of clear plastic on which were marked locations of all friendly and enemy troops in the area. Blue grease pencil was used to mark the American units and red to mark the German units. I was curious to see if there were any markings for the Russians. I saw none, so I asked one of the G2 lieutenants where we were supposed to meet the Russians.

He said he didn't know. "We can pick up their voices on the radio and know they must be within a range of fifty miles. We've assumed they're on the other side of the Elbe River to the east of us."

I realized that high-level decisions must have been in progress. This uncertainty was compounded by rumors: Certain irresponsible and uninformed commanders were making brash statements that we could go into Berlin tomorrow without any trouble. The press picked this up and magnified it even further.

Although I had no idea what was transpiring at the high levels of command, I felt that the frontline combat troops had been stretched to the limit. The 3d Armored Division had spearheaded the VII Corps, which had in turn led the First Army across central Germany. Since crossing the Roer River at Düren on February 23, the VII Corps had captured Cologne, crossed the Rhine River at the Remagen bridgehead, and completed the envelopment of the Rose Pocket. The division had then led the corps eastward and enveloped the southern flank of the Harz Mountains. They arrived in the vicinity of Dessau on April 16 and attacked and surrounded the city; by April 21 it surrendered.

We now awaited orders to advance toward Berlin. We had lost many tanks and other armored vehicles, and all the equipment was in dire need of heavy maintenance. The personnel casualties had been heavy, and the men were completely exhausted.

General Eisenhower supposedly asked General Bradley what it would take to capture Berlin. Bradley reportedly said it would take 100,000 British and American casualties. Some felt that Bradley's estimate was high; however, it cost the Russians at least this many. Because the Russians had already been slated to occupy the territory around Berlin, Eisenhower had obviously made a wise decision not to attack Berlin.

When the order came to cease the attempt to bridge the Elbe River, a great relief came over the troops. Many remained in the vicinity of Dessau until April 26. We spent these last few days examining the airport and the surrounding facilities.

We discovered a gold mine of German military secrets. Dessau appeared to be the main Luftwaffe research and development center. The airport, hangars, and surrounding buildings were filled with models and experimental aircraft. Partially completed drawings were still on the boards. The cabinets were filled with drawings, letters, documents, and research reports describing in detail many advanced weapons systems.

The Germans left so rapidly that they apparently did not have time to destroy these secret documents. We immediately impounded them and put guards on them. Our ordnance reports went back to the First Army G2, and they immediately sent military intelligence people to collect these documents before we turned the area over to the Russians.

The division held its position in Dessau at the confluence of the Mulde and Elbe Rivers and for an area several miles south of there. A large Agfa film factory at Tornow had been set on fire. In spite of the flames and fumes, some of our troops managed to get into the factory and evacuate considerable quantities of film and other photographic equipment before the plant was consumed. Because such equipment was considered military contraband, it became "legal loot" and could be confiscated and used by our troops.

On April 26, our troops had drawn up along the west bank of the Mulde River; the Russians were about twenty miles away on the east bank of the Elbe River. We had been ordered to hold these positions until further notice.

That morning, a lieutenant from the 69th Division, just to the south of us, took a patrol across the zone between the Mulde and Elbe Rivers at Torgau, which was supposed to be strictly off-limits. He contacted the Russians, in the first joining of Russian and American forces in World War II. This joining eliminated any possibility of the Germans withdrawing from Berlin.

On this same date, the division was finally relieved by the 9th Infantry Division, and we withdrew to the vicinity of Sangerhausen. The 3d Armored Division had fired its last shot against the German army.

13
The Aftermath

V-E Day

Our feelings were mixed as we withdrew from the line "for the last time", because we were not sure that it would be for the last time. We were delighted to move out of the range of enemy artillery; however, pockets of Germans holed up in small villages fought bitterly to the very end. Our answer was to overwhelm these villages with our highly mobile and devastating artillery fire.

The Germans' resistance reinforced the idea that the war wasn't over yet. There were rumors that Hitler and his entourage escaped from Berlin to Berchtesgaden, his summer hideaway. Previous experience had taught us that fighting in the mountains can be vicious and drawn out, and a relatively small force can extract enormous casualties.

The maintenance battalion headquarters company moved into an old sugar mill in Sangerhausen. For the next two weeks, we relaxed in relative ease. We lived inside covered buildings, and no one worried about digging foxholes every night. The maintenance battalion was busy getting our vehicles back in shape for whatever came next. There was a large German minefield on the forward slope of a hill in front of the sugar mill and the remains of an 88mm antiaircraft battery on a hill behind the mill. This battery had been neutralized by our artillery when we came through Sangerhausen the first time.

We cautioned the men about the possibility of booby traps in the minefield and the battery. Although the looting instinct was uppermost in the minds of some GIs, and the demand for Lugers, P38s, and other weapons was great, most of the men realized the danger of rummaging around in these abandoned German positions. The words of caution must have been taken seriously, because no one in my battalion was injured by these mines.

During this period, First Army sent ordnance intelligence people to Dessau to examine in detail the Luftwaffe research and development facilities we had reported. They searched the hangars, model shops, and drawing rooms. Several of the drawing rooms contained safes, and these were blown open. Anything that appeared to have any ordnance intelligence value was taken. Thousands of drawings, files, and models of all types and descriptions were crated and loaded on the trucks. Our men realized that anything left there would be turned over to the Russians.

Back at Nordhausen, the collection of ordnance intelligence data was on a much larger scale than at Dessau. Colonel John Medaris, First Army's chief of ordnance, immediately recognized the bonanza we had uncovered at the V2 rocket manufacturing and supply center. The group he sent to study the installations found that the underground plant was more extensive than we had thought. The tunnels extended in layers some six hundred feet below the surface, completely impervious to bombing. The V2 had been in full production, and thousands of them had been turned out. Prior to our capture of the plant, London and the south coast of England had suffered devastating damage from the rockets. Now, however, all the launching sites in France, Belgium, and Holland had been taken.

Medaris organized a massive effort to load fifty railroad cars with rockets and rocket assemblies. In addition, there were many truckloads of smaller rocket motors, parts, and documents evacuated before we turned the area over to the Russians.

After the war, Medaris was promoted to major general and organized the Army Ballistic Missile Agency at Redstone Arsenal in Huntsville, Alabama. Working with him in developing ballistic missiles and the nucleus of our space technology was the group of German rocket scientists, led by Dr. Werner von Braun, who had surrendered to our troops in southern Germany as we were evacuating the V2 assembly plant material from Nordhausen. Although the cost of capturing these facilities had been high, the action allowed the United States to win the Cold War and develop a space program.

• • •

Because the division constantly sent information to the troops, and we could pick up the BBC news broadcasts, we knew that the Russians had reached the outskirts of Berlin and had begun the final assault on the city. The rubble of a heavily bombed-out city can make formidable defense positions, and the Germans loyal to Hitler made the Russians pay dearly. We were glad that it was the Russians instead of us doing this fighting. Finally, we heard that the city had fallen to the Russians and that Hitler was dead.

My first reaction was that Hitler had been killed by the Russians; I learned later that he had died by his own hand. On May 7 we got the word that General Jodl had surrendered. On May 8 the ceremony was repeated in Berlin for the Russians. For the 3d Armored Division, the war in Europe had finally come to an end.

Darmstadt and the Army of Occupation
Shortly after V-E Day, the division was ordered south to Darmstadt. We proceeded down the autobahn over the gently rolling hills of western Germany south of Kassel.

The road was intact except for the bridges. Most of them had been blown; in some instances only one span going north was gone. Perhaps the Germans didn't have time to mine both spans. It was a simple matter to cross over to the other lane of the road.

When we reached the northern outskirts of Frankfurt, it was obvious that the city had been heavily bombed but had not taken as much punishment as Cologne. The primary streets had been cleared of rubble, and we continued south past the railroad station to the Main River.

In moving through the northern part of the city, we passed near a large, low-lying brownstone complex that had been the headquarters for I. G. Farben, the largest chemical company in Europe. The complex was soon to become SHAEF headquarters. We crossed the Main River on a Bailey bridge, reinforced to take our M26 tanks. All the bridges across the Main had been blown, and our engineers were working feverishly to replace the major ones as quickly as possible with temporary bridges.

After crossing the river, we passed a large airport. The woods around it had numerous small indentures cut into them about two hundred feet wide and six hundred feet deep. The tarmac had been extended into the indentures, which were used to park aircraft. Although the airport had been bombed and strafed, more than two thousand planes, including Me109s, FW190s, and Ju88s, had survived in these spaces completely unscathed. I was amazed that with this many planes intact, the Luftwaffe didn't put up a better showing in combat during the last days of the war. Although there was a shortage of aircraft fuel, it appeared that the shortage of pilots was the main reason for the collapse of the Luftwaffe.

As we threaded our way through Darmstadt, I was shocked to see the degree of destruction. The British had bombed the city during a night raid in February. The target was the Merck Chemical Works, on the northern outskirts. On the night the raid took place, strong winds blew from north to south, carrying the flares that were dropped over the chemical plant southward over the center of the city. When the first bomber dropped its incendiaries and started fires in the center of the city, the remaining bombers dropped their incendiaries on the same flaming targets.

Once a fire of this size got started, the tremendous heat generated by the flames caused the smoke and other combustion gases to rise rapidly. This in turn caused air to rush in, bringing in oxygen to further accelerate the rate of combustion. This miniature hurricane, known as a firestorm, not only consumed all the oxygen from the area but replaced it with carbon dioxide and carbon monoxide. These combustion gases, being heavier than air, cascaded around the entire area surrounding the fire. In the residential area that we moved into, approximately a mile south of the fire ring, the people either suffocated or were asphyxiated by the falling gases. The effect was devastating. Of a total population of about sixty thousand people, more than forty thousand died in this inferno.

The maintenance battalion moved into a lovely suburban residential area about a mile and half south of the damaged city. We set up our shop in a large, modern brick and stone building that had been designed as a repair garage for the city streetcar system. Across the street from the shop was a handsome park with a large swimming pool surrounded by numerous playing fields. Adjacent to this was an arboretum of several acres with numerous walking trails.

Many tasteful homes surrounded this park, and we took them over as our living quarters. Most had been abandoned because the people who lived here were high in government and business circles, and with their Nazi connections they were afraid of American reprisals.

We lived in a large home near a swimming pool that was half full of water with a lot of dead leaves and tree branches in it; we were afraid to swim in it because of possible contamination. Battalion headquarters took over the largest home in the area, across the park from us. It had been the home of the Merck Chemical Works director general and was probably one of the finest homes in Darmstadt.

After ten months of combat, we tried to relax in our new quarters and take advantage of every amenity. Captain Ellis, commander of headquarters company, obtained the services of two Latvian women to cook at the officers' mess. They were both large, heavyset peasant women who had been taken forcibly from their homes and made to work as slave labor in German war plants. Not knowing the whereabouts of their families or friends, or if any of them had survived, they were waiting to return home. They soon became good cooks and learned to speak passable English.

One day a German woman in her middle thirties came to the back door of the officers' mess. Although her dress was somewhat shabby, she looked neat and composed. She asked to speak to the commanding officer. The cooks called Captain Ellis, and he talked with her. The army had imposed a strict ban on any contact with German civilians unless it was absolutely official. The nature of her request appeared to be official business. She spoke good English and was obviously educated.

She said that this had been her home and that her father, now deceased, had been the director general of Merck Chemical Works. She was living with the nuns at the Catholic hospital nearby and was helping take care of wounded German soldiers. While living in this house, she had planted a vegetable garden in the backyard and wanted to know if she could tend the garden and take some of the vegetables back to the hospital to supplement her patients' diet.

She seemed immensely grateful when Ellis gave her permission to do this. She came every day thereafter to weed and water the garden and keep the edges neatly trimmed.

Although we were not supposed to fraternize with German civilians, it was difficult to ignore her, and gradually her tragic story came out. Her father's position was comparable to that of the president of a corporation in the United States. All high-ranking German industrialists were either members of the Nazi Party or were strong Nazi supporters. As the daughter of a relatively high German official, she had grown up in an aristocratic society. She had attended the best schools in Germany and as a young lady had gone to both France and England to attend finishing schools. She was fluent in French and English. After school in England, she returned to the ranks of high Nazi society. She married a young captain in the German army and had two daughters. While her husband was away on the Russian front, she and her young daughters lived in this house with her mother and father. They received word that her husband was killed on the Russian front a few months prior to the end of the war.

Her father had been convinced by Hitler and the continuous stream of German propaganda that Americans were barbarians. He was told that if the Americans ever occupied Darmstadt, he and his entire family would be brutally tortured and put to death. He, his wife, and daughter made a pact that if such came to pass, they would all take cyanide capsules before the Americans arrived.

In late February 1945, when the American Third Army crossed the Rhine at Oppenheim, her father called the family together in the living room. He told the daughter to leave the two little girls, approximately three and five years old, in one of the bedrooms behind a closed door. He then distributed five cyanide capsules. The mother and father took their capsules and died quickly. She took the capsules for the children and put them in candy that she had prepared. She gave the candy to the children and stayed with them until they became unconscious. When she was convinced they were dead, she took her capsule and collapsed.

Shortly afterward, American troops reached Darmstadt and found the five bodies in the house. She apparently had regurgitated the capsule in her unconscious state and was still breathing when the troops arrived. The medics revived her, then took her to the Catholic hospital and turned her over to the nuns. When she finally revived sufficiently to realize what had happened, she was in a state of shock. How could she possibly have believed the Americans were barbarians when they instead had saved her life. She had become such a pawn of Nazi propaganda that she had killed her own children. This was more than she could cope with, and she cut her wrists with a razor. The German nurses found her in a pool of blood and managed to save her again.

It's relatively easy to accept the fact that propaganda can be a powerful weapon among backward, uneducated people. This young woman, on the other hand, had had all the privileges of an aristocratic upbringing in a modern nation and had even gone to school in France and England. How could she possibly believe Americans were barbarians who would torture and kill her little girls?

One would think that after ten months of combat, nothing would shock you. As I was fortunate not to have been a tanker or infantryman exposed to terror on a twenty-four hour basis, I was perhaps more sensitive to shock. In any event the death camps in Nordhausen, Belsen, and Auschwitz and incidents such as this were bound to shock even the most insensitive person. How could any civilized people, on the face of this earth, possibly have been brought to do what the Germans did in this war? Man's inhumanity to man seemed limitless. To this day, I've never heard a reasonable explanation of how this could have happened in a modern civilized world. I have no answers to this terrible question.

After two weeks at Darmstadt, we had caught up on our maintenance and had time to relax. The photographic equipment we had found in the Agfa plant came in handy. We set up our own lab and started developing pictures, not just our own but also film that we had found in many captured German cameras.

One roll of film, apparently taken by a German guard in one of the death camps, showed the slave workers in the process of burning the bodies. The corpses were stacked in piles along the wall at the end of the crematorium vault. There appeared to be fifteen to twenty furnaces in the crematorium. The workers used large clamps to grab the head and feet of the naked corpses and drag them across the floor to a small conveyor in front of each furnace. They loaded the corpses on the conveyor head first and used a long poker in the crotch to push the bodies into the furnace.

As soon as the first conveyor was loaded, the workers would load the next one. By the time they had loaded all the furnaces, they would come back to the first one and start all over again. Any bits of bone or residue remaining on the conveyor were brushed into the ash pit. The workers' faces appeared void of any emotion. Several years after the war, a set of these pictures appeared in the holocaust museum in Atlanta, Georgia.

Major Arrington had us bring our final combat loss reports up-to-date. He told each liaison officer to review his records and those of the maintenance battalion shop work order clerk to make sure we had not missed anything. We went through all the records and tried to recount as accurately as possible every incident of vehicles being knocked out or damaged and repaired. After many hours, the final record was compiled and turned over to the division, which in turn sent it to the War Department for historical documentation. A summary copy of these records appeared in the 3d Armored Division history, entitled *Spearhead in the West*.

During this period, I received a ten-page V-mail letter from my Aunt Betty in Nashville, Tennessee. She was my grandmother's youngest sister, and I had fond memories of the summers that she and the young grandchildren spent together in my grandfather's house on the mountain in Huntsville. She would show us postcards of her trip to Europe many years before and would tell us stories about castles on the Rhine and knights and their exploits in great battles in the glorious past. Little did I realize as a little boy that I would someday be involved in similar exploits in this same land.

In her long letter, Aunt Betty described a trip she had taken with her father to Germany in the early 1890s, when she was seventeen years old. They had been invited to visit the family of a German music teacher in Rüdesheim, a small village on the east bank of the Rhine across the river from Mainz. The day they arrived in Rüdesheim on the train from Berlin, the Germans were celebrating the dedication of the Germania Denkmal (monument), a huge bronze statue cast from French cannon captured by the Germans during the Franco-Prussian war in 1871. The statue represented Germania, the German goddess of war, and was the largest statue in the world at the time.

The American ambassador and his daughter, who had been invited to participate in the dedication, were supposed to arrive on the same train from Berlin but had missed the train. My great-grandfather and aunt were mistakenly identified as the ambassador and his daughter and were given seats as guests of honor. While the *bürgermeister* and other high German officials gave numerous speeches, my aunt was given a beautiful bouquet of flowers and a red, white, and blue cockade to wear on her hat. Not until the ceremony was over did she finally comprehend what had taken place.

After reflecting on this event for some fifty years and through two world wars, she felt that this statue represented the height of German-Prussian militarism and wanted me to blow it up. This was the purpose of her letter. I was shocked to read that the woman I had regarded as a sweet little old lady music teacher had harbored such aggressive thoughts all these years. I looked at my map and discovered that Rüdesheim was only about seventy-five miles from Darmstadt. I decided to go there.

My aunt had described in the most minute detail the layout of the village and gave me the address of the house where she had stayed, number ten Schmidthoff. I soon found the street and the little courtyard with a small chapel and a fountain, which my aunt had described; she remembered having seen it from her bedroom window. I went around to the front of the house and found the number ten almost covered by an overhanging thatched eave. I took several pictures of the house, clearly showing the address.

We found the road that wound up the hill through the Niederwald to the Germania statue, still standing in all its majesty. Including its large stone pedestal, the statue was well over a hundred feet tall. From the shell craters around it and from the blasts on the stone base, we could tell that the area had been subjected to heavy shelling. The statue itself did not appear to have taken any direct hits, but there was great evidence of strikes by shell fragments. Perhaps the Germans had used this as an observation post, and the shelling was an attempt to neutralize it. On the front of the stone base was inscribed in large letters *Wacht am Rhein* ("watch on the Rhine").

I took several pictures of the statue, then found a number of battered postcards in the little tourist center at the base of the statue. I later gave them to Aunt Betty, who was angry that I hadn't blown up the statue. I explained that a quarter-ton Jeep loaded with TNT wouldn't have been enough to destroy it. That seemed to assuage her fury.

German soldiers were being repatriated as rapidly as possible. If their background and personnel data showed no possible record of war crimes or high Nazi connections, they were dismissed immediately. Many of the high-ranking officers, particularly in the SS, were held for further questioning.

Although the war had been over for about a month, we still saw groups of German soldiers in uniform walking along the road heading toward their homes. Even though they were disarmed, they had to wear their uniforms because that was their only clothing. The men were either very young, many in their early teens, or in their late fifties and sixties. There was an almost complete absence of men in their twenties, thirties, and forties; they had been killed or wounded long ago.

My Christian background told me that I should have sympathy and understanding for the defeated enemy, but the memory of the devastation they had caused made me feel hatred instead, even for the women and children. Although we had accepted war as a terrible barbaric tradition, the Germans breached all bounds of humanity: the machine-gunning of disarmed American soldiers at Malmédy; the wanton slaughter of Belgian civilians in Stavelot; the deliberate starvation, torture, and the killing of millions of innocent civilians at Nordhausen, Belsen, and Auschwitz revealed the ghastly genocide that Hitler inflicted on an entire generation. These terrors were incomprehensible to the American mind; there was no answer.

The First Industrial Survey of Postwar Germany

The joint Allied high command ordered a preliminary survey of all German industries to determine what each one made before and during the war and what it was capable of making after the war. The survey would produce a rough listing of German facilities, with particular emphasis on military technology, sources of raw material, and the status of utilities. It would seize and impound all documents and technical information.

The American sector of occupied Germany was divided into division areas. The primary function was to feed and clothe the civilians in each area and get industry and agriculture going as a productive enterprise as quickly as possible. The 3d Armored Division area was divided into three segments, one for each liaison officer. My area was a pie-shaped segment extending northwest from Darmstadt at the apex, with the Rhine River on the west and the Main River on the north. It included the cities of Gross-Gerau and Rüsselsheim plus numerous other small towns and villages.

Our liaison group reported to division headquarters to receive our instructions for the survey. We were given lists and locations of major German industries in our area and were told to be on the lookout for other industries not listed and to survey them if we felt they had any significant value. We received printed forms, several pages each, on which to record all pertinent information plus any comments we might choose to add. In addition to my driver and my Jeep, I was assigned an American soldier who was fluent in German. We also had a copy of a SHAEF order written in both English and German directing German civilians to cooperate with us fully.

As a young engineering student, I could understand some of the intricacies and problems of organizing a major industrial economy for war. At Gross-Gerau I surveyed a medium-sized plant that manufactured 40mm ammunition for Bofors antiaircraft guns. The plant's several rambling, older buildings contained about fifty thousand square feet of space. The roofs of several had been damaged by bombing, but the machinery, covered with tarpaulins, seemed intact. The director general and owner of the company took us through the plant and described in detail his production process. He opened his books and records and gave us all the pertinent information we needed to fill out our forms.

He said it was not until February, when the bridges across the Main River were destroyed, that he experienced a shortage of steel bar stock, which came from the Ruhr. He was able to operate with the considerable stock he had on hand, but in late February the bombing destroyed the roof and disrupted his main power feeders. Although the power was restored, he could not obtain materials to fix the roof. When his machinery started rusting because of the inclement weather, he had to shut down.

He told me that the 40mm Bofors shells he was making would fit our navy's 40mm antiaircraft guns. I knew this to be true, because both the United States and Germany had licensed the design from Sweden. In good English, he offered to make a deal. If the U.S. Army could get him roofing material to make repairs, he would assemble enough men to start up the plant and manufacture shells. He seemed to have no qualms about producing shells to destroy his former allies, the Japanese, if he could make a fast buck doing it.

I explained that, although the United States had adequate shell production of its own, I would include his suggestion in my report. I recommended that the plant be tooled for automatic screw machine parts, because I knew that postwar Germany would have a great demand for them.

It took several days to complete our survey of the General Motors Opel plant, the largest automobile manufacturer in Europe, which had been taken over by the German government and converted to war production. Although the plant manufactured many items, its major products were trucks and the FW190 fighter plane's radial engine for the German Luftwaffe.

Because of the plant's location at the confluence of the Main and Rhine Rivers just west of Rüsselsheim, it was easy to identify from the air. The bombing of December 1944 damaged the roofs of several production buildings, although making quick temporary repairs and moving some of the machinery to less damaged areas enabled full production to resume quickly. The plant operated continuously until February 1945, when bombing destroyed the Darmstadt gas works, which supplied the gas for the annealing furnaces and foundries.

All German plant managers had to be regarded with suspicion, because their position hinged on being Nazis or Nazi sympathizers.

One of the Opel plant's assistant directors, who worked with us on our survey, was cooperative in showing us all the records and documents (which we immediately impounded), but he appeared more interested in covering his tracks and protecting himself than in helping us. All the managers knew about the forthcoming war crimes trials and wanted to make sure that they would not be accused of atrocities against slave laborers. They wanted their names cleared. Although it was not our job to get involved in the politics, we did note whether or not the various managers were cooperative.

Each evening, all three liaison officers got together in our quarters at Darmstadt to compare notes. An air force team from SHAEF headquarters who lived in the house next door was also surveying the bombings; however, their focus was on the physical extent of the bomb damage as compared to the afteraction reports from the flight crews.

From these surveys and earlier observations, I began to develop reservations about how and why the air force chose targets. There is no question that their efforts were a primary factor in the defeat of Germany. Strategic bombing had completely devastated all the major German cities and many of the industries. Severe damage to the infrastructure had made it extremely difficult for the Germans to move troops and matériel during the last stages of the war.

In spite of this, there were questions. For at least two years prior to the war's end, both American and British bombers had made deep raids into central Germany. These flights passed right over the plants that contributed about 70 percent of all the electric power for the Ruhr and for German industry. The flights also bypassed the chemical by-product plants that manufactured lubricants for the army and briquettes to heat German homes.

During the deep raids, the air force suffered terrible losses, because they had to go without fighter protection. Yet many of the more accessible large power plants went untouched. The large Fortuna plant at Oberaussem and many others around it were still operational two months before the war ended. The destruction of the ballbearing plant at Schweinfurt, which was extremely costly to the air force, may not have been necessary if the power plants in the Rhineland had been destroyed and the Opel plant in Rüsselsheim had been shut down. The FW190 engines manufactured at the Opel plant used ball bearings made at Schweinfurt.

Why these power plants remained operational until ground forces captured them was debated at length at the higher levels of command. There was, no doubt, a great deal of political maneuvering involved. Although the air force planners tried to do what they thought best, it appears that they made some serious errors in judgment.

Reflections on the Aftermath

The pain, suffering, and losses of our tankers, infantrymen, artillerymen, engineers, and other combat arms affected me deeply and profoundly. I came on active duty in June 1941 at Camp Polk in a cadre group of about four hundred officers. During the next three years of training in the States and in England, I got to know many of them and became close friends with some of them. Of all those assigned to the infantry, tanks, or engineers, or as artillery forward observers, I did not know of a single one who survived without being seriously wounded.

As a young ordnance ROTC cadet in August 1939, I was shocked to find that our total tank research and development budget for that year was only $85,000. How could the greatest industrial nation on earth devote such a pittance to the development of a major weapons system, particularly when World War II was to start in two weeks?

Development of the M4 Sherman was further hindered by bickering and rivalry between the infantry, artillery, and armored officers about the characteristics of this tank. The infantry wanted a heavy tank that they could use for breakthroughs. Armored officers wanted a fast, mobile tank with adequate armor and a high-velocity gun. These requirements conflicted with those of the artillery, who felt that the tank was essentially a mobile artillery piece and therefore they should dictate the characteristics of the gun. It should be capable of firing at least five thousand rounds before being replaced. To do this, it was necessary to use a low-velocity gun. Artillery won on this point; the tank carried the short-barreled 75mm M2 gun.

Apparently, it hadn't occurred to anyone that there was only a remote possibility that a tank would last long enough in combat to fire five thousand rounds. Ordnance intelligence had indicated that the Germans were rapidly replacing their short-barreled 75mm howitzers in the PzKw IV tank with long-barreled, high-velocity KwK41s for greater penetration against enemy tanks. There was also information that the Russians and Germans both were using tank against tank in massive battles. This information, which should have been the handwriting on the wall for future trends in high-velocity tank-gun design, was either misunderstood or completely ignored. It appeared inexcusable to me that our troops were furnished with such a deficient main battle tank. The M4 appeared to have been designed by a committee, and many young Americans bled and died as a result.

As the middle of July 1945 neared, the tension became more acute. Although the war in Europe was over, everyone knew that the war with Japan still had to be won. Future plans had to be put on hold.

Although we were never formally briefed, there were many bull sessions going on similar to those held before D day. Speculation ran somewhat along these lines: Two American armies, the Eighth and the Tenth, were already in the Pacific and were being reinforced with additional units. The First Army would be added to this new army group. The final assault would be on the main island of Honshu. The Eighth Army would land on the north and the Tenth Army on the south. The First Army would then land both north and south of Tokyo Bay and attempt to cut off the city before the Japanese command could escape.

Whereas the Germans, when they were cut off and completely isolated, had eventually surrendered to save further loss of life, I was not sure that the Japanese would do this; in many instances in the South Pacific, they had fought to the last man. In Japan itself, the casualties could be horrendous. Some estimates put American casualties at a million and Japanese casualties at perhaps 10 to 20 million. This, of course, was speculation, but the rumors became wilder as time went on.

14
The Survivors

The French Riviera

The division was tentatively scheduled to go to Marseilles in late August and early September, preparatory to shipment to the Pacific. About this time, Major Arrington told us we could all take two weeks' leave, either in Paris or on the French Riviera. Although I wanted to see Paris, I'd had enough of the ice and snow of the Ardennes and the frigid weather of northern Germany. I was looking forward to warm sunshine.

We were still in winter uniforms: wool shirts, wool trousers, long underwear, lightweight combat jackets, and combat boots. At least we had done away with the steel helmet and wore only the helmet liner. The loss in weight made us feel about ten feet tall. Our footlockers had caught up with us by this time, and I could hardly wait to get out a summer uniform. I packed my GI knapsack for the trip with two sets of khaki shirts and trousers and GI underwear. After wearing long underwear for more than a year, putting on lightweight cotton boxer shorts made me feel buck naked.

We took the truck convoy from Darmstadt to Luxembourg to catch the train to Marseilles. Four company-grade officers were assigned to a compartment. Even though the roadbed was rough in places, because the tracks had just been repaired, our accommodations were comfortable, and I enjoyed the trip down the Rhône Valley to Marseilles. From Marseilles we went by truck convoy to Cannes. We were assigned quarters at the Gallien Hotel, a medium-sized, luxurious French hotel in the foothills above Cannes and about half a mile from the beach. My traveling buddies were Capt. Cecil Martin, a medical officer in the 45th Medical Battalion, and Joe Lykes, a first lieutenant in the 33d Armored Regiment.

We soon settled into a routine of pure pleasure. We were issued tickets for all meals and upon request could get additional tickets to take guests to dinner. The tickets were good at any hotel except the Breakers, which was off-limits to all but general officers. The army never forgot RHIP (rank has its privileges). The routines for field-grade officers (colonels, lieutenant colonels, and majors) and company-grade officers (captains and lieutenants) were much more relaxed than they had been when we were on garrison duty back in Germany. The uniform of the day was khaki shirts and trousers and dress shoes. We didn't have to wear ties and could leave our collars open. We removed our rank insignia from the right side of our collar but kept our branch insignia, which in my case was a flaming bomb, for ordnance. We wore our division patch on our sleeve. We could go bareheaded or wear our overseas cap.

We would get up at about ten o'clock in the morning and have a leisurely breakfast. The food was primarily GI 10-N-1 rations, but prepared by French chefs it certainly didn't taste like GI chow. Omelets made with powdered eggs and powdered milk tasted like gourmet creations. I understand that adding a tablespoon of bacon grease to one quart of milk was the key to the flavor. After breakfast, we would promenade down the main avenue to view the lovely French mademoiselles. Every mademoiselle in France who could beg, borrow, or steal a ride to Cannes headed there. It did not take long for the war-weary young Americans to get acquainted with them.

One morning as Doc Martin and I walked past the Carlton Hotel, I heard a familiar voice cry out, "Hey, Cooper what the hell are you doing here?"

I immediately recognized one of my old fraternity brothers, Marshall Stringer, from Michigan. One of the first members of our fraternity to be called to active duty, he was now a lieutenant colonel in the air force and was stationed in Naples. His squadron had been downsized to one B25 bomber, a Jeep, and a master sergeant.

Stringer told me that he and the sergeant would sign the morning report in Naples on Monday morning, stash the Jeep (first having removed the wheels) in the bomb bay of the B25, and fly to Nice.

The sergeant and the plane would stay in Nice, and Marshall would take the Jeep to Cannes. They would stay the entire week enjoying themselves, then fly back to Naples on Sunday night in time to sign the next Monday morning report. This had been their routine for the last six weeks.

Marshall asked if we had met any girls. When I replied that we had not, he invited us inside to meet "the Baroness."

We entered a small bar next to the hotel, and he introduced us to "Baroness Olga from the Volga," a tall, handsome woman with aristocratic bearing. She was a White Russian married to a French attorney and had a beautiful villa at Cannes, where she stayed during the week. Her husband came on weekends. She appeared to be in her middle forties and spoke several languages, including perfect English.

This was the first season that the French had been allowed to return to the Riviera since the German occupation. She had come early to reclaim her prewar title as the grand dame of French society in Cannes. Many of the mademoiselles who had come to Cannes gravitated to her, because she seemed to have the right connections to enhance their social standing.

She made a couple of phone calls, and in a few minutes a tall, good-looking redhead wearing red-and-white polka-dot shorts and a halter top rode up on a bicycle. The baroness introduced her as Ginnerret. She was a medical doctor and had worked with the French underground during the war. The baroness thought she might make a good date for Doc Martin.

A few minutes later, a beautiful, tall blonde rode up on another bicycle. In white shorts and a halter, and with golden bronze skin, she looked as though she had just stepped off the cover of *Vogue* magazine. Michelene would be my date. I thought I'd hit the jackpot.

We all sat down at a little table in the back and enjoyed a few drinks together. We seemed to be the envy of all the young GI lieutenants.

One afternoon we took the girls on the bus to Eden Rock, a large promontory projecting into the Mediterranean. The Breakers Hotel was located at the extreme tip of the promontory. Although it was off-limits to all but general officers, junior officers could use the pavilion next to the hotel. The pavilion was located on the upper level of the cliff and contained dressing rooms, a bar and grill, a dance floor, and an open patio looking over the beautiful blue Mediterranean. The patio was enclosed with a decorative steel railing and steps that led to lower levels. Each level contained a diving platform. From the patio we could see the bottom; although the water must have been twenty feet deep, it was crystal clear. It was the only place we were allowed to swim, because the sewage treatment facilities had been damaged during the war and raw sewage was discharged directly into the bay. Barbed-wire entanglements on the beach marked the possible site of remaining mines.

The four of us sat on the patio at a little table with a brightly colored umbrella. We were enjoying our drinks and the view, particularly the mademoiselles in their new bathing suits, the skimpiest I had ever seen. They consisted of a G-string and a minimal bra that barely covered what it was supposed to cover. The suits were flesh colored, just a shade lighter than the tanned body of the owner. Ginnerret explained that when a mademoiselle went into a store to purchase a bathing suit, she followed a strict procedure. She placed the bra over her forearm and wet it with a glass of water. When the bra darkened sufficiently to match the color of her skin, she chose that one. This meant that bathing suit shops had to carry many different shades, and that whenever a mademoiselle got a darker tan she had to come back and buy a new bathing suit. The idea was to make the mademoiselle look as though she was wearing nothing at all when she came out of the water.

Any skepticism I might have had over this explanation was erased when one of the young officers standing near the rail hollered, "There's a naked woman lying down there on the rocks."

There was a mad scramble as everybody rushed to the rail to see for themselves. Sure enough, on the platform about fifty feet below was a lovely young mademoiselle lying on her back apparently nude. She opened her eyes and smiled, got up, and came slowly up the stairs. When she got within about ten feet of the top, I realized that she had on a wet bathing suit. This was the beginning of the famous bikini.

Eden Rock was a beautiful resort. In the afternoons a small string combo played dance music on the patio. One afternoon as we were sitting there, I heard a particularly lilting melody. When I inquired, I was told that the song was written by a local musician and was entitled "C'est Fini" (it is finished). The song, which became popular with the American soldiers, told about the problems of the war and the sense of relief that it was finally over.

One evening we were making the rounds of the bars along the beach. We had visited the bar at the Carlton Hotel and the Miramar, which was an air force hangout. We finally wound up in the Martinez Hotel, near the east end of the beach. This was the general routine for everybody; the more bars that were visited and the more liquor that was consumed, the more rambunctious the party became.

When the liquor flowed, the soldiers loved to brag about the heroic exploits of their particular unit. Exaggeration increased with the number of drinks consumed until the bragging eventually degenerated into arguments about who won the war. Sometimes these became heated. When this would happen, a group of 3d Armored Division soldiers would raise their arms, bring their hands together at a point over their heads, and shout, "Just call me Spearhead and I'll pass on through."

One young lieutenant of the 101st Airborne became obnoxiously loud. As far as he was concerned, the 101st Airborne had won the war almost single-handedly. Four young lieutenants from the 1st Infantry Division, one of the crack infantry divisions, finally had enough. They escorted the young airborne lieutenant off the patio. Some thought they were taking him home and tucking him into the sack. Such was not the case.

Suddenly, there was a great commotion overhead. Each of the four 1st Infantry lieutenants had grabbed an arm or a leg of the airborne lieutenant; they were swinging him back and forth over the fourth-floor-balcony railing. At the count of four, they threw him off the balcony and screamed, "Geronimo! Fly, you S.O.B.!"

To the amazement of those below, the lieutenant flew in a spread-eagle position from the fourth floor toward the patio, but he landed in the middle of a large awning that stretched from the edge of the building, then rolled off one side and fell into a cactus bed. He was so drunk that he was completely limp; the only injury he sustained was a few cactus needles in his butt. The fall apparently sobered him up enough to navigate back to his hotel alone.

The Bomb

Our leave was rapidly drawing to an end. In a few days we would return to Darmstadt and prepare to depart for the Pacific. About half past ten one morning as we were sitting on the patio of the Miramar Hotel drinking coffee and relaxing, a young French boy came down the street distributing the *Stars and Stripes* newspaper, a GI publication free to all servicemen. He was hawking it at the top of his lungs just like an American newspaper boy selling an "extra." I got a paper and brought it back to our table. The date on the paper was August 6, 1945, and the headline read, "Americans drop atomic bomb on Hiroshima, Japan."

The article said we had developed a secret atomic bomb with an explosive capacity of twenty thousand tons of TNT. Everyone looked at me; they knew that I had gone to bomb disposal school.

I was just as shocked and surprised as they were, and I had no idea what it really meant. My first reaction was that we had indeed developed some kind of super explosive; however, I did not believe that it was an actual atomic explosion. Talk of nuclear power and nuclear bombs appeared to be Buck Rogers–type thinking; I thought that those developments would be at least a hundred years away. It never occurred to any of us that this new bomb might appreciably shorten the war.

Early on the morning of August 9, we boarded trucks to head back to Marseilles to catch our train to Luxembourg. When we arrived in Marseilles, the French newsboys were hawking another *Stars and Stripes* announcing that an atomic bomb had been dropped on Nagasaki. Gradually, I realized that this was more than just a super explosive, that maybe we had developed a real atomic bomb, but I was convinced that we would still have to invade Japan to finally bring the country to its knees. I think that most of the soldiers felt the same way.

On the trip up the Rhône Valley, I was jammed into a compartment with seven other junior officers. After we had completely ex-

hausted our repertoire of stories about whiskey, women, and pleasure, the conversation finally turned to war. I realized that all the ex-
aggerations were a reflection of the pain and suffering that these
men had been through and that this was their way of letting off
steam. Somebody finally broke out a deck of cards and some dice,
and the crapshooting and poker games went on late into the night.

The Survivors

We arrived in Luxembourg about midmorning and were told that
3d Armored Division trucks would pick us up about half past four
that afternoon. We would have the rest of the day to explore the city.

Other than some shelling during the Battle of the Bulge on the
northern outskirts, this medieval city had been relatively undamaged
by the war. We walked around, crossed the stone bridge over a big
canyon park formed by the river running through the middle of the
city, and had a leisurely drink and lunch at one of the many bars and
sidewalk cafes. Then we visited the Luxembourg Theater, which had
been taken over by the army and showed free movies twenty-four
hours a day.

The theater, the largest in Luxembourg, was typical of the large
movie palaces built in the late twenties and early thirties. Elaborately
decorated like a Moorish palace, it had two balcony levels and two
rows of box seats on the sides. We got good seats in the middle of
the first balcony and settled down to relax and enjoy the movie, *Dark
Victory*, starring Betty Davis. The film was interrupted about every fifteen minutes with announcements for such and such a unit to report to Plaza Square.

I had already seen the film, so I let my mind wander to our terrible tank losses. Major Arrington's order to prepare final combat loss
reports had given us the losses for the entire division. Of 158 M5 light
tanks, we lost more than 100 percent. (Although the M24 light tank
that replaced the M5 was far superior in both firepower and armored
protection, it was still too light for major assaults.) Of a total of 232
medium tanks (including 10 M26 Pershings), 648 were totally destroyed in combat and 1,100 needed repairs. Of these 1,100, approximately 700 had been knocked out in battle. This meant that
we lost 1,350 medium tanks in combat, or a total loss of 580 percent.

It was obvious why we soon ran out of trained tank crews and had to substitute raw infantry recruits during the Battle of the Bulge.

I had mixed thoughts about the capability of Japanese armor. Japanese tanks were reportedly extremely light and much inferior to ours in firepower and armor, but the Japanese reportedly had gotten the complete plans and specifications for the German Panther tank some time ago. If the Japanese could manufacture Panther tanks in large numbers, this could pose a major threat. But even if Japanese armor posed no major threat, we had every reason to believe that if the Japanese infantry fought as tenaciously as it did in the South Pacific islands, it would inflict severe losses on us. Our men felt that an invasion of Japan would be extremely bloody and costly to both sides.

Suddenly the screen in the movie theater went blank and the lights started to brighten. We all stood up to look around, at first I thought that this was merely another announcement telling a particular unit to meet their trucks in the plaza. But then the theater manager's voice came over the speaker loud and clear and in perfect English. "We have just received a BBC broadcast that the Japanese have agreed to unconditional surrender."

The effect was stunning. Some of the men stood speechless and in a daze; some fell on their knees and started praying; some broke down and cried. I said a silent prayer, thanking God for my deliverance. It was as if we had all been on death row and had suddenly been given a reprieve. Time seemed to stand still and merge into eternity while three thousand young soldiers realized that by the grace of God we had all at last become survivors.

Epilogue: The Coin

During World War II, *The Huntsville Times* published the names of the young men when they were sent overseas. In early September 1943, when the 3d Armored Division was sent to England, my name appeared. An elderly lady, a long time family friend, called my father and said, "George, I see your son Belton has gone overseas." After replying affirmatively, she asked that he come by, as she had a gift for me. My father called on her the next day and she gave him an 1825 fifty-cent coin. (This was not a particularly rare coin at the time; it had an appraised value of $38.00.) She said the coin had a story behind it and that my father should pass the story on to me with the coin.

It so happened that this coin was carried by her husband's great great grandfather as a good luck piece in the Mexican War in 1840. It was then passed on to his grandfather, who carried it in the Civil War in 1862. It was passed on to her husband's father, who carried it in the Spanish American War in 1898, and he, in turn, passed it on to her husband who carried it in World War I, in 1917. As they had no more sons in her branch of the family, she wanted my father to send it to me. She hoped that I would carry it safely and that I would not have to pass it on to any future sons who I might have in any future wars. I carried the coin as a good luck piece throughout World War II in Europe, and I still have it today.

Thus, this coin was carried by five different American soldiers, in five different American wars, and they all survived without being killed or seriously wounded. I believe this is unique, and is the only coin in existence that has had this history.

Appendices

Panzers Versus American Armor

The M4 Sherman that we took into Normandy weighed thirty-two tons and had two and a half inches of armor, inclined at forty-five degrees, on its front glacis plate. It had a short-barreled, low-velocity (2,050 feet per second) 75mm gun. Later, about 15 percent of the tanks we received had the new 76mm gun with a higher muzzle velocity (2,650 feet per second).

When the war began in Europe, a confused debate was raging between American tank designers in ordnance and senior officers in the army ground forces. In the summer of 1939, when I was at Aberdeen Proving Ground as an ordnance cadet, our main battle tank was the M2A1 medium tank with a 37mm gun mounted in the turret. After the Germans invaded Poland in September, the debate became more intense. The armored and cavalry officers favored a large-caliber, high-velocity antitank gun mounted in the turret. The infantry officers still thought of the tank as an infantry assault weapon. The artillery officers thought that if a tank was going to carry a gun larger than a 37mm, the gun should conform to artillery specifications, which required a gun to be capable of 7,500 service rounds in combat. To meet this, a 75mm gun and larger would require a relatively low velocity. It apparently never occurred to the artillery officers that few tanks would ever survive in combat long enough to fire 7,500 service rounds. The result of this was the new M3 battle tank, designed by a committee.

This committee chose the new tank's basic features. It had the M2A1 lower hull and track system, powered by the R975C1 400-horsepower radial engine, and a transmission and final drive similar to that of the old M2A1. The side and frontal armor were increased, and an angular-shaped hull was devised using riveted connections. The front glacis plate, approximately two and a half inches thick, started out at forty-five degrees where it connected with the transmission and extended about halfway up the front. It then had a knuckle riveted joint in the middle and extended upward at about sixty degrees. The riveted joint was used because some officers felt that the welding would weaken the armor plate. This decision was disastrous. When a small-caliber, armor-piercing bullet struck the head of one of these rivets, it sheared it off and drove the internal part of it into the tank, where it ricocheted like a projectile and killed the crew.

The committee decided to put a 37mm antitank gun in the turret, coaxial with a .30-caliber machine gun. The 37mm was already obsolete and had practically no effect on the frontal armor of German tanks. The turret also had a .50-caliber ring-mount, dual-purpose machine gun. The main armament, conforming to the artillery board's specifications, was a low-velocity 75mm M2 gun mounted in a barbette enclosure on the right side of the tank. With approximately forty-five degrees of lateral traverse and its low muzzle velocity (2,050 feet per second), it seemed to satisfy the infantry board as a good assault tank.

The tank had a much higher silhouette than any comparable German tank and could be easily spotted from a considerable distance. To make matters worse, the committee was apparently dominated by Yankees, who decided to name this tank the "Grant," after the Union general and later president. The Southerners were aggravated further by the later naming of the M4, known as the "Sherman," after the Union general who burned a path through Georgia.

Opposing us were three types of German panzers. The PzKw IV, which we usually called the Mark IV, weighed twenty-three tons and had four inches of vertical armor on the front and a high-velocity (3,000 feet per second) 75mm gun. Next came the PzKw V Panther, weighing fifty-three tons with three and a half inches of armor on the front glacis plate at thirty-eight degrees, below the critical angle of ricochet. The Panther carried a long-barreled, high-velocity (3,300 feet per second) 75mm gun. Finally came the PzKw VI King Tiger, weighing sixty-four tons with six inches of armor at forty-five degrees on the glacis plate and a long-barreled, high-velocity (3,250 feet per second) 88mm gun. The German tanks had a qualitative superiority of as much as five to one over our M4 Sherman.

The combination of superior firepower and heavier armor allowed the German tanks to engage and destroy the M4 Sherman at long range. There were many cases where Shermans would score multiple direct hits on the front of a Panther or a Tiger, only to see the shells bounce off harmlessly. In comparison, the German high-velocity guns could not only penetrate the lighter armor of the Sherman with a single shot at long range, they could knock out a Sherman even after shooting through a brick wall and, in at least one instance, by shooting through another Sherman tank. Whereas the Sherman had to get within six hundred yards of a Panther and hope to catch it on the flank, the Panther could knock out a Sherman at two thousand yards head-on.

Before the Normandy invasion, some U.S. armored commanders assumed that because the Sherman was lighter than the Panther, it would be more mobile. This assumption was incorrect. The key to a tank's off-road mobility is its ground bearing pressure: how the weight of the tank is distributed over the ground. Because the Panther had a wider track than the Sherman, it actually had a lower ground bearing pressure and could go places where the Sherman could not. More importantly, the narrow track on the Sherman could not negotiate muddy terrain and snow.

The M4 Sherman's inferiority was by no means predestined; we enjoyed a great superiority in other weapons systems. After a twenty-year period of isolationism between the wars, in just four years the United States was able to produce superior weapons in vast quantities, including rifles, artillery, motor transports, and aircraft.

As the only officer in the maintenance battalion who had been to the tank maintenance school in Fort Knox, I was knowledgeable about tanks, particularly their technical capabilities. At tank school, I took copious notes and read every field manual I could get my hands on. I also read any G2 ordnance reports we had on German tanks. Unfortunately, this information was limited. I saw no reports on German tanks larger or more powerful than the PzKw III and the PzKw IV with the short-barreled 75mm howitzer. We had no information about the German Panther tank, either, although I had read a newspaper account of the Tiger tanks that were used in North Africa against the 1st Armored Division. Because the M4 Sherman, with the 75mm gun in the turret, was far superior to the old M3, and because our knowledge of comparable German armor was limited, we felt that the M4 was a good tank.

Meanwhile, the Germans were replacing all the short-barreled 75mm guns on their Mark IV tanks with higher velocity guns, and they were developing the Panther and Tiger. The Sherman could not compare with these. American tank designers also failed to give proper consideration to the latest Soviet advances in armor. Their medium T34 and heavy Josef Stalin tanks were both equipped with more powerful guns, heavier armor, and wider tracks than the M4 Sherman.

The U.S. Army did finally develop the M26 Pershing tank, with heavier armor and wider tracks than the M4, and with a long-barreled 90mm gun. This tank was far superior to the Sherman and would have placed us on a more level playing field with the German armor. However, due to the arrogance of certain high-ranking officers it was recommended that this tank be given a low priority, and production concentrated on the M4 Sherman. Many observers at the time believed that had we had the M26 Pershing during the November 1944 offensive east of Aachen, we might have been able to break through the last vestiges of the Siegfried line, exit onto the Cologne Plain, and outflank the German troops building up in the Ardennes. Had this occurred, the Battle of the Bulge might never have taken place and the war would have ended months earlier.

APPENDIX II

Adding More Protection

I first became aware of the deficiency in the M4 Sherman's armor
in England in November 1943. Major Arrington told me that ordnance had prepared a field service kit to put additional armor plate
on all the M4 Sherman tanks, and I was to be in charge of the project. The work was to be performed at Warminster, the main British
armored depot. Army ordnance, at Aberdeen, had sent over a technical observer (TO), who was an expert on welding armor. He was
on loan from General Motors and had a good background in production welding techniques.

It was my job to work with the British depot commander and secure the necessary labor and facilities. The TO's job was to work with
the British foreman to figure out the necessary jigs and fixtures and
welding procedures. After several screwups and near disasters, we finally got things worked out and the job went along smoothly.

From combat experience in North Africa, Sicily, and Italy, we had
learned that the M4 Sherman had inadequate armor and was vulnerable in several critical areas. It was felt that the application of this
additional armor would overcome some of its vulnerability. The tank
carried a combat load of eighty-nine rounds of 75mm ammunition.
It was stored with sixteen rounds in each of two racks in the right-
hand sponson (the area that overhangs the track) and one rack in
the left-hand sponson. There were thirty-two rounds stored in a rack
under the turret, in the main fighting compartment, and nine
rounds in ready rack clips in the turret itself.

If the tank was penetrated in any of these areas and a fragment
penetrated the soft brass case of a 75mm round, the round was likely
to detonate and set off the other rounds. A one-inch-thick patch of
armor plate approximately eighteen inches by twenty-four inches was
welded on the outside of the sponson immediately over the ammunition boxes. Inside the sponsons we fabricated small boxes of quarter-inch armor plate with doors to go around the ammunition, in
case a fragment struck the ammunition from the inside. We fabricated another quarter-inch armor plate box with doors to go underneath the turret. On the right forward side of the turret, the cast

armor had been thinned out to accommodate the control mechanism for the turret's hydraulic powered traverse. We welded a two-inch-thick bulbous contoured patch approximately two feet square over this area. On the M4 Shermans with cast armor, the contour of the glacis plate changed radically to an almost perpendicular position right in front of the driver and assistant driver. We welded two large inch-and-a-half-thick tapered patches over these areas.

After several days of experimenting, we finally got a good assembly line set up. We were fortunate to have a large fabricated steel shop building with plenty of floor area, overhead cranes, and heat. The building was large enough to accommodate eight tanks at a time. This was unusual for us; we had been used to working in the fields in the rain, sleet, and mud up to our butts.

We would bring the tanks into the long bay and space them about thirty feet apart. Our tank maintenance mechanics got in the tanks and disconnected all the wiring and hydraulic mechanisms from the tank turret. We removed the bolts from the turret rings, and the crane picked up the entire turret with its attached bottom cage and set it on a fabricated steel stand to one side of the tank.

Three welding crews started tacking the side patches into position, then the regular welders came in and finished the job. Welding armor plate is tricky, but our TO welding expert set up an efficient procedure and trained the British welders in effecting a good weld, using the right kind of alloy rod and making small multiple passes. The heat from each pass tended to stress-relieve the bead underneath to produce a relatively stress-free joint.

One of the first tanks off the assembly line ran over a six-inch timber used for blocking, and this slight jar caused one of the welded patches in front of the driver's position to crack loose. The British welder had apparently made too large a weld, which built up excessive stress and caused the patch to crack. This condition was corrected, and we proceeded without further incident.

In the meantime, other crews fitted the preassembled ammunition boxes inside the tank sponsons and underneath the turret. Some crews repainted the interior and others repainted the exterior. The turrets were then reinstalled, and the wiring and hydraulic mechanisms were hooked up. Once the production problems were worked out, we were able to turn out eight tanks a day. By working around the clock, we completed the entire division in approximately one month.

Due to my complete ignorance, I got into a hassle with some of the British workmen; it was blown completely out of proportion and almost became an international incident.

Things were hectic during our first few days of operation. One morning, just as things began to settle down, I noticed that at about ten o'clock the lead British foreman signaled the men to stop working. At first I thought this was similar to the incident that happened on board our troop ship at Liverpool, when the stevedores went on a short strike and refused to unload the rest of the ship until a British dock officer got them straightened out.

When I asked the British foreman what was going on, he replied that the men were taking a thirty-minute tea break.

"I've got my men working around the clock trying to get these tanks out, and you guys are taking a damn break? Don't you realize there's a war going on?"

Here was a young American lieutenant who had just gotten overseas and was telling the British that a war was going on while they had already been in it for four years. Some of these men had had sons at Dunkirk and in North Africa; others had lost members of their family to the bombing.

The tension heightened as I continued to make a fool of myself. I could see that we were getting nowhere, and I walked away to report the work stoppage to the British base commander. The British foreman returned to his men and finished his tea break.

It was finally explained to me that these men worked ten- to twelve-hour shifts. There was insufficient labor in England for war workers to work three shifts, as they did in the United States. The men came to work at seven in the morning and finished at seven in the evening, when the night shift replaced them. The British had five meals a day: breakfast, morning tea, lunch, afternoon tea, and supper. They didn't eat supper until about eight in the evening. Thus, tea was actually one of their regular meals. Once I understood this, work proceeded smoothly. I never apologized to the British foreman;

however, we understood each other, and before the project was finished we became good buddies.

The entire project, involving more than 232 medium tanks, was finished in approximately a month. When we left Warminster, the assembly line was set up for the 2d Armored Division. In addition, several thousand tanks at Tidworth Downs came through the same assembly line that we had established. I recall being at Tidworth Downs when the sixty thousandth tank was unloaded from the transporter. Detroit had painted 60,000 in large numerals about two feet high on the sponson of the M4 Sherman tank. Everyone cheered as the tank was unloaded from the back end of the trailer. I was amazed that this many tanks had been built. The experience of learning how to weld armor plate became an invaluable one later on when we got into combat.

APPENDIX III

Field Deployment of an American Armored Division

During World War II, the U.S. Army had two types of armored divisions. The 1st and the 4th through the 20th Armored Divisions were "light" divisions, each with approximately 11,000 men and 168 medium tanks. The 2d and 3d Armored Divisions were "heavy" divisions, each with approximately 13,500 men and 232 medium tanks. Both types of division had a number of light tanks; because of their extremely limited capability, they were used primarily for reconnaissance. Some felt that the light divisions, based on the highly successful German panzer divisions, would be more effective than the heavy divisions. This was a highly controversial issue among the armored force staff. It was finally decided to leave the 2d and 3d as heavy armored divisions.

The thinking behind the light armored divisions was based on quantitative numbers instead of the qualitative capability. In relative qualitative comparisons of the strength of the main tank forces, the Germans held an edge of at least five to one. Although the light armored divisions did an excellent job, it was soon discovered, after the Normandy invasion, that they did not have the staying power to take horrendous casualties and recover as rapidly as the heavy divisions. As a result, it was decided that in assault operations the 2d and 3d Armored Divisions had to be used to a much greater degree than the lighter units.

Armored Force Tactical Doctrine called for the operation of two types of armored units. The first was the GHQ tank battalion, designed to work with and support infantry divisions. The second was the armored division, a completely self-contained unit containing tanks, self-propelled artillery, and mechanized infantry. In addition, the armored division contained all the necessary support arms, including reconnaissance, combat engineers, supply, medical, and maintenance. This provided a single unit with the firepower, mobility, and shock capability necessary for independent combat operations. The mission of the armored division was not to make the initial breakthrough but rather to exploit the breakthrough made by the GHQ tank battalions and infantry divisions.

The armored division had the capacity to supply itself for three days without outside assistance. Its immediate objective was not to engage other enemy armored units but instead to bypass them and attack artillery and supply units and destroy enemy infantry reserves before they could deploy. By not dissipating its armored striking power by engaging enemy tanks, the division would maintain its full capability.

This tactical doctrine was developed simultaneously by a group of young British and American officers in the late 1920s and early 1930s. By adopting the tactics and basic mission of horse cavalry and modernizing it with tanks and other mechanized units, an entirely new type of combat unit was created. The Germans obviously came upon the same idea.

An American heavy armored division deployed in the following manner: The basic unit consisted of a division headquarters, three combat commands, and the division trains. The division headquarters consisted of the headquarters company, a reconnaissance battalion, and a signal company. Each combat command consisted of a headquarters, a recon company, two tank battalions with two medium tank companies and one light tank company each, an armored infantry battalion, an armored field artillery battalion with eighteen M7 self-propelled 105mm howitzers, an armored combat engineer company, an ordnance maintenance company, a medical company, and a supply company. The division trains consisted of their headquarters, the ordnance battalion headquarters company, the medical battalion headquarters company, and the supply battalion headquarters company. In addition, a heavy armored division had attached to it an antiaircraft battalion, a tank destroyer battalion, and a heavy artillery battalion of 155mm GPF rifles mounted on an M12 tank chassis. This gave the division a total strength of approximately 17,000 men and 4,200 vehicles. Had the division ever gotten on the road in single file, in normal march order interval, it would have stretched 150 miles from the head of the column to the end.

Once the division deployed to exploit a breakthrough, it moved out with two combat commands abreast and one in reserve. Each combat command contained two separate task forces, moving as much in parallel as the contours of the land would permit. The front of a heavy armored division could vary in width from several hundred yards up to twenty miles depending upon the terrain. During the daylight hours, each task force had available four P47 fighter-bombers under the direct control of an air force liaison officer who rode in the lead half-track with the task force commander. The task force's mission was to advance rapidly toward its objective, leaving any resistance to be cleaned up later by the infantry, which might arrive within the next few hours to two days.

At night the combat elements would coil off the road and form a circular perimeter. The tanks and infantry would form the outer perimeter, and the maintenance, medical, and supply units would be inside, where they could do their work. At daybreak, when the combat units moved out, the maintenance unit commander had to make certain critical decisions. All vehicles repaired and ready for action would be returned to their units. All others would be towed to the next stopping point. If there were more vehicles than the wreckers could accommodate, a vehicle collecting point (VCP) was established. The ordnance company commander would detach a maintenance platoon to establish the VCP and repair the vehicles that were left behind. This could take several days. During this period, the maintenance platoon would be completely isolated behind enemy lines and be responsible for its own security.

After the vehicles were repaired, they returned to their original units, and the maintenance platoon went forward to rejoin the ordnance company. In some instances, there would be several VCPs along the route of advance. As soon as any platoon finished its repairs, it would leave the others and return to the company. By utilizing this system, plus the replacement vehicles brought up each day by the ordnance liaison officer, the combat command was able to maintain its effectiveness during long, continuous operations.

Suggested Reading

Ambrose, Stephen E. *D-Day June 6, 1944,* Simon and Schuster 1994.
———.*Citizen Soldiers,* Simon and Schuster 1997.
Arend, Guy Franz. *Bastogne.*
Blumenson, Martin. *Breakout and Pursuit.* Washington, D.C.: United States Army Center for Military History, 1981.
Bradley, Omar N. *A Soldier's Story.* New York: Henry Holt & Co., 1951.
Cole, Hugh M. *The Ardennes: Battle of the Bulge.* Washington, D.C.: United States Army Center for Military History, 1988.
Eisenhower, Dwight D. *Crusade in Europe.* Garden City, N.Y.: Doubleday & Co., 1948.
Green, Michael. *M4 Sherman.* Osceola, Wis.: Motor Books International, 1993.
Houston, Donald E. *Hell on Wheels: The Second Armored Division.* Novato, Calif.: Presidio Press, 1977.
MacDonald, Charles B. *The Mighty Endeavor: The American Army in Europe.* New York: Oxford University Press, 1969.
———. *The Last Offensive.* Washington, D.C.: United States Army Center for Military History, 1981.
———. *A Time for Trumpets.* New York: William Morrow and Co., 1985.
———. *The Siegfried Line Campaign.* Washington, D.C.: United States Army Center for Military History, 1989.
MacKinder, Sir Halford. *Democratic Ideals and Reality.* London: Royal Historical Society, ca. 1921.
Mellenthin, F. W. von. *Panzer Battles: Classical Account of German Tank Warfare in WW II.* New York: Ballantine Books, 1956.
Normandie Album Memorial: 6 June–22 Aug 1944. Editions Heimal.
Scott, Wesley W. *Tanks Are Mighty Fine Things.* Detroit: Chrysler Corp., 1946.
Written by the men of the Third Armor Division. *Spearhead in the West: The Third Armored Division.* Frankfurt am Main: Schwanheim, 1945.
Weigley, Russel F. *Eisenhower's Lieutenants.* Bloomington, Ind.: University Press, 1981.
Zumbro, Ralph. *Tank Aces: Stories of American Combat Tankers.* New York: Pocket Books, 1997.

Index